NOTORIOUS AUSTRALIAN
Women

NOTORIOUS AUSTRALIAN
Women

KAY SAUNDERS

ABC
Books

The ABC 'Wave' device is a trademark of the Australian Broadcasting Corporation and is used under licence by HarperCollins*Publishers* Australia.

First published in Australia in 2011
This edition published in 2013
by HarperCollins*Publishers* Australia Pty Limited
ABN 36 009 913 517
harpercollins.com.au

HarperCollins*Publishers*
Level 13, 201 Elizabeth Street, Sydney NSW 2000, Australia
31 View Road, Glenfield, Auckland 0627, New Zealand
A 53, Sector 57, Noida, UP, India
77–85 Fulham Palace Road, London W6 8JB, United Kingdom
2 Bloor Street East, 20th floor, Toronto, Ontario M4W 1A8, Canada
10 East 53rd Street, New York NY 10022, USA

National Library of Australia Cataloguing-in-Publication entry:

Saunders, Kay, 1947-
    Notorious Australian women / Kay Saunders.
    978 0 7333 3216 6 (pbk.)
    978 0 7304 9479 9 (ebook)
    Includes index.
    Women – Australia – Biography.
305.40994

Cover design by Christa Moffitt, Christabella Designs,
adapted by Alicia Freile, Tango Media
Cover images: Lola Montez © Bettmann/CORBIS; pattern by istockphoto.com
Typeset in 11/16pt Adobe Garamond Pro by Kirby Jones
Printed and bound in Australia by Griffin Press
The papers used by HarperCollins in the manufacture of this book are a natural, recyclable product made from wood grown in sustainable plantation forests. The fibre source and manufacturing processes meet recognised international environmental standards, and carry certification.

6 5 4 3 2 1   13 14 15 16

To

Louise Bass Saunders and Harolda Sizer,
my English great-grandmothers who fought valiantly in the WSPU
and
my granddaughter Gabriella Hilder who inherits their legacy

Contents

Introduction 1

Chapter 1 Mary Broad Bryant 5

Chapter 2 Mary Cockerill and Walyer 28

Chapter 3 Eliza Fraser 49

Chapter 4 Lola Montez 71

Chapter 5 Ellen Tremaye (Edward De Lacy Evans) and Marion ('Bill') Edwards 90

Chapter 6 'Madame Brussels' Caroline Hodgson 108

Chapter 7 Helena Rubinstein 118

Chapter 8 Adela Pankhurst 139

Chapter 9 Annette Kellermann 157

Chapter 10 Lady Maie Casey 178

Chapter 11 Florence Broadhurst 194

Chapter 12 Pamela Travers 213

Chapter 13 Enid, Countess of Kenmare 233

Chapter 14 Tilly Devine 251

Chapter 15 Sunday Reed 266

Chapter 16 Rosaleen Norton 285

Chapter 17 Charmian Clift 302

Chapter 18 Lillian Roxon 320

Endnotes 337

Acknowledgments 375

Index 377

Introduction

Australian history is replete with rebels, rousers, eccentrics and plain bad girls who have not received the sort of attention they deserved. From its earliest days when convict Mary Broad Bryant escaped with her husband, Will Bryant, and children across more than 5000 kilometres in an open boat to Timor, through the nineteenth century with its bushrangers, madams and cross-dressers – to wit Ellen Tremaye and Marion Edwards – to the twentieth and characters such as standover merchant Tilly Devine and satanic artist Rosaleen Norton, Australia has been rich in women who had an eye for an opportunity and ran with it.

In the nineteenth and early twentieth centuries, gender roles in most of the Western world were restricted and options for women few and stark – usually marriage or work as a domestic or teacher. Yet in the fluidity of colonial Australian society some women carved out profitable and successful careers, though not perhaps conventional ones – for example, Caroline Hodgson, aka Madame Brussels, the proprietor of Melbourne's most exclusive brothels.

Others were able to remake themselves altogether. Distance from the mother country meant that reputations could be discarded and better origins manufactured. Who was to dispute a woman like Helena Rubinstein, who said she had learned from a distinguished chemist? Or Florence Broadhurst, who claimed tutelage by a Parisian couturier?

In some cases it operated in reverse and a woman could flee scandal in Australia or profit from wild frontier stories back in Europe. This seems to have been the case with Eliza Fraser, who, with encouragement from her new husband, toured England relating an exaggerated story of her time with the Indigenous people on Great Sandy Island following her shipwreck.

Eliza Fraser's story has inspired many creative endeavours. Some of the women documented here have left a much fainter print on the historical record and their stories are consequently harder to effectively dramatise. Little snippets appear in the official records about 'Black Mary', or Mary Cockerill, the partner of Van Diemen's Land bushranger Michael Howe, who raided and robbed in the Hobart and central Tasmanian districts in the mid 1810s. This enterprising young woman was an active bushranger in her own right rather than just the partner of a well-known male. Her life as an Indigenous woman brought up by English settlers and her decision to become a bushranger reveal defiance and a singular vision that is both remarkable and unique.

Researching these women has taken me on a journey through many worlds, ranging from the stinking and foul prison hulks to Lady Kenmare's aristocratic boudoirs. From many different backgrounds have our notorious sisters emerged, some to flourish in their fame or infamy, some to meet inglorious ends. I have frequently marvelled at their audacity, pluck and wickedness. Each of the women described here has added considerably to the fascinating texture of the Australian experience. I salute their verve and adventurousness, and their courage in breaking free of the strictures that confined a woman.

CHAPTER 1

Mary Broad Bryant
(1765–UNKNOWN)

The highway robber and First Fleeter who rowed from Sydney to Timor with her husband and two children.

Mary Bryant was Australia's first authentic celebrity. The *Dublin Chronicle* of 4 June 1793 brought fascinated readers up to date with her remarkable story:

> The female convict who made her escape from Botany Bay, and suffered a voyage of 3000 leagues, and who afterwards was taken and condemned to death, has been pardoned and released from Newgate. A gentleman of high rank in the Army visited her in Newgate, heard the details of her life, and for that time departed. The next day he returned, and told the old gentleman who keeps the prison he had procured her pardon, which he shewed him, at the same time requesting that she should not be apprised of the circumstances. The next day he returned with his carriage, and took off the poor woman who almost expired with excess of gratitude.[1]

The description of Mary in the records of London's
Newgate Prison for the year 1792 reads: 'Mary Bryant,
alias Broad, age 25 [sic], height 5'4", grey eyes, brown
hair, sallow complexion, born in Cornwall, widow'.[2]
Neither this nor the *Dublin Chronicle* account reveal much
of the drama, courage and despair that characterised this
young woman's life. Her extraordinary story might have
been a sensation soon forgotten but for the advocacy of
her benefactor, the Scottish aristocrat and barrister, also
ninth Laird of Auchinleck and author of the famous *Life of
Samuel Johnson*, James Boswell.

Mary Broad was born in Fowey, a small fishing village
on the English Channel side of Cornwall, the daughter
of mariner William Broad and his wife, Grace, and was
baptised on 1 May 1765. Cornwall is a distinctive part
of Britain, having far more in common with other Celtic
regions in Brittany and Wales than the neighbouring
English counties. Until the end of the eighteenth century,
the Cornish spoke their own Celtic language, Kernewek.
English language, customs, laws and ways of life were
often seen as foreign impositions. Like the people in
the maritime villages of nearby Devon, the Cornish
were renowned for smuggling, which they regarded as a
legitimate form of free trading. Looting and plundering
wrecked vessels off the rocky coastline were also common
practice. Indeed, the local economy along these coasts
depended upon smuggling and looting luxury goods
from France bound for the more urban centres of Bath,
Plymouth and London. The historical novels by Daphne
du Maurier, *Jamaica Inn* (1936) and *Frenchman's Creek*
(1942), along with Winston Graham's *Poldark* series,

capture the atmosphere of Cornwall at the time of Mary Broad's childhood.

As a mariner, William Broad would presumably have participated in smuggling, safe in the knowledge that this was a protected industry among his local community. However, Mary's biographer C. H. Currey has claimed the Broad family were also 'prominent sheep stealers'. Cornwall was an extremely poverty-stricken area of Britain in the eighteenth century, with little industry apart from fishing and smuggling. Stealing food and animals to sell was part of a folk culture that eluded the stronger claims of the law.

As a child, Mary spent many hours on her father's small vessel, learning the ways of the sea, an education that would later help preserve her life, but like girls of her class and region, she was illiterate. Free compulsory education did not arrive in Britain until a century after her birth. Despite her considerable nautical skills, life at sea, or as a smuggler, was not the province of a female, yet we do not know how she was employed once she was old enough to work. We can surmise that, like her sister Dolly – whose trade was mentioned much later in a letter of James Boswell – she was a domestic servant. Mary later worked as a cook in London after her escape from Botany Bay, so this might have been her occupation.

Mary came to public notice when she was convicted, at the Exeter Assizes in Devon on 29 March 1786, along with two female accomplices, of the highway assault of spinster Agnes Lakeman of Plymouth, the nearest large town to Fowey. They stole her cloak, bonnet and other personal items (presumably jewellery) to the value of £11/11s. It was a bold and daring crime, performed in broad daylight in full public view. Most transported convicts were found guilty of petty property crimes such as theft, selling stolen goods or pickpocketing, but this was an audacious assault and robbery. It was also conducted without much forethought and on the spur of the moment. Coming across the well-dressed woman of wealth and standing, who was without family or maid in attendance, Lakeman provoked envy among the three young women, whose lives were dictated by poverty and relentless hard work. But lacking discretion and cunning to successfully pull off such a bold move, they were easily apprehended.

All three young women were given a capital sentence, as thefts over the value of 40 shillings warranted the death penalty if undertaken with threats or violence. Mary would have felt terrified and alarmed – she had presumably only wanted to wear some beautiful clothes and jewellery, and soon she would be dead. Not only executed, but hanged in public to the shame of her family.

Fortunately, the sentence was later commuted to transportation for seven years (which was itself a fearful outcome). At twenty-one years of age, Mary was not a juvenile offender, so the comparative leniency of her sentence attests to her otherwise good character and disposition before the court. Certainly she had no previous convictions.

Nevertheless, transportation was the second most feared and severe punishment after execution. Introduced in 1717 – although suspended following the independence of the American colonies – transportation was devised to 'deter wicked and evil-disposed persons from being guilty of crimes'.[3] By 1786 the Secretary of State, Lord Sydney, had announced that transportation would resume in earnest, as places like Newgate Prison in London and the disused hulks of old sailing vessels moored in the waterways of England and used to house felons for years on end, were criminal training grounds rather than places of reformation.[4]

Mary was first confined in the decrepit and unsanitary hulk *Dunkirk*, off Plymouth. Convicts like Mary were sent from the hulks to work during the day, returning to the cramped, dank locations in the evening. But now as a member of the First Fleet, she was destined to be part of this new experiment, leaving the familiarity of Plymouth for an unknown destination at the end of the earth for a life of exile and compulsory, unremitting work.

The Governor of the new convict settlement at Botany Bay and commander of the First Fleet, Arthur Phillip, was at the end of a long but not particularly illustrious career. He was a man of probity, humanity and solid qualities. A professional naval officer who rose through the ranks, Phillip had seen action in the Seven Years' War and at Havana.[5] He also farmed successfully in Hampshire between bouts of active service, though this experience did not prepare him for the new conditions in the colony he was to establish. He commenced his complex and unique task of founding a colony with a surprising optimism and charity that seemed misplaced, considering his new charges were mostly habitual metropolitan criminals who preferred robbery and theft as a way of life.

Phillip spent the time between October 1786 and May 1787 preparing for the voyage and the establishment of the settlement. He penned his thoughts on the future direction of the settlement, wherein he imagined a robust civil society forming out of the Empire's criminal outcasts. His gift for level-headedness and sound administration can be appreciated in his dispatches.[6] He did not, however, provide for basic necessities, such as needles and threads to mend clothing, nor cutlery for the felons – hardly an inducement to reformation and manners. Yet, despite these oversights, he was a man of sympathy and humanity, unlike his deputy, Lieutenant Governor and Vice Admiralty Court Judge Major Robert Ross, who described New South Wales' felons as 'the outcast of God's works'.[7]

The First Fleet left Plymouth on 13 May 1787 for close to a nine-month journey.[8] Like other felons embarking into this unknown, Mary on board the *Charlotte* must have wept bitter tears of sorrow and fear as she lost sight of land and the fleet headed for the Azores – on their way to live among cannibals and monsters for all she knew. It would have been natural for her to assume she would never see her homeland or family again. She might die on the voyage from scurvy, or perish in a tempest, or languish in the new colony. Like most of the women felons, she was young, robust and healthy, a potential founder of new lines of residents in the penal colony, not that such thoughts of lineages, re-establishment and hope could have been much in their minds as they left behind all that was familiar.

Once underway on their journey, the convicts sought any comfort they could. Naval and civil officers decried the conduct of many of the convicts, particularly their sexual licentiousness, drunkenness and gambling, and sermons by the chaplain, the Reverend Richard Johnson, about penitence, reformation, the atonement of sins past and present and the perils of bad behaviour, were not heeded. This is hardly surprising given the character of the felons and the soldiers sent to guard them. Life on the transport ships was bleak and brutal; any pleasure that could be found could be seen as a small reward for life's precariousness and inequities.

Because of incomplete records, Mary Broad's name does not appear on Captain Arthur Phillip's list of transportees.[9] Her first official appearance in the New South Wales chapter of her life came when Surgeon John White, now remembered for his extraordinary zoological and floral depictions of the Antipodes, noted that 'Mary Broad, a convict, delivered of a fine girl at sea'.[10] The baby was named Charlotte, presumably in honour of the vessel on which they sailed, and given the surname Spence. There was a seaman on board named Spence, but he is undoubtedly not the father, as Mary would have been pregnant when she left Plymouth. Charlotte was baptised by the Reverend Johnson on 13 November 1787. If some officers despaired of these 'damned whores',[11] Mary was presumably not one of them. She was pregnant and then had the responsibility of tending to her new baby.

During the nine-month voyage to the new penal settlement, Broad met several other felons with whom her fate would be later entangled. Her future husband, William Bryant, a Cornish fisherman convicted of smuggling at the Launceston Assizes in March 1784, was originally sentenced to seven years' transportation to the American colonies. When the American War of Independence curtailed this outlet for the criminals of England, Bryant was sent to

Botany Bay. Mary and William shared a lot in common as Celtic Cornish people from maritime villages. Their life experiences were very different from the majority of the convicts who came from large, overcrowded urban centres, such as London. Mary also met James Martin, an Irishman who stole from his employer Viscount Courtney; and James Cox, given a life sentence and exile through transportation, although the records do not reveal his crime.[12]

On board the *Charlotte*, Mary Broad also met Captain Lieutenant Watkin Tench, a veteran of the American War of Independence in which he was a prisoner of war of the American colonists for three months. His insightful and well-written *A Complete Account of the Settlement at Pt. Jackson in New South Wales* (1793) later brought the rigours of establishing a penal settlement in a hot, alien world sharply to life for readers on the other side of the world. His earlier volume, *A Narrative of the Expedition to Botany Bay* (1789), described the voyage of the First Fleet. A keen ethnographer and naturalist, Tench recorded his observations of the new world and the new arrivals with humanity rare among naval and military officers of the day. Later, he was the only senior officer who wrote kindly of Mary and William Bryant after their escape.

Among the people who disembarked at Sydney Cove in January 1788 were: 548 male and 188 female convicts, along with the civil and naval officers and their family members. There were nineteen officers, eight drummers, twenty NCOs, 160 privates, twenty-seven wives and thirty-seven children.[13] Arriving in the heat and glare of summer, we can assume Mary looked out from the *Charlotte* with deep apprehension; all she would have been able to see was wilderness, without a house, church or horse. Her only security lay in the familiarity of William Bryant's similar life experience. Indeed, Broad and Bryant married less than three weeks later in a mass ceremony with nine other couples, without the reading of banns – customary in the Church of England as a prelude to the ceremony of marriage – on 10 February 1788, conducted by the Reverend Johnson. Married felons received more privileges than single felons, such as their own hut with a garden rather than living in mass camps with no privacy and no degree of comfort, and these privileges may have been William Bryant's motive for undertaking a formal union.

In the new penal colony, the young couple was perhaps the most privileged of all the felons. William must have been well educated for his humble origins, for he signed his marriage certificate in a clear and confident hand. As a skilled sailor and fisherman he was placed in charge of the boats used for fishing to supplement the inadequate and mouldy rations brought from England and the Cape of Good Hope. Judge Advocate David Collins wrote in his book *An Account of the English Colony in New South Wales* (1798) that:

> From his having been bred for from youth
> to the business of a fisherman in the western
> part of England, William Bryant was given the
> management and direction of such boats as were
> employed in fishing; every encouragement was held
> out to keep him above temptation; a hut was built
> for him and his family; he was always presented
> with a certain part of the fish which he caught ...

Mary kept busy with her baby and tending to her garden, a difficult undertaking in the hot and unfamiliar environment, but with a husband, she had some protection, unlike most of the convict women who were eagerly sought out by predatory men, both felons and the military.

But within two years William Bryant had abused the trust bestowed on him: he was caught trading some of the catch bound for the public store in exchange for liquor. His punishment was severe – 100 lashes and the loss of his hut and private garden. Mary and Charlotte thereby lost their privileged positions and extra fresh food. Collins again depicted the scene:

> As, notwithstanding his villainy, he was too useful a
> person to part with and send to a brickcart, he was
> still retained to fish for the settlement; but a very
> vigilant eye was kept on him and such steps taken
> as appeared likely to prevent him from repeating
> his offence, if the sense of shame and fear of
> punishment were not of themselves sufficient to
> deter him.[14]

For Mary, William's punishment was harsh and humiliating. Her husband had risked all the family's comfort and necessities for his own pleasure in a drink of rum. Her feelings of anger and resentment must have been great during this period.

Meanwhile the early years of the colony progressed precariously in the extreme. The *Sirius* brought provisions from the Cape of Good Hope in May 1789. The following year it was lost at sea.[15] Another supply ship, the *Guardian*, was lost also when it struck an iceberg in December 1789. Phillip was forced to cut the already lean rations as of November 1789. Tench noted that the struggling farms that had been established were hit by drought, describing them as 'in a wretched condition'.[16] Along with others in the colony, Mary must have wondered where the next meal was coming from. As starvation loomed, all the officers and even the chaplain were forced to go out fishing at night.[17] Amidst all this deprivation, Mary Bryant gave birth to a son, Emanuel, who was baptised by the Reverend Johnson on 4 April 1790.[18] Several weeks later the *Supply* sailed for Batavia (as Jakarta was then known) in the Dutch East Indies for food, and in June the *Justinian* arrived with provisions, unappetising as they were. The prospect of starvation was staved off for the present but could not have been far from everyone's mind for the future.

On 18 October 1790 the *Supply* returned to Sydney with provisions, and later in December the 350-ton Dutch vessel, the *Waaksamheyd*, under the command of Detmer Smit, hired by one of the NSW officers, a Captain Bell, arrived loaded with pork, beef, flour, rice and sugar. Smit was later recompensed with £100 from the English Treasury.[19]

Smit's arrival also provided an opportunity for escape for Mary and William Bryant. Judge Advocate David Collins, a man far less charitable in his judgments of human frailty than Tench or Phillip, recorded:

Bryant ... was overheard consulting in his hut, after dark, with five other convicts, on the practicality of carrying off the boat in which he was employed [in late February 1791]. The circumstances being

> reported to the Governor, it was determined that
> all his proceedings should be narrowly watched,
> and any scheme of that nature counteracted.[20]

What Collins and Phillip did not know was that William Bryant had obtained a compass, quadrant and nautical charts from Smit, along with two muskets and ammunition.

According to Collins, Bryant's escape was delayed by an accident when he was caught in a squall with the fishing catch and his fishing boat – and prospective escape – swamped, with the boat needing some repair. Interestingly, Charles Currey notes that Bennelong's sister and her three children were on board, perhaps helping with the fishing.[21]

We may speculate why a far more vigilant eye was not kept on William and Mary Bryant. We may also wonder why William Bryant wished to flee. His seven-year sentence was completed and he could return to England if he had the fare, though he would have had to wait until Mary finished her sentence in 1794 – regulations prevented jailers or their charges from abandoning legal wives and legitimate children. He may have been influenced by reports of Captain William Bligh's successful trip to Timor in an open boat after the *Bounty* mutiny. Detmer Smit may also have encouraged him in some way.

Even more interesting is to consider Mary's motives. William had already betrayed the trust placed in him and jeopardised the comfort and security of her family. Yet she bound her fate with his in the desperate undertaking of rowing to Batavia, thousands of kilometres away. Additionally she risked the lives of her two small children in this hazardous bid. Her faith in his nautical and navigational skills, along with her own, must have overcome any hesitation that this would destroy them all. But perhaps it was she who was the driving force behind the escape. After all, no one could be certain how long the supplies of food and clothing would last in the fledgling colony.

On 28 March 1791 the *Waaksamheyd* set sail for England, arriving in April 1792. That night, with *Waaksamheyd* gone and the *Supply* en route to Norfolk Island, and therefore no ships in the harbour, the party of eleven escapees departed under a moonless sky at 11pm in the Governor's six-oared open boat on which William Bryant had been working. One of the sailors in the settlement, John Eastey, left an account of the remarkable event in his diary, and perhaps provides a bit of an answer as to why the party risked all. He wrote:

> Between the hours of 9 and 12 it was supposed that they intended for Bativee but having no vessel in the harbour there was no Persuing them so thay got clear of but its a very Desparate attempt to go in an open Boat for a run of about 16 or 17 hundred Leags and in pertucular for a woman and 2 Small Children the oldest not above 3 years of age but the thought of Liberty from Such a place as this Enoufh to induce any Convicts to try all Skeemes to obtain it as thay are in the same as Slaves all the time that thay are in this Country ...[22]

Tench, Collins and the Governor also recorded the escape. Sergeant James Scott noted in his journal that a party raised the alarm at 6am the next morning.[23]

Nine adults and two children escaped in the flimsy, uncovered craft. Each adult brought valuable skills to the enterprise. As Watkin Tench noted, William Bryant was an excellent sailor in charge of the vessel he stole. William Morton was a skilled navigator; James Martin, William Allen, John Butcher (aka Samuel Broom), James Cox, Nathaniel Lilley and John Simms (aka Samuel Bird) were experienced sailors. As a mariner's daughter, Mary was an experienced and proficient sailor. Tench also noted that Mary Bryant had gathered provisions and extra clothing for the voyage. In 1926 Ralph Isham found in the records of James Boswell a curious artefact labelled 'Leaves from Botany Bay used as Tea'. This was the only memento that Mary Bryant gave to her generous benefactor.[24] Undoubtedly it was the sole souvenir, if we could call it such, from her whole ordeal. The so-called 'sweet-tea' or 'sarsaparilla', *Smilax glyciphylla*, is a member of the eucalyptus family, used by the Eora people as a medicinal. Tench observed that '[t]o its virtues the healthy state of soldiery and convicts may be greatly attributed. It was drunk universally as "sweet-tea".'

The trip to the Dutch settlement at Koepang in Timor, a distance of 5240 kilometres, was a feat of navigational skill matching that of William Bligh. What is astounding is that the escapees were not trained naval officers like Bligh, who later expressed his admiration at their achievement.[25] With two small children aboard, and no sails for protection from the tropical sun and torrential rain, the voyage is even more extraordinary. Mary Bryant recounted her tale of endurance and suffering to the journalist who set down her story in the *London Chronicle* of 30 June–3 July 1792:

'During the first weeks of the voyage they had continual rain, and being obliged, in order to lighten the boat, to throw overboard all their wearing apparel. Etc, were for that time continually wet. They were once eight days out of sight of land.'

The rations Mary had so carefully garnered at great peril to her own safety in the penal colony were now ruined and inedible. For the other escapees, the children, who cried constantly in fear, driven by intense hunger and thirst, were excess baggage. Did thoughts of throwing them overboard ever surface? Yet all knew it was William's procurement of the vessel and the navigational instruments, and Mary's provision of the food, that had allowed them to undertake this hazardous enterprise in the first place.

They were kept from starvation by eating turtles and their eggs and calling into land at various places for water and whatever food they could obtain. Off Cape York they were attacked by Indigenous warriors and pursued by canoes filled with thirty to forty angry men. They survived one attack by firing their muskets. The narrative in the *London Chronicle* revealed they were 'much distressed for food and water … expecting every moment to go to the bottom'. While Bligh praised William Bryant who '… must have been a determined and enterprising man', he acknowledged that Mary and the children '… bore their sufferings with more fortitude than most among them'.[26]

William Bligh and his loyal *Bounty* seamen had found refuge at the Dutch settlement of Koepang two years before the escapees arrived. When Mary and her companions arrived, the decrepit and destitute band of convicts portrayed themselves as survivors of a whaling shipwreck, though the presence of a woman and two children should have raised some suspicions that this was not true. The Provincial Governor, Timotheus Wanjon, gave them hospitality, accommodation, and secured work for some of the men. James Martin stated that:

> We remained very happy in our work [in Timor]
> for two months till Wm Bryant had words with his
> wife, went and informed against himself, wife,
> children and the rest of us ... We was immediately
> taken prisoner and was put [in irons] in the
> castle ...[27]

What could explain this action? C. H. Currey, one of Mary Bryant's more reliable biographers, mentions William Bryant as never having seen the marriage as binding because no banns were read. Moreover, Charlotte was not his biological daughter. But he also quotes Watkin Tench's suggestion that one of them gave the party away when drunk.[28] For Mary, she had risked her children's safety and wellbeing on a journey of unimaginable horror and privation, only to be betrayed at the distant Dutch settlement.

On 7 September 1791, Captain Edward Edwards arrived in Koepang with some survivors of the *Pandora* wrecked off the Great Barrier Reef, along with a party of *Bounty* mutineers he had arrested in Tahiti. He added the convict escapees to his human cargo on 5 October, all to be dispatched to England for due process of the law. His memoirs cover these momentous events and provide some estimation of the fate of the convict escapees: [29]

William Allen, John Butcher, Nath'l Lilley, James Martin and Mary Bryant were transported to HMS *Gorgon* at the Cape of Good Hope in March 1792; William Morton died on Board Dutch East India Com'y's ship, *Hornway*; William Bryant, died 22 December 1791, hosp'l, Batavia; James Cox (fell overboard), Straits of Sunda; John Simms, died on board the Dutch East India Comp'y's ship, *Hornway*; Emanuel Bryant, died 1 December 1791, Batavia; Charlotte Bryant, died 5 May 1792 on board HMS ship, *Gorgon* (children of the above Wm and Mary Bryant).[30]

Mary Bryant lost her two children and her husband all within six months following the most gruelling deprivations of the journey to Timor. She must have reflected on the comparative safety of the convict settlement at Port Jackson. She had risked and lost everything – her liberty, her family, and her carefully won independence. All that faced her now, in her sorrow and grief, was further incarceration or possible execution. The account of her travails in the Irish and London newspapers only hinted at her suffering and despair. The report in the *Dublin Chronicle* of 4 June 1793 did not mention that her two children died, though her entry in the Newgate Prison records has her as a widow but not that she had lost her children. Written in the language of bureaucracy, her tragic personal story was hidden.

Newgate Prison, where she was sent on arrival in England, housed a series of famous felons including Jack Shepherd, Dick Turpin and Casanova, who described his surroundings there as 'an abode of misery and despair, a Hell such as Dante might have conceived'. Lawyer James Boswell earlier in the 1760s felt Newgate 'hanging upon my mind like a black cloud'.[31] Yet the escapees from Botany Bay '… thought this prison was a paradise, compared to the dreadful suffering they endured on the voyage [to Timor]'.[32]

Built originally during the reigns of King Stephen and Henry II, and situated on Newgate Street near the Old Bailey in the western part of the old city of London, Newgate housed prisoners, those awaiting execution, debtors, and the mentally ill. In the late eighteenth century there were over 200 capital offences, ranging from treason to murder and even impersonating an Egyptian. Children over the age of twelve could be executed. As late as 1772 the decapitated heads of two Jacobites (executed in 1746) fell off their spikes in public view at Temple Bar, near today's modern barristers' chambers. Tyburn, the site of public executions by hanging, was situated on Edgeware Road, where Marble Arch stands now. Some fifty public hangings occurred there every year in the 1770s. Boswell was addicted to the spectacle of the public execution with all its ritual, solemnity and horror. 'I had a sort of horrid eagerness to be there,' he admitted. His friendship with Richard Ackerman, the Keeper of Newgate, allowed him to watch many private executions conducted there from December 1783. Considering his fascination with death and the spectacle of execution, Boswell's later assistance towards Mary Bryant is both commendable and inexplicable.[33]

The first clue to historians concerning Boswell's interest in Mary Bryant was detected in a letter written by James Boswell to his brother David in November 1793:

> Be so good as to give Mrs. Bruce five pounds more
> and Betsy a guinea, and put into banking shop of
> Mr. Devaynes and Co. five pounds from you to
> the account of the Rev. Mr. Baron at Lostwithiel,
> Cornwall, and write to him you have done so. He
> has taken charge of paying the gratuity of Mary
> Broad.[34]

Mrs Bruce was Boswell's housekeeper and Betsy his daughter; but who was this mysterious Mary Broad? When Professor Chauncey Tinker of Yale University began his edition of Boswell's letters in 1922, he had no idea who she was and what her relationship with Boswell involved. The substantial collection of Boswell's records had not yet been retrieved from Lord Talbot at Malahide Castle in Dublin where they were stored. These were later obtained by the suave Anglo-American Ralph Isham in 1927 and purchased by Yale University in 1929.[35] When the papers were examined and catalogued, the mystery that had puzzled Tinker was solved. In his journals Boswell revealed his charity and beneficence towards Mary Bryant, whom he referred to by her birth name: Mary Broad. He also acted for her surviving co-defendants who had suffered the traumas of escape from Botany Bay to Timor.

Unlike William Bligh, who endured a comparable feat of navigation and deprivation on a voyage to Timor under challenging circumstances after the mutiny of the *Bounty*, Mary Bryant was illiterate and therefore unable to adequately present her case. She signed her marriage licence to William Bryant in February 1788 with an X. Bligh, on the other hand, was a prolific author and memorialist of his achievements and sorrows. James Boswell recorded in his diary entry of 12 October 1793 that 'I went to see her [Mary Broad] in the forenoon and wrote two sheets of paper of her curious account of her escape from Botany Bay.'[36] Unfortunately for later researchers, Mary's account in her own words was not found among Boswell's disordered manuscripts, journals and papers. The original report in the *London Chronicle* of 30 June–3 July 1792, where her case came to public attention, did not directly quote the survivors of the escape from Botany Bay and contained some inaccuracies.

Boswell wrote to his former college acquaintance George Dundas, the Secretary of State, about the 'adventurers from New South Wales, for whom I interest myself'. By using the term 'adventurer' Boswell began the process of romanticising Mary and her fellow escapees, though the term is a little jaunty for what they endured. The notorious highway robber and seafaring escapee was a free spirit in this scenario. He also approached Under Secretary of State Evan Nepean and the Chief Clerk, Mr Pollock.[37]

On 7 July 1792 Mary Bryant, James Martin, William Allen, John Butcher and Nathaniel Lilley went on trial at the Old Bailey and were ordered to complete their sentences. This was a particularly lenient punishment and no doubt owed much to Boswell's interventions on their behalf. As Nepean wrote to Boswell, 'Government would not treat them with harshness but at the same time would not do a kind thing to them, as they give encouragement to other escapees.'[38] Governor Phillip expressed similar concerns.[39]

There is a gap in Boswell's journal in early 1793, and researchers cannot track exactly what happened to Mary

Bryant in Newgate. On 2 May 1793 Mary was given an unconditional pardon and settled in Little Titchfield Street between Great Portland Street and the less salubrious Tottenham Court Road in London, where the School of Law for the University of Westminster is now located. This was a pleasant area near Cavendish Square and both a spatial and symbolic distance from the St Giles' area near Oxford Street and the vice-ridden Rookeries where Mary might have found herself but for her benefactor. Boswell arranged and paid for her accommodation and found work for her as a cook to Mr Morgan in Charlotte Street, Bedford Square. As Mary, after her ordeals, found the work difficult, he arranged an annuity for her of £10 per annum 'as long as she behaved well, being resolved to make it up to her myself in so far as subscription should fail ...'[40] Boswell went to considerable trouble to reunite Mary with her sister Dolly, who was working as a domestic servant in a grand house in London. He showed an immense concern for her emotional wellbeing, confiding in his diary: 'I had a suspicion he [Mr Castel who knew Dolly Broad] might be an impostor ... It appeared he really did know her relations [in Cornwall] ... I cautioned Mary not to put any trust in anything he said until he had brought her sister. I sauntered restlessly ...' This said Castel alleged Mary's father, William Broad, had come into a great inheritance and this knowledge made Boswell protective and suspicious in case of fraud.[41] Mary's legacy may not have been a large sum to Boswell, but to someone of the Broad family's social rank even £200 would seem a great fortune. Mary was duly appreciative of all Boswell had done so unstintingly on her behalf, telling him, 'if she got a share [of the legacy] she would reward me for all my trouble'.

On 2 November 1793 the remaining escapees were
freed by proclamation, due largely to Boswell's strenuous
representations on their behalf. William Allen served on
a warship against Napoleon; Nathaniel Lilley returned
to work in London as a weaver; John Butcher joined the
New South Wales Corps and received a land grant at
Parramatta.[42] Mary Bryant's last correspondence with her
benefactor, the Laird of Auchinleck, occurred in November
1794 acknowledging the receipt of her allowance.
Boswell died the following May. Mary may have later
married her childhood sweetheart, Richard Thomas, at
St Bartholomew's Church at Lostwithiel.[43] A couple with
those names married in 1805 when Mary Bryant would
have been forty years of age and have lived in the area
for some twelve years. The vicar in this village parish was
the Reverend Mr Baron to whom Boswell entrusted the
dispersal of her gratuity.

Few convicts were inclined or had the navigational skill
to attempt such a hazardous undertaking as the Bryants
and their fellow escapees did. Thomas Watling, the
Scottish forger and artist briefly escaped en route to Port
Jackson at Cape Town in 1791 but this was within an
urban environment, hardly a difficult feat.[44] In November
1794 Molly Morgan escaped from Port Jackson on the
store ship *Resolution* and got back to England. She next
came to official attention when she was arrested for theft
and resentenced to transportation in October 1803. Unlike
Mary Bryant, Morgan became a wealthy landholder in

Maitland.[45] The most spectacular escape, apart from Mary Bryant's, occurred among the Fenian political prisoners held in Western Australia in 1868. One of them, John O'Reilly, escaped on an American whaler, going first to Liverpool and then immigrating to Boston where he became a noted newspaper editor. His novel about his experiences as a convict escapee, *Moondyne* (1879), is perhaps too florid for modern tastes.[46] But none of these escapees enjoys the enduring notoriety of Mary Bryant.

CHAPTER 2

Mary Cockerill
(C1800–1819)

Walyer
(C1810–1831)

One daring outlaw and bushranger, and one frontier warrior.

Frontiers are deadly places with no rules or terms of engagement, but a complexity and flexibility that are at once profoundly unsettling and liberating. As two societies first encounter each other, the possibilities of mutual respect, wonder and accommodation, alongside negotiation, domination and violent struggle, are all present. Australian history has many stories about how Indigenous men and the invading British followed complicated paths of uncertainty, fear and aggression. In this narrative, women are often shadowy, hidden figures or the victims of male combat for supremacy over territory, resources and, ultimately, survival. Several Indigenous women in Van Diemen's Land in the years 1814 to 1831 defied these stereotypes of passivity, assuming new roles as bushranger, outlaw and warrior.

'Black Mary', as Mary Cockerill was often called in historical records, is a romantic figure of passionate loyalty, revenge and defiance, a young woman possessing remarkable intelligence, ingenuity and bush skills. Convict Thomas Worrall, in his contribution to *The Military Sketch-book* (1827), provided an image of Mary gained from an encounter in the 1810s that has been hard for later researchers to counteract:

> We could hear the fellows [bushrangers] through
> the bushes, cursing, swearing and laughing. Some
> were cooking pieces of mutton, others lolling
> on the grass, smoking and drinking, a pretty,
> interesting-looking native girl sat playing with
> the long and bushy ringlets of a stout and wicked-
> looking man seated by her ... Her dress was neither
> Native nor European, but a very pretty sort of
> costume made of skins, feathers and white calico.[1]

Worrall could not have met Mary in the Tasmanian bush, as claimed, as she was captured in April 1817 and he only arrived in Hobart Town in October 1817.[2] We do know she was a notorious bushranger, the lover of Michael Howe, Van Diemen's Land's most famous early bushranger, the self-styled 'gentleman forester', and that, some time after Howe shot her when they were ambushed, Mary led the army to his hiding place deep in the forests of the Shannon River. Although one part of Worrall's account is inaccurate, he was with the party that captured and killed Howe.

We do not know Mary's real name, nor where or when she was born. There was no drawing made of her in her lifetime, or other images, as she lived before photography was invented. Mary most likely was a member of the Mouheneener band who lived near the Derwent River and Hobart in the southern areas of Van Diemen's Land, as Tasmania was called until 1855. She was born in the late eighteenth century, the latest probable date being 1800. Marcus Clarke, in his celebrated book *Old Tales of a Young Country* (1871), thought Mary was seventeen in 1817.[3] Written records about her adopted family, the Cockerells, are easier to locate. Their name also appeared in the 1818 muster (or census) spelled 'Cockerill'.[4] They were among the first white settlers who came to this outpost of the British Empire in 1804. Londoners by birth, William Cockerell and Mary Crisp were married in May 1787 at St Martin's in the Field Church. They decided to try their luck in the new settlement of Port Phillip in 1803, accompanied by their three children, Ann, William and Arabella, and niece, Sophia Chivers. Setting sail from Portsmouth on the *Ocean* in early 1803, the family was full of hope that this dangerous adventure would reap them good fortune and prosperity.

Port Phillip was a disastrous experiment plagued by too few resources. Undeterred by the enormity of the tasks faced by the original colonisers, the Cockerells again joined the fleet of the *Ocean*, *Lady Nelson* and *Calcutta*, carrying the first batch of felons from England to the new settlement at Hobart Town. On 29 February 1804 the passengers, both free and in chains, left the vessels to start a new endeavour in Van Diemen's Land.[5] The Cockerells were granted 100 acres (40 hectares) at Stainsforth Cove (now New Town), on the western bank of the Derwent River.[6] For the Indigenous people of the island, isolated for thousands of years from the mainland, this was to prove the beginning of horror and near total destruction.

Initially, relations between the incomers and the traditional owners were amicable. In the 1860s the historian James Bonwick interviewed Salome Pitt, who as a child had been a neighbour of the Cockerells and their adopted daughter, Mary Cockerill. Salome recalled that she and her brother had tried to walk to Mount Wellington and, getting lost, were rescued by the Mouheneener, who treated them kindly and returned them to their home. She also visited their camp sites and played with the children there. British boys were often taken out hunting with the Mouheneener men, or 'the dark skins', as Pitt called them.[7] Mary was undoubtedly one of the children informally adopted into a white family. Like other dependent relatives of the time, she was expected to work for her keep. As the Cockerell children were no longer infants she would not have worked as their nursemaid but as a domestic. We know that she spoke excellent English, as her deposition in 1817 about her experiences as an outlaw was told in sound grammatical English. This would indicate she learned the language as a small child, a time that coincided with the arrival of the Cockerells.

Mary's life changed forever in late 1812 or early 1813 when she saw the handsome convict Michael Howe (1787–1818), who was assigned to John Ingle, a rapacious and rough wealthy merchant who had arrived with Lieutenant Governor David Collins in 1804.[8] Howe had been a deserter in both the British navy and army, though he was transported for highway robbery in 1812 from the York Assizes. Unrepentant in exile, Howe told Ingle 'he would be no man's slave' and promptly absconded.[9] Howe began a career as a robber and burglar, attacking the house of Richard Pitt, the Chief Police Constable of New Town and Salome's father. Mary first saw this handsome, proud man who called himself 'the Governor of the Ranges' when she was a child.[10] She most certainly saw him when he was employed by John Ingle as she lived nearby.[11] She did not, however, elope with him until late 1814 or early 1815.[12] This suggests that they had regular contact in the intervening couple of years. Presumably Mary had resisted returning to the Mouheneener for marriage, as would be expected in traditional Pallawah society, where the girls wed young, although such a marriage would not be consummated until the girl matured. It would also seem that Mary's defiant and headstrong ways were firmly established by the time she was thirteen.

In 1813 Howe absconded from his assignment, originally joining the Whitehead gang of twenty-nine army deserters and runaway felons at large around Hobart. He saw Dick Turpin as his hero and was described by the colonial historian J. E. Calder in 1873 as 'one of Byron's ruffian heroes'.[13] Though uneducated he had a 'taste for ceremony' and fine words, with a revolutionary turn of phrase. He 'borrowed' a dictionary from the farmhouse of Lieutenant Governor Thomas Davey, promising to return it.[14] Howe loved words, and the Old Testament in the King James Version of the Bible was a constant companion on his travels and adventures. It is no wonder that a beautiful, high-spirited young woman like Mary Cockerill found him irresistible. Howe was charismatic, charming when needed, quick-witted and audacious. These qualities mirrored

Mary's own: she was articulate, brave and resolute, which, along with her personal beauty and physical stamina, made her an ideal partner for a bushranger.

The nature of bushranging in this period of Tasmanian history needs some explanation. The settlement was largely lawless, with the army hard pressed to maintain any sort of order. At first it was not conflict with the Indigenous people that made the society unstable but the presence of so many convict 'absenters' who became bushrangers.[15] The convict settlement was poorly provisioned, so from soon after the outset of British occupation in 1804, convicts and soldiers alike were armed with muskets and dogs and allowed to hunt kangaroos. A good hunting dog was a prized possession. The Reverend Robert Knopwood, the Anglican priest and magistrate of the convict settlement, offered a £10 reward, the equivalent of an English labourer's annual wage, in return for his bitch, Miss, who had been stolen by bushrangers.[16] By 1806 kangaroos were in short supply around Hobart Town and the New Norfolk area. The traditional owners, without dingoes to assist in hunting, had been careful harvesters of game, so the depletion of kangaroos and the superior weapons of the new arrivals meant far more conflict between the invaders and the Pallawah. It also meant that the British ventured further north into the island looking for game themselves.

'Bushranging' at first meant searching or ranging for food, often to sell. Indeed, the early bushrangers frequently saw themselves as canny traders rather than thieves and outlaws. When he robbed her family farm, Howe told one Mrs McCarty that 'we are bushrangers and freebooters, but not thieves'. A police magistrate in October 1814 reported to Lieutenant Governor Thomas Davey that the Howe gang '… were consummate bushmen, they dressed completely in kangaroo skins from cap to moccasin; they jokingly called themselves gentlemen foresters'. (The Pallawah also wore beautiful kangaroo capes to protect themselves against the cold winds from Antarctica.)[17]

These references to the English rural tradition of protest and resistance, like that of Robin Hood, were reinforced by the Howe gang's deployment of blackface, like protesters of England and Wales a century before. The *Waltham Black Act* (1722) specifically outlawed the practice with heavy penalties for any infringements. Blacking of the face in disguise was employed by the early convict bolters as early as 1807.[18] This deployment of potent symbols is not surprising; England was undergoing enormous transition with displacement and poverty caused by the Industrial Revolution as well as the prolonged wars with France and her allies. Many of the convicts, like Howe, exiled to the antipodean colonies were the direct casualties of these two massive social and economic dislocations.

Howe took this traditional symbol and gave it new meaning. He had enormous admiration for the Indigenous people, appreciating their bushcraft and ability to thrive in an often unforgiving environment. He meted out harsh punishment to anyone in his gang who mistreated the local people.[19] Howe was not alone in these alliances and attitudes. Sealer James Kelly in the north-east region reached an understanding with Indigenous leader Tolokunganah and his band, though this may have been to the detriment of the Indigenous man's kinswomen who were frequently traded to white men.[20] Bushranger

Archibald Campbell made a home with his Indigenous wife and lived amicably with her kin.[21] Mary Cockerill's relationship with Howe, when considered in this context, is not so unusual; what marks it as extraordinary is her role as an armed and active bushranger, not just as a helpmeet and supporter.

Many settlers, whether former felons themselves or people employing former convicts, attempted to stay on amicable terms with the marauding bushrangers. Unlike later bushrangers, these gangs travelled on foot, as horses were a rarity in the early days of colonisation on the remote island. Military detachments were foot soldiers as well, thus, knowledge of the land and how to survive in it was a prerequisite for successful bushranging. Despite the hardships, the outlaw life on the island flourished. The difficulty of policing and cost of conducting trials in Sydney proved prohibitive for the tiny administration and defeated enforcement of the law.[22] By May 1814, the island was so infested with outlaws and absconders that Lieutenant Governor Davey was forced to issue an amnesty against their depredations.[23] Many of Whitehead's former gang took advantage of this amnesty and returned to Hobart Town. Michael Howe, however, wrote to Lieutenant Governor Davey detailing the specific terms of his amnesty. The letter was forwarded to Governor Macquarie who promised to dispatch it to the Secretary of State for the Colonies in London. Unfortunately, this bizarre document, written in kangaroo blood, has not been located.[24] There is no doubting Macquarie's word, for he acted with a degree of humanity and judiciousness unusual in colonial management.

With his demands as yet unmet, Howe continued his marauding, taking over the leadership of what remained of the gang and acting as its master strategist. He robbed homes in Hobart Town, attacking the home of the Cockerells' neighbour Richard Pitt, where he stole a book which was found in his kangaroo knapsack after his death. Called 'the Captain' by other members, Howe organised the gang with military precision, attempting to impose the discipline required by war. To inculcate moral virtue among his fellow outlaws he regularly read from the scriptures.[25]

Emboldened by his successes, Howe sent a challenge, again written in kangaroo blood, through the agency of the Reverend Knopwood to Lieutenant Governor Davey on 30 August 1814, reminding him that his troupe consisted of former soldiers who had seen active service in war, adding '… were we As Much Inclined to take Life As you Are … We could Destroy All the Partyes you can send out …'[26]

His fame spread, spoken of in whispers in the homes of the free settlers. No doubt Mary listened to the fears and anxieties expressed by the Cockerells, smiling secretly to herself as she thought about her own relationship with this audacious man. Howe had undoubtedly risked capture by visiting Mary on many occasions in 1813 and 1814. We do not know when Mary left the Cockerells, but presumably, given that the documents say she cohabited with Howe, she had left by the end of 1814. Despite the considerable age and cultural differences, Mary and Howe formed a strong alliance.

Howe's attacks on property, like the one against Police Magistrate Adolarias Humphrey at Pittwater on 24 April

1815 and on settlers at New Norfolk, became more daring. The 24 April attack is the first time the records mentioned 'a black native girl called Mary with whom Howe cohabited'. Mary took part in the attack on a Carlisle property in New Norfolk and the murder of Richard Carlisle, after the Pittwater robbery.[27]

The gang, including Mary, robbed Richard Pitt again in July 1816, taking his valuable hunting dogs, two muskets and ammunition.[28] This was territory that she had grown up in, and though kindly treated by her adoptive family and their neighbours, she had no hesitation in robbing and marauding her former neighbourhood. The thrill, danger and sheer audaciousness must have appealed to her wilful spirit.

Violence by the gang against settlers escalated, going from robbery with threats and burning of crops and buildings to cold-blooded murder, including that of James O'Berne, the captain of a vessel in the Derwent River.[29] The bushrangers also began roaming a wider territory, suggesting that they may have been aided by Mary's bush skills. Although she had lived with the Cockerells, it is more than likely she rejoined her band at various times, for she was an excellent bush woman and there were traditional routes and passageways that Mary must have known about from her own people or other friendly bands. Her relationship with the neighbouring Panninher, Pangeeninghe and Leenowwenne would also have assisted their progress. These 'Big River' bands kept on amicable terms with their neighbours and were the most travelled of all the Tasmanian clans.[30] Another possibility also presents itself. William James Cockerell, the son of William and

Mary Cockerell, received a grant of land in 1813 at what is now Brighton, far closer to the Shannon River area than Hobart Town. Mary may have accompanied William and his bride, Mary Ann Peck, to their new home for a visit. This would have given her a familiarity with the wider region where Howe made his headquarters.[31]

Over the summer of 1816 and 1817 several members of the gang were waylaid and killed by soldiers of the 46th Regiment disguised as civilians. Mary led the bushrangers further along the Shannon River, where they established a base camp. Thomas Wells, Private Secretary to Lieutenant Governor William Sorell (who succeeded Thomas Davey in 1817), in 1818 wrote the first book published in Australia, *Michael Howe: The Last and Worst of the Tasmanian Bushrangers*. In it he stated that the 'site was chosen in taste, in an open undulating country, stretching to the western mountains: the spot was secluded from observation; was covered by large honeysuckle and on a rise sloping to the stream'.[32] Here the bandits corralled fifty-six sheep they had stolen with other provisions, and from this hideaway they continued their assaults into the Oatland, Jericho and Norfolk regions.

In the meantime, Howe was confident that Mary's bush skills and ability to negotiate with Indigenous bands, together with his military training, made him untouchable. He wrote a series of provocative letters to Lieutenant Governor Davey identifying himself as 'Lieutenant Governor of the Woods'. Mary, in this scenario, was hardly a Maid Marion – chaste, demure and wise – rather, she was active, aggressive and daring in these joint enterprises. In September 1816, Mary, Howe and the rest of the bandits raided Davey's farm of 3000 acres (1200 hectares), taking muskets, ammunition, tea, sugar, flour, needles and thread, as well as six bottles of fine wine from the cellar.[33] Just to annoy the Lieutenant Governor even more, the gang again raided his farm on Christmas Day 1816 and forced the servants and convict workers at gunpoint to dance and drink with them. They stole blunderbusses, pistols and ammunition, tea, 12 pounds of sugar and the overseer's trousers. Leaving the farm in a state of great excitement and intoxication, and shooting off their pistols, they headed for the nearby farms of Richard Troy and James Stynes to continue their terror.

Mary and another older Indigenous woman who is not named in the records were by this time core members of the gang. We do not know when this other woman joined the gang, as initial reports identified only one Indigenous girl, and Mary would have been at this time aged fifteen or so. A document of November 1816 records earlier horrific incidents during which some members of Howe's gang cut the throats of their confreres. According to this document Mary purportedly said to the chief perpetrator, 'Hillier, you killed my sister too!'[34] The two women were close, but 'sister' in the Western sense of the word may be too restrictive. This unnamed woman who apparently died a violent death at the hands of a fellow bushranger may have been Mary's putative sister, as Pallawah kin systems were highly complex, but she was a not a leader like Mary and this may account for her anonymity in the accounts. For Mary, this scene of one man dead with his throat cut, another severely wounded, and her sister dead, must have been traumatic in the extreme. Indeed, Van Diemen's Land

society, both in its treatment of felons and conduct of the
frontier war, was deeply violent and cruel.

The detailed deposition made by John Yorke, who was
captured by the gang for a few hours on 27 November
1816, said the gang consisted of four men and two women.
They informed him they could 'set the whole country on
fire with one stick'. As mentioned, Howe conducted a
strange prayer meeting where male gang members were
made to swear oaths on the Bible. This behaviour, reflecting
the dominant evangelism of the time, sits uneasily with his
lawlessness and cruelty. Yet perhaps he took justification
from many parts of the Old Testament that stressed
violence, retribution and vengeance. Yorke believed they
had recently forced settlers to render down the fat from
the sheep they had stolen from various farms. This means
that the bandits moved the sheep a considerable distance
across the midland plains region of the island.[35] No doubt
the dogs were useful as guards, hunters and herders.

The army increased its operations to locate and arrest
the bandits. In March 1817 Mary and Howe decided to
head out on their own with their hound, Bosun. In this
desperate move, as the gang disintegrated amid rumours
that the aforementioned Hillier had slit the throat of
one of the men, the pair was more vulnerable to attack.
Surrounded by the army and convicts armed with muskets,
Mary and Howe tried to flee their pursuers. In the ensuing
melee Howe shot Mary.[36] In early documents such as
Thomas Wells' account, Mary was 'shot at by Howe ...
receiv[ing], however, little injury'. Yet Worrall's account
in *The Military Sketch-book* a decade later has her severely
wounded in the shoulder and the back. K. R. von Stieglitz

wrote Howe's official entry in the *Australian Dictionary of Biography* in 1966. In this Mary is said to have been heavily pregnant and severely wounded. This is entirely unlikely, as commentators at the time would have remarked upon her pregnancy, and the chance of surviving a gunshot wound and advanced pregnancy in 1817 was remote.

Wells and later authors were outraged with Howe, 'being hard pressed, in order to facilitate his own escape, he fired at this poor female companion, who, from fatigue was unable to keep pace with him ...'[37] Howe displayed a cruel cowardice towards his partner by leaving her wounded and at the mercy of the army to save his own skin. The treatment of bushrangers by the military was severe, and the soldiers might have raped, tortured or killed Mary, as she was an outlaw condemned in absentia for serious crimes. In June 1816 captured bushrangers were summarily executed and their bodies gibbeted on the wharf at Hobart Town. Executions and gibbeting also occurred at the Cascades where female convicts were housed.[38] It was rumoured that after his execution, the head of Whitehead, the former leader of Howe and Mary's gang, was impaled and put on public display. This had been common practice in England, though in 1746 two Jacobites supplied the last impaled heads shown at Temple Bar.

In 1871 Marcus Clarke wrote in his book that 'Mary relates that Howe was kind to her – after the manner of his sex – whenever "things went right for him"; but that if anything "crossed his temper he was like a tiger". He was very jealous of her, she says; when Edwards, one of the gang, gave her a shawl which he had stolen from Captain Tonnson, Howe pistolled him on the spot.'[39] How Clarke, writing almost sixty years after the events, could quote Mary Cockerill, remains unexplained. These words do not appear in any other records of the time though like Tasmanian colonial writers John West and Edward Curr, Clarke interviewed elderly people who remembered the events. This hint of domestic violence is consistent with Howe's cowardly, selfish behaviour in the moment of crisis when the army was upon him. He lost his valuable dogs and ammunition, but, most significantly, he lost Mary, his guide and confidante.

The *Hobart Town Gazette* of 12 April 1817, in a report on Captain Nairn's company of the 46th Regiment, stated that 'a Native Black Girl, named Mary Cockerill', having been wounded by Howe, led the soldiers deeper into the woods for 17 kilometres, where they found four huts which they promptly burned. Attempting to locate Howe and other gang members Geary and Septon, Mary now led the military search party. With her superior bush skills and knowledge of the area, she led the chase for two days until the trail weakened. But they recovered some of the sheep the gang had stolen from farmers. Mary later provided much information on the gang and its operations. This suggests she had been only slightly wounded, though her sense of outrage and betrayal at Howe's callousness spurred her on to wreak vengeance upon him.

Davey's earlier proclamation of martial law against the outlaws had not proven effective against the bushrangers, and was overruled by Governor Macquarie in Sydney. Davey's replacement, William Sorell, a man of moderate temperament and good sense, offered Howe a pardon for all his crimes bar murder, and a strong recommendation for clemency on that matter if he turned King's evidence. He also offered a considerable reward for the capture of the gang members still at large. Alone and vulnerable, Howe retreated further west. In his solitude he put to paper – made of fine kangaroo skin – his dreams and fantasies, penned in kangaroo blood. He wrote a message to his sister, alongside a list of the flowers and vegetables he wished to plant in his garden when he had done with bushranging. This expression of deep feelings and romantic longings perhaps gives us a clue as to what attracted him to Mary. Howe does not mention her in this strange and sad memoir,[40] nor does he say that he wanted to return to England, instead seeing his future in Van Diemen's Land. These writings were found when he was captured the following year.

For over a year Howe stayed on the run, forced to live in remote hideouts with no comforts or companionship. With Mary's assistance, he was captured, only to kill several of his captors. He was sent to Hobart Town, where he escaped again. On 21 October 1818, Howe was located and clubbed to death. He was decapitated and his head taken to Hobart Town where it was displayed as a moral lesson to other bushrangers.[41] Convict Thomas Worrall was pardoned for his role in Howe's capture and death.[42]

Mary Cockerill had been pardoned for her crimes as an outlaw in return for her cooperation and information. On her own request she went to Sydney, as she had no intention of rejoining any gangs. No doubt her own people did not want her to return to them, given her notorious reputation and criminal behaviour. Mary was fed, clothed and housed by the colonial authorities in Hobart Town before she left for Sydney. Once there, Governor Macquarie took a personal interest in her welfare, writing that 'I had a private decent lodging provided for her here ... and she is about to get some decent apparel ...'[43]

In Sydney Mary contracted pulmonary disease. She returned to Hobart Town and was admitted to hospital, where she died on 29 June 1819.[44] She did not record what she thought of Howe's demise and the indignity of his rotting and putrid-smelling head on public display. Mary was buried at St David's cemetery with a service conducted by the Reverend Robert Knopwood. Her burial with the full rites of the Church of England implies she was a communicant and raised in the Church.

The story of Walyer (or Tarenorerer, as she is sometimes called), a Pallawah warrior from the Plair-Leke-Liller-Plue band from Emu Bay on the north-west coast of Van Diemen's Land, reveals dramatically transformed race relations since the childhood of Mary Cockerill. Walyer was probably born around 1810, when few Europeans had ventured across the Bass Strait to live and work. Until the 1820s bushrangers were a far greater threat to stability and expansion by the pastoralists than the Pallawah.[45] In fact, Lieutenant Governor Thomas Davey had proclaimed martial law in 1816 – against the bushrangers, not the Indigenous peoples. By 1823 and 1824 this scenario had changed dramatically, with far more attacks by the Oyster Bay bands against stock keepers and pastoralists. The new Governor, William Sorell's successor, George Arthur, arrived in May 1824 after a posting in British Honduras, where he had ruled with a benign concern for the slaves. His attitudes to the Pallawah at first expressed this humanitarianism. Yet by 1826 they had hardened, as the original landholders refused to voluntarily relinquish their lands and embrace Christianity. On 26 November the Governor issued a notice allowing any settler to drive off Aboriginal 'intruders', using any degree of force. Moreover, the military could be summoned to assist in this process of dispersal and possible extermination.[46] Not altogether unsympathetic to the claims of Indigenous peoples, Arthur suggested that the north-east region, where pastoralists had not yet intruded, might be set aside as a permanent reserve. He saw this as a voluntary process whereby groups would enter the safety of the reserve of their own free will.

On 15 April 1828, the Governor divided the colony into the settled and unsettled districts, marked by the notorious Black Line. By this he meant, of course, settled by British occupation. Thus began the terrible Black War. As the violence escalated on the frontier, Arthur began to renounce his earlier moderation and declared a state of martial law on 1 November 1828. Reminiscent of the bounty parties that hunted bushrangers from 1815, military expeditions were now sent to find and destroy Aboriginal groups.[47]

This was the broad context within which Walyer operated. There were factors that exacerbated her situation. The sealers stationed in the islands of the Bass Strait frequently kidnapped women and forced them into raw and savage bondage. This process was aided by Pallawah men who caught Indigenous women from across northern coastal areas and sold them to the sealers. Walyer was one of those kidnapped and sold at a young age to work for the sealers and mutton birders. She was purchased for a few bags of flour and several dogs.[48] In 1828 she escaped from the island she was confined to and returned to the mainland of Van Diemen's Land, fired to wage war on the invaders. With her skills in using weaponry, particularly the use of firearms, she set about establishing herself as a warrior leader, teaching the men of the Emu Bay region how to use the British weapons. Walyer was the strategist of operations, directing some eight men, a boy and a woman to conduct raids against settlers. Often she called from a rise or hill, directing the manoeuvres and taunting the Europeans to come out of their huts and face spears and other weapons.

In June 1830 Walyer and her group met George Augustus Robinson, who had been commissioned by Arthur to conciliate with the Indigenous population and establish missions, as he was rounding up those Pallawah not dead or defeated. Robinson was taken aback by a woman warrior but believed that it was Walyer's aggressive raids that were causing a lot of the troubles west of the Tamar River.[49] In December 1830, Walyer was again captured by two sealers and taken to a small island in Bass Strait. She refused to work in any way for her captors, with intractable resistance. The sealers then proposed to isolate her on Penguin Island. On the way over she attempted to murder them and take control of the boat. For once the sealers were delighted to relinquish one of their captives to an emissary of Robinson.[50]

Robinson was a determined and methodical man who forced Walyer to go to the Swan Island Aboriginal

Reserve, situated on a small island between Cape Portland and George Bay on the north-east coast. On Swan Island, Walyer was disruptive to Robinson's order as soon as she alighted from the boat. He then feared she would incite rebellion and revolt, so he determined to banish her. But her experience as a leader came to the fore and she warned the other internees that the soldiers would head out of the garrison at Launceston, perhaps to kill them all as had already happened to the Oyster Bay and Midlands peoples. She taught other women how to use firearms and conduct efficient warfare, and boasted of the many whites she had raided and killed. They were no doubt astounded, as women in traditional society never assumed the role of warrior or combatant. Walyer told an amazed Robinson that she liked *lutetawin* (white men) as much as she liked the black snake. She dealt with them in the same manner – death at all times when she was able.

Strangely, Walyer did not publicly denounce the Pallawah men who had originally sold her into servitude. Perhaps she did and it was not recorded, as the rhetoric of the frontier hardened the racial lines. Although a young woman, Walyer contracted influenza and died on 5 June 1831. Her role as a warrior and resistance fighter made her a notorious, indeed feared, woman. She broke every taboo about what it meant to be a woman, black or white. No other Indigenous woman in colonial Australia took on a similar leadership role to fight and resist the invaders.

Mary Cockerill and Walyer were products of the Van
Diemen's Land frontier and both were aggressive, violent
women who embarked upon crusades. For Mary, her role
as a bushranger was entangled with her relationship with
a white charismatic rebel and outlaw. For Walyer, her
life in a frontier that had advanced and hardened in its
resolve to subdue the Pallawah was dominated by capture,
enforced slavery and servitude. Yet she too fought against
the strictures of sexual and racial confinement, becoming a
warrior and a challenge to all those who oppressed her.

CHAPTER 3

Eliza Fraser
(1798–1858)

*The shipwreck survivor dressed in her fringe of leaves whose
'rescue' from Fraser Island continues to rock race relations
in Queensland to this day.*

Eliza Fraser remains the most intriguing and notorious
woman in the Australian imagination. She has been
immortalised in Patrick White's novel *A Fringe of Leaves*;
as the crouching, naked figure, her hair falling over her
face to hide her identity in Sidney Nolan's painting; as
a disembodied head in a dark sky in artist Fiona Foley's
depictions; and as an assertive voice in Barbara Blackman's
libretto for Peter Sculthorpe's music-theatre piece *Eliza
Fraser Sings*. In 1836 she survived a mutiny on board a ship
under her husband's command and a shipwreck off the
coast of what is now Queensland. She perhaps gave birth
to a baby who died in a lifeboat, and she was reputedly
'captured' and tortured by 'cannibals' before being rescued
by 'wild white men', escaped convicts who had merged
into Indigenous societies, thus making them doubly
'savage' and vengeful. She was lionised in Sydney, the
United Kingdom and the United States and was eventually
revealed as an exaggerator, if not a liar, and reduced to
giving public accounts of her ordeal for payment. Her life
story holds no parallel for adventure and notoriety.

Eliza Fraser's version of her protracted ordeal magnifies the sensational aspects and makes it difficult to identify the central veracity of the events. She was at times courageous, resourceful, self-sacrificing, as well as manipulative, deceitful and hungry for celebrity and its attendant rewards. Even at her story's outset, the birthplace of Eliza Ann Slack is clouded in conjecture. Several versions appear in the historical records. According to one, Eliza was born in 1798 in Derbyshire in the English East Midlands, famously portrayed as the home county of Jane Austen's favourite hero, Fitzwilliam Darcy. The medieval centre of the lead-mining industry, Derbyshire was the first area to transform under the Industrial Revolution of the later decades of the eighteenth century.[1] Other sources suggest Eliza was born in the British settlement of Ceylon, now Sri Lanka. Colonised by Portuguese Jesuits in 1505, the Dutch in 1658 and the British East India Company in 1769, before recognition as a British colony in 1802, Ceylon was a beautiful, mysterious multicultural outpost of several European empires. Eliza's father may have been an officer in the British East India Company, as her birth date is consistent with the arrival of officers' families to the operation.[2] Eliza Fraser never publicly commented on her birthplace nor on her parents' origins. Rather, she kept her public pronouncements solely focused on her ordeal in the tropical hell of Great Sandy Island, now Fraser Island.

When she married Captain James Fraser at age twenty-one, he was already sickly and twenty years her senior. As an educated and articulate woman without family connections or her own money, few possibilities for independence existed for her at the end of the Napoleonic

Wars. The life of a governess, in which she would reside in an ambiguous limbo between servant and accepted member of a rigidly hierarchical household, held little attraction for the spirited, intelligent young woman. But the marriage took her to an unlikely spot for someone of her character and inclinations. Stromness, in the Orkney Islands to the north of Scotland is a bitterly cold place blasted by the winds off the North Sea. Far more Norse and Danish than Celtic or Scottish – as the islands only came to Scotland in 1468 from Denmark – Stromness would have been a difficult home for a young woman from Ceylon, accustomed to the vitality, colour and heat of the tropics. With its small dark-stoned buildings, Stromness would have been made even worse by an older ill husband and a narrow-minded, strict Calvinist community.

When James Fraser was offered the chance to captain a vessel to Hobart Town, Sydney and Singapore in 1835, Eliza begged to accompany him. Despite the responsibilities of her three children, she felt he needed her reassuring presence. The captain had damaged the *Stirling Castle* in the previous year, which came on top of the loss of the *Comet* in the Torres Strait in 1830. This voyage was his last chance at professional redemption. No doubt he was filled with reservations, for women did not accompany the crew or officers on long, perilous voyages in small sailing boats. Convincing the island's stern Presbyterian minister to take care of her children, Eliza showed her first display of talented persuasion. In her rendition of the biblical story of Ruth and Naomi, she implored the minister to heed her cry: 'Whither thou goest, I will go; and where though lodgest, I will lodge ...' What she did not pledge was the final part of the biblical pact of fidelity: 'Where thou diest, will I die …' Rather, like Job's unnamed wife, Eliza was forced to endure a journey of unimaginable travail, despair and loss.

Travelling down to London, Eliza delighted in the expensive shops in the handsome area of Mayfair around Regent and Old Bond streets. Gazing at the fashionable patrons in their finery, she felt a dowdy provincial in her bland, modest outfits appropriate for the Orkney Islands; Calvinist strictures there dictated plain garb, plain manners and a stoic demeanour.

Leaving London on 22 October 1835, the *Stirling Castle* initially made good progress to Hobart Town in far away Van Diemen's Land. The vessel brought new immigrants and manufactured goods to this distant British settlement at the edge of the known world. The boredom of so many days at sea and the even duller confined evenings were dispelled when she saw the beauty of Hobart Harbour and its brilliant light.

In Hobart Town the venture faltered. The *Stirling Castle* collided with another vessel on departure – in the eyes of the sailors an omen of disaster to come. Already they had little confidence in the sickly captain with his stomach ulcers, bad temper and erratic judgment, and they had heard rumours of his negligence on past voyages. Many of them left when the vessel reached Sydney. With the crewmen replaced, joining the captain's young nephew, midshipman John Fraser and Second Officer John Baxter, already on board, they set sail for Singapore. This should have been a calm passage, as the torrential rains and cyclones of summer off the east coast of Australia were long past, yet, on 21 May 1836, the brig was caught in a storm 500 kilometres off what is now Queensland.[3]

Eliza's report to Foster Fyans, the Superintendent of the Moreton Bay penal settlement, captured the panic of the shipwreck that ensued:

> [Captain Fraser] ... gave orders [not to abandon ship] ... the men however insisted ... some of them said if he would not come they would leave him behind, he then consented. He now ordered beef, bread and water be brought up ... some of the crew said that if he wanted it he could fetch it himself ... They became very mutinous ...[4]

Two lifeboats were launched. For Eliza in her skirts and petticoats, just to clamber into a tiny life raft was perilous. Women did not commonly wear underpants until later in the century and this would have been an embarrassment to overcome.

Without adequate food or water – though the captain took his charts and compass – the survivors headed southward to find Moreton Bay. After drifting for ten days, the mutinous crew departed in the faster lifeboat, taking with them the captain's nephew.[5] This left the Frasers with steward Joseph Corralis, first mate Charles Brown, second mate John Baxter, and the seamen Robert Darge, Henry Youlden, William Elliott, John Major, Michael Doyle, Robert Carey and Robert Dayman in the lesser vessel. The mutineers were not fortunate and only one survived.

The Frasers' lifeboat took a month to find shelter on Great Sandy Island. How anyone survived this ordeal is a miracle. It is possible that Eliza also gave birth during this time. In 1838 reporter John Curtis gave an account of the event in his book *Shipwreck of the Stirling Castle* and claimed Eliza had given birth at sea. However, in the first two narratives she gave after her rescue – including the report to Foster Fyans at Moreton Bay – she made no mention of a pregnancy or birth. The humiliation for a woman to give birth among men in such cramped conditions can be imagined, and Eliza may have felt reticent about relating news of this to men. However, in her later versions of events, related in Moreton Bay and Sydney, she did mention it to the ladies who offered their support. She could have done so and not breached decorum. We can assume the story was a fabrication in the English press and in Curtis' book, and not one of Eliza's making. Interestingly, Olga Miller, a Butchulla elder, upon recounting the stories of her family, believed that Eliza had not given birth when her ancestors cared for her back in 1836,[6] and in an account seaman Henry Youlden published about his experiences some twenty years after the events no mention of a birth and death is made.

Youlden spared no sympathy for Mrs Fraser. He portrayed her as 'a very vixen … the most profane, artful wicked woman that ever lived, coming very near in my idea of the Devil'.[7] His vitriol is directed to the 'She-Captain' in an attempt to show her as a controlling female with a desperate and ineffectual husband who should have been there to command. Youlden failed to point out that Eliza had prepared food for the fourteen-month voyage, a difficult undertaking in Stromness. She had also insisted on the trunk of food going into the lifeboat along with her two trunks of clothing and china. Eliza also took turns at bailing out water when James was too ill to take his turn. In *Shipwreck of the Stirling Castle* Curtis paints her as a devoted companion, risking her own safety for her husband's welfare.

The party first landed on some rocky islands. In one of the illustrations in Curtis' book Eliza is depicted in her dress and shoes climbing rocks in search of water (hardly the activity of a woman who had recently given birth). What it does display is the pluck and resourcefulness that Youlden so despised. Continuing southward they spied Great Sandy Island. The crew insisted on going ashore, although Captain Fraser wanted to keep sailing to Moreton Bay. He had a morbid fear of cannibals, saying 'in all probability they would be eaten ...'[8] Ironically, the only threat of cannibalism came from the British sailors: the seamen went so far as to threaten to kill and eat one of their number if he did not accede to their demands.

Landing on the northern end of Great Sandy Island with great difficulty in the high surf after a month at sea in the lifeboat, Eliza must have wondered if this was truly deliverance. Though spectacularly beautiful, there was little vegetation and sand dominated the landscape.[9] In the distance they spied some 'natives' waving spears at them. When no attack ensued, they focused on trying to mend their leaky boat, but without tools this proved impossible.

The local Butchulla clan approached the strangers with some trepidation. Could they be the return of the beings in long ships their ancestors had spoken about? Were they returning spirits of their ancestors, lost and bewildered to be on land again? Certainly they did not look like ancestors with their pale, reddened skins and strange adornments around their bodies and they already knew – from the nearby Kabi people – about strange beings with firearms that could kill or maim instantly. Offering some of their clothes for barter, Eliza was horrified to learn they merited only two mullets, and that she had virtually given away some precious protection against the sun. She had jeopardised the safety of the boat and incurred the wrath of the crew for two fish.

The landing had not yielded the safety or security the crew had hoped for, and this added substantially to the hostility among the group. Those who opposed the captain – Youlden, Dayman, Carey, Elliott and Darge – set out to walk to the Moreton Bay settlement. The power struggle between the seamen and the now enfeebled commander reached its climax when the men took the party's muskets and ammunition by force. Realising that their safety lay in numbers, the others reluctantly followed. They left at night to avoid detection and began the 100-kilometre walk down the island. With only berries and pandanus fruit to eat, they were beset by 'flux' (diarrhoea), which further weakened their already depleted bodies. Even in winter the sun along the coast of Great Sandy (Fraser) Island is hot.[10]

Eliza had endured so much indignity, pain and humiliation since leaving Hobart Town, and now she was racked with diarrhoea, sunburn and dehydration. Her pale skin was blistered and sore. Walking along the seashore, the bedraggled party was met by Butchulla warriors who confiscated their clothes and weapons. Stripped of their clothes, the bodies of these strange beings were examined by the Butchulla, who marvelled at their colour and thinness. The standards of dress for a woman of Eliza's status in 1836 were rigid and modest. Her portrait in the State Library of Queensland shows her modesty of dress, with lace cap and her shawl hiding her contours. Eliza was mortified that these wild savages not only gazed at her body but had the audacity to touch her skin, feel her hair and examine the inside of her mouth as if she was an animal. This was a deep affront to her identity as a middle-class Englishwoman. Whatever her later embellishments to her story, the destruction of her modesty on the island must have been insufferable. According to Second Officer John Baxter, Mrs Fraser was left only with 'an article of underdress after this encounter'.[11] This was presumably a light chemise or petticoat. Along with the affronts she had already suffered, the group was deprived of their blankets, making the cool winter nights even harder to bear.

Moving slowly along the coast of K'gari, as the Indigenous owners called this territory, the castaways reached Hook Point on its southernmost extremity. Here the mainland was tantalisingly close, visible but difficult to get to without a raft in the shark-infested waters. In any case, few people could swim in the 1830s. Seamen William Elliott and Michael Doyle later drowned when attempting to swim the channel to the mainland. By this time James Fraser and Charles Brown had become ill and exhausted. Strangely, Eliza became the most determined to survive the almost biblical afflictions. Whether she resorted to the lamentations of Jeremiah is not recorded, but her relative strength once again suggests that she had not recently given birth.

The Butchulla people, watching the pathetic strangers' slow progress down their lands, debated what course of action was appropriate. Clearly, if they were returning spirits they had completely forgotten how to survive even at the most elemental level. And if they were indeed these alien white beings they had heard about, they were not frightening in their power but weak and stupid. After much discussion, the Butchulla agreed to assist them. Henry Youlden and John Baxter later reported they were surprised to be offered food and water by the warriors, who seemed concerned for their welfare.[12] Their accounts of their treatment are completely different from Eliza's, who saw her time with the Butchulla as torture and hardship. Her account omitted that it was their many kindnesses that allowed her to survive.

The presence of these white beings presented a huge strain on the resources of the Butchulla. The island lacked good soil, and few fruits and berries grew in the sand. This was in contrast to the abundance on the mainland. But the territory did offer good fishing. The elders decided to divide the strangers into more manageable groups, so that a clan would be responsible for a few rather than one overwhelming group. With around seventy people in a clan and six clans on the island with prescribed territories, this was a sensible move.[13] In return, these reddened white men were expected to search for firewood and to fish.

Eliza was the odd one out in this arrangement. What should be done with a woman – this emaciated, burned wreck of a human being? When the Butchulla women conferred, they decided Eliza should join them in the women's area in the north-west of the territory at Moon Point. A middle-class European woman accustomed to weak sunlight, always covered in protective clothing, Eliza had no defences against the subtropical sun. Her skin was raw and blistering. Her arms lay 'across her bosom, to shield her person as much as possible from the fierce oblique rays of the setting sun, which had a powerful effect, of course, upon a delicate skin so recently denuded of clothing'.[14] As an act of ritual cleansing, the Butchulla women threw sand over her body causing her excruciating pain. To heal the sunburn they applied charcoal and fat sealed with feathers, vines and twine to stop further penetration of the sun's rays and to offer a modicum of protection against the winter chill at night.

For Eliza these attempts to heal her spirit and her body were horrifying. In her eyes the Butchulla were trying to turn her into an uncivilised savage, naked, degraded and barbarous. Even more confronting was that she was expected, indeed forced, to dig in the dirt for roots and nuts, gather berries, care for babies and search for firewood. At Stromness she had a maid, as befitted her status as a captain's wife, and here in the wilds she was expected to work with her hands in the dirt and sand.

Eliza later reported to Superintendent Foster Fyans:

> During the whole of my detention among the natives I was treated with the greatest cruelty, being obliged to fetch wood and water for them and then constantly beaten when incapable of carrying heavy loads they put upon me; exposed during the night to the inclemency of the weather, being hardly ever allowed to enter their huts even during the heaviest rain.

It is interesting to note Eliza regarded her period as a castaway as a 'detention', without understanding she was incapable of leaving unaided and supporting herself with the basic elements of food, water and shelter. Indigenous societies contained small-scale hunting and gathering groups in which everyone had to work together, albeit in strictly gender-specific roles. No one had the luxury of leisure and not contributing to the communal effort.

James Fraser and First Officer Charles Brown were also made to gather firewood and undertake work they considered below their status as British officers. But as shipwrecked castaways their former identities and status were irrelevant. Why would the Butchulla care about what was in the past, or comprehend what an officer was, and why this person might merit special treatment? Butchulla elders were respected for their knowledge of law and religion, but even they worked. Fraser and Brown resisted this imposition to work, thereby angering their saviours. The ordinary seamen, accustomed to hard menial work, did not complain or resist, as we know from later testimony, and they coped far better and fitted in more easily to their radically new circumstances.

In her first report to Fyans, Eliza described her husband's condition:

> In consequence of these hardships my husband soon became so much weakened so as to be totally incapable of the work that was required of him, and being on one occasion unable through debility to carry a large log of wood one of the natives threw a spear at him which entered his shoulder just below

the blade-bone. Of this event he never recovered and being soon seized with a spitting of blood he gradually pined always until his death which took place eight or nine days afterwards. During this time when he was laying on the ground incapable of moving, I was always prevented from approaching him or rendering him any assistance. When he died they dragged him away by the legs and buried him.[15]

Brown died also. In her testimony Eliza stated that he died a painful death. She acknowledged that his feet were so burned and torn that the bones showed through and his knees protruded through the skin. The Butchulla had attempted to heal his sunburn and wounds with clay heated by firebrands to seal the skin, but this was interpreted as gross cruelty. These wounds would have proven a challenge to heal in European society, as antiseptics did not then exist. Again, according to Eliza, she was prevented from helping Brown, reporting that when she tried to give him some cockles '… some of the natives came up, and taking them from me, they knocked me down and dragged me along the ground. After this I saw him no more …'[16]

Baxter, who was not present at this incident, later told the London enquiry into the case that Brown was 'inhumanely tied to a stake and, a slow fire being placed under him, his body, after the most excruciating sufferings, was reduced to ashes'.[17] This report added to the already sensationalised account of the shipwreck survivors that had appeared in the Sydney Gazette of 17 October 1836. Far from being saviours, the Butchulla were portrayed as monsters who tortured and incinerated decent British men. Undoubtedly, the Butchulla did treat the men harshly and were exasperated at their feeble attempts at work, but theirs was a hard life and this was the punishment they meted out to their own for infringements of the rules of group survival. The Sydney newspaper article was the first public discussion of the men's deaths. Eliza further clouded the issue by saying the Butchulla were very friendly to Brown just before his death and concerned about his welfare. She interpreted this behaviour as cowardly, savage treachery.

In this second account of the deaths of Brown and Fraser, she embellished the gory details and used terms like 'savages' and 'cannibals', rather than 'natives'. She acknowledged that both men were already weakened and depleted from the ordeals of the shipwreck and its aftermath. Taking up this theme in her third rendition of the tale, in 1837, the image of the cannibal was firmly established. In an anonymous broadsheet ballad called 'Wreck of the *Stirling Castle* Horrib [sic] Treatment of the Crew by Savages', Eliza appeared in an accompanying illustration somehow miraculously fully attired in clean clothes, beset by stereotypical cannibals, replete with nose bones and surrounded by decapitated heads. Similarly, in an American pamphlet, 'Narrative of the Capture, Sufferings and Miraculous Escape of Mrs. Eliza Fraser', Eliza, again fully attired with her hair neatly coiffured, is seen in the process of capture by the Butchulla who now are represented as Native Americans. This piece added to a substantial popular literature on captured white women taken by savage Indians, tortured, kept as slaves, raped and made to perform unspeakable indelicacies. It was a type of sensational forerunner to today's stories of outlandish and bizarre traumas seen in *The Enquirer* and the like.[18]

Eliza Fraser and the other survivors of the *Stirling Castle* were neither captured nor enslaved by the Butchulla people. These concepts were entirely foreign to Indigenous societies. The references to slavery were more relevant to current debates in the British Empire and the official abolition of slavery in 1833.

Taken in canoes to Butchulla territory on the mainland, Corralis, Darge, Dayman, Carey and Youlden decided to walk to the Moreton Bay penal settlement – if proof were needed that the group was not in captivity. Corralis and Darge stumbled across Lieutenant Charles Otter, who was out shooting game on Bribie Island. He recorded that he was astounded to see two 'black and perfectly naked' men coming towards him who spoke to him in English. Astonished, he realised they were not Indigenous people but castaways. They had been guided down this far by two Indigenous men who had spent a lot of time and effort passing through others' territory to assist the strangers. Youlden was resting nearby, unable to walk, as his feet were so torn. Isolated from the other men, Dayman and Carey were also resting at Lake Cooroibah on the Noosa River. An escapee from the detention centre in Moreton Bay, John Graham, who had lived with the Kabi people for many years, found Dayman and Carey 'in an abject state', naked, sunburned and deeply afraid.[19] On 19 August 1836, a search party was organised to find the rest of the survivors.

At this point it was thought that Baxter and Eliza Fraser still remained on Great Sandy Island. Graham, as an initiated man of a nearby tribe, made enquiries about their whereabouts and organised a search party with his friend and ally Gormondy, the only Indigenous person ever directly named in all the evidence and testimony. Near death, Baxter was found on the southern end of the island and rescued. Graham and Gormondy assumed Eliza was living in the women's camp on the far north. Returning to the mainland, after much negotiation and bartering they located Eliza's whereabouts at Fig Tree Point, 50 or so kilometres south of Great Sandy Island, at the northern tip of Lake Cootharaba, also attached to the Noosa River. When Graham located her Eliza was wandering around the huts at a large feast. Graham convinced the assembly that Eliza was the ghost of his dead wife and that he would assume control for her welfare. Taking her to his country at nearby Teewah Beach, he and four of his putative kin travelled in two canoes to the safety of a secluded beach where the party met up with Otter.

Graham recalled his first sight of Eliza:

> On her head was a Southwester, the smell of the paint kept the blacks from taking it. Around her loins were part of the legs and waistband of a pair of trousers, which covered part of her thighs, wound around with Vines twenty fold as well for delicacy as the preservation of her marriage ring and Earrings which she concealed in the vines.[20]

It was from this description that Patrick White wove his tale *A Fringe of Leaves*. Although we know all the castaways' clothes were confiscated on the trek, some may have been returned to Eliza. Graham had also previously been given clothing for Eliza in case she was naked.

Charles Otter provided an extraordinary picture of his first glimpse of Eliza after fifty-two days with the Butchulla:

> You never saw such an object. Although only thirty-eight years of age, she looked like an old woman of seventy, perfectly black and dreadfully crippled from the sufferings she had undergone. I went to meet her and she caught my hand and burst into tears and sunk down quite exhausted. She was a mere skeleton, skin literally hanging on her bones, while her legs were a mass of sores, where the savages had tortured her with firebrands.

In just a few months, all the frail vestiges that marked her sex, class, marital status and nationality had disappeared, shrouded within the fringe of leaves and charcoal.

The group set out for Double Island Point, their progress hampered by Eliza's debilitated state. As they were without horses, she had to walk along with the men. They rested for a few days, and then left after some minor altercations with the local people, arriving in Brisbane on 21 August 1836.

Arriving at the penal outpost, where she gave her first short account, Eliza wept tears of joy at her deliverance, despite its rudimentary dwellings and convict population. Like Job's wife, she had survived her travails. She had lost her husband in tragic circumstances, but she still had her three children in Scotland who knew nothing of their parents' ordeals. With her mind focused on her husband's reputation and her children's welfare, she knew she had to compose herself and recover. Under the careful nurturing of the officers' wives for two months, she recuperated and transformed herself slowly back to a middle-class Englishwoman. These kind ladies provided her with clothes and money they could ill afford, before she set off to Sydney to be proclaimed a hero of the Empire.

By mid October 1836 Eliza was a *cause célèbre* in Sydney. As a guest of the Colonial Secretary, she repeated the story of her ordeal to thrilled and shocked audiences, embellishing each detail in the retelling. The surviving crew members were also in Sydney but receiving treatment different from Eliza's. A service in St James' Church in Macquarie Street – which Eliza did not attend – was held to raise funds for the survivors. During proceedings four of the seamen were forced to sit bare-chested in the aisle in some strange symbol of the shipwreck.[21] The crew was each given £5, held in trust for them until departure for England. Only after the intervention of the Governor was Second Officer Baxter given a new suit and passage home to England. These men all harboured deep resentments towards Eliza, whom they saw as unduly profiting from their shared trauma. To them the cause of their ordeal was her husband's gross incompetence, and they conveniently forgot their own insistence on landing on Great Sandy Island.

Eliza thus received both public acknowledgment and considerable largesse in Sydney. Her status as a respectable mother and widow who had suffered unimaginable hardship elicited deep sympathy and prurient curiosity.

Yet there were whisperings undermining her reputation too. Was she molested by the 'cannibals' or the convict absconders who saved her? Charlotte Barton, a talented English gentlewoman separated from a brutal husband, wrote a curious book, *A Mother's Suffering to her Children* (1841), defending Eliza's reputation as a genteel victim. There were hints in Barton's narrative, and in the earlier book by Curtis, that Eliza Fraser was deranged from her ordeal. But more lasting in their consequences were Eliza's negative depictions of the Kabi and Butchulla peoples as 'savages' when in reality they had done their utmost to assist the survivors.

On 3 February 1837, only five months after her rescue, Eliza married naval captain Alexander John Greene. This was a shocking disavowal of her status as a respectable widow, for one year was the customary minimum of mourning expected before remarriage. How she met this new Scottish captain was a subject she kept to herself. The couple departed on the *Mediterranean Packet* on 16 February 1837, leaving Eliza's Sydney benefactors wondering about the honesty of the castaway. Had Eliza played the role of a docile, genteel woman driven to near insanity by her suffering to tug on their heartstrings and their purses?

Reports of the ordeal, including the questionable dead baby incident, preceded Eliza's arrival in Liverpool on 16 July 1837. Since this was before the invention of the telegraph and radio, news must have been prepared while she was still in Sydney and sent ahead on an earlier vessel to burst out sensationally on 3 July 1837. Greene was also a competent journalist who was fascinated by stories of women shipwreck survivors. He knew the details of Betty Guard and her two children who were stranded in New Zealand with Taranaki Maoris. A teenaged bride, Betty and her former convict husband, Captain John Guard, were shipwrecked in 1834. On returning to Sydney they recounted tales of torture and humiliation.[22] Tales of the even more horrific wreck and murder of survivors of the *Charles Eaton* in the Torres Strait had reached Sydney by 1836.[23] Curtis' book on Mrs Fraser also contained the story of this latter drama. Greene was thus entirely familiar with the narrative of the chaste, vulnerable Englishwoman thrown on the mercy of 'savages'. And so Eliza docked in Liverpool a fully created celebrity, again arousing much morbid curiosity and sympathy.

By the time Eliza Fraser – as she presented herself, with Greene merely as her agent – arrived at Liverpool docks, her story had been refined. She was a destitute widow with three children, cast upon wild and alien shores and subjected to unspeakable torture at the hands of 'cannibals'. Even when rescued, she alleged she battled on alone without resources or aid. This very understated nature allowed readers to flesh out their own details of sexual violence, torture and the eating of human flesh. That she travelled to London to capitalise on her fame, rather than rejoining her children in Scotland, gives a hint of her motives. Perhaps as she wandered the fashionable streets of Mayfair she saw herself in beautiful gowns and jewels now so tantalisingly within her grasp. A considerable subscription was taken up for her, with the support of the Lord Mayor of London. Feeding the appetite for sensation, lurid accounts of her ordeal appeared in the broadsheets:

Eliza had been forever marked with hideous disfiguring tattoos; John Major was tortured, decapitated and eaten, his head forming a fine ornament for a war canoe.[24] In the United States, *Tales of Travelers* (1837) fed the demand for sensational adventures. Yet, as the editor of the *Sydney Gazette* wrote on 25 January 1838, Eliza Fraser had been showered with money and gifts in Sydney. Middle-class Britons in the Antipodes were outraged that their generosity and kindness had not been acknowledged. She had been amply assisted in both Moreton Bay and Sydney. Indeed, she was now married to a naval captain and no longer a widow.

As other stories emerged the Lord Mayor withdrew his patronage and ordered an enquiry into the shipwreck of the *Stirling Castle* and the experiences on Great Sandy Island. He directed that all the subscription funds go to her children in Stromness. In 1838 John Curtis published his account, in which any discrepancies lay in Eliza's derangement from grief and torture. Eliza was depicted not as an impostor or perpetrator of a fraud but as an innocent victim of circumstances. An interesting sideshow to the affair was a performance in Hyde Park in which Mrs Fraser supposedly told her tale. The wealthy squatter and Old Etonian Henry Stuart Russell, who knew the convict renegades and other participants in the rescue, recorded in his memoirs that he had a handbill for the show.[25] Russell was a good researcher and documenter of his own life and the society around him. There was undoubtedly a sideshow; whether Eliza performed is unlikely. The strong constraints of her class and sexual identity suggest that the performer was an actor capitalising on Eliza's notoriety.

Yet Eliza was a manipulative embellisher of her tragedy as well as a strong, resolute and courageous woman. She revelled in publicity, seeing it as the means to a fortune. Eliza and Alexander Greene eventually migrated to New Zealand.

Eliza died in a carriage accident in Melbourne in 1858. Her complex notoriety also had diverse historical rewards; her story, with all its twists, turns, ambiguities, exaggerations and retellings, is the primary material for great art in the twentieth century.

CHAPTER 4

Lola Montez
(1818–1861)

The Irish-born grande horizontale *who destroyed King Ludwig I of Bavaria through extravagance.*

In the year of revolution, 1848, Lola Montez was the most famous and recognised woman in the world after Queen Victoria. Whereas the later Empress of India and head of the British Empire grew into the role of wise monarch and devoted wife and mother, Lola was an infamous courtesan who ruined the life of the monarch of Bavaria, on top of conducting other scandalous liaisons and entering two bigamous marriages. Her notoriety far outlived her own time; Aldous Huxley once remarked that every time he thought of Lola Montez he thought of bedrooms – and this was nearly a century after her death in 1861.

Lola's origins are clouded in uncertainty. She wrote in *The Times* on 9 April 1847 that she was born in Seville in the year 1823: 'My father was a Spanish officer in service of Don Carlos, my mother a lady of Irish extraction … and married for the second time to an Irish gentleman, which I suppose, is the cause of my being called Irish and sometimes English, "Betsy Watson", "Mrs. James" etc etc. My name is Maria Dolores Porris y Montez.'

There is little truth in this declaration, aside from the facts that her mother was Irish and Lola was technically Mrs James. How did a young Irish dancer of little talent, although an accomplished courtesan, come to make such an important announcement in the press? By 1847 Lola Montez was a household name across Europe and the English-speaking world. The Australian colonial press was already full of her doings, as she lurched from scandal to scandal. By the time she came to Sydney in 1855, she was the most notorious woman in the world.

Baptised Maria Delores Eliza Rosanna Gilbert, Lola was born in Limerick, Ireland, in 1818 to her fourteen-year-old mother, Elizabeth Oliver. Elizabeth, a milliner's assistant, was born in 1805 to Mary Green and Charles Silver Oliver, MP, a pillar of the Irish Protestant ascendancy and former sheriff of the County of Cork. This long-term alliance produced four children, before Charles Oliver married a woman of his own class background. He did, however, acknowledge his four illegitimate children and provided modestly for their welfare. Lola's father, Ensign Edward Gilbert, was a handsome young officer in the 25th Foot Regiment which had recently seen service in India. He met Lola's mother in Cork and they married on 29 April 1819 in Christ's Church, Cork, soon after Elizabeth discovered she was pregnant. Unlike her own mother, she was able to marry the father of her child, thus avoiding the stigma of illegitimacy that had affected her own life and chances.[1]

In 1823 the family went to India, where Edward was stationed with the British East India Company's troops. He died of cholera in September 1823, an event that was to change his young, high-spirited daughter's life forever. Her mother married a kindly Scotsman, Lieutenant Patrick Craigie, a scion of a bourgeois Montrose, Scotland, family. And it was only these two men that Lola ever truly loved, as her later life revealed. Sent home to Scotland, the young Lola was wild. She wrote in her autobiography, she was a 'queer, wayward, little East India girl' sent to the coldness of eastern Scotland.[2] Her book spoke at great length about the colours and vibrancy of India, so this exile, along with her beloved father's death, cast a terrible shadow over her spirits. After a brief period with her stepfather's sister in Durham, Lola was sent to Bath, where she attended the Misses Aldridge's Academy, and learned the graces and accomplishments of a young lady. This was an expensive exercise for Lieutenant Craigie to undertake.

The lessons in propriety and modesty were entirely lost on the stubborn teenager who had spurned the advice of her stepfather's friend Lieutenant General Sir Jasper Nicolls. Her extravagance and impetuousness were already apparent. In 1837 Lola saw her mother again after a six-year separation. Elizabeth proposed an arranged marriage with a 64-year-old widower, Major General Sir James Rutherford, a friend of her stepfather. Repulsed by this suggestion, Lola eloped with the handsome Lieutenant Thomas James, aged thirty-one. They were duly married by his brother, the vicar of a Protestant parish in Dublin. As Lola later wrote, '[r]unaway matches, like runaway horses, are almost sure to end in a smash up'.[3] The couple then went to Simla (now Shimla) in India, where Lieutenant James' regiment was stationed.

The nineteen-year-old bride, despite her childhood in India, was singularly unsuited to the constraints of an officer's wife in a tiny British outpost. The marriage faltered quickly. There is some speculation as to whether Lola or James abandoned the marriage, but evidence suggests that perhaps it was Lola who strayed from the marital bed, as she had an open affair on the ship returning to England. Caroline Marden, a female steward on this vessel, reported that 'I more than once saw Captain Lennox lacing up Mrs. James' stays.'[4] George Lennox was the aide-de-camp to Lord Elphinstone, and once in London Lola met with him in her hotel, again breaching the rules of decorous behaviour. By the age of twenty, Lola's life was characterised by scandal and notoriety – she had eloped and then abandoned her husband, and had now taken up publicly with another man. Meanwhile, Thomas James obtained a judicial separation in the Church of England's Consistory Court; divorce at this time was only by an Act of parliament.

Lola needed some way of supporting herself and by now she was estranged from her mother. The thought of working as a milliner's assistant, as her mother had done, never entered her head. Rather, Lola – or Mrs Betty James as she was then called – needed to reinvent her whole identity. She went to the Fran Kelly Academy in Dean Street, Soho, to learn dancing, before taking a trip to Cadiz, Spain, to learn Spanish language and dances.[5] Lola later wrote in her autobiography that 'we poor women are such helpless creatures that we do not always have the choice of means. Often we are forced to achieve our goals by whatever is available to us, even if we recognized that we are thus put in an unflattering light.'

Billed as Donna Lolah Montez, Lola made her theatrical debut on 3 June 1843 at Her Majesty's Theatre in Haymarket, London, performing 'El Oleano', an early version of her famous Spider Dance. What reviewers remarked upon was not her proficiency in the art of dance but her spectacular appearance. With thick raven-black hair, intense blue eyes, a perfect porcelain complexion and superb figure, Lola was an extraordinary beauty.

The performance was marred by shouts of 'Betty James' when she was recognised from the audience. Her run at the theatre was short-lived. She fled to Hamburg and from there toured extensively in Germany, Poland and Russia, where she could be spared such ignominy and abuse. In early 1844 Lola met Franz Liszt, the Hungarian piano virtuoso with whom she conducted a barely concealed liaison, even scandalising the tolerant band of artists and intellectuals who populated the demimonde they inhabited. When the affair faltered, Lola went to Paris, armed with letters of introduction, to reignite her career. On 28 March 1844 she made her debut at the Paris Opera. Again the audience of men – ladies did not attend theatrical performances – admired her beauty and vivaciousness while lamenting her lack of talent and expertise in Spanish dancing.

After her limited artistic success, Lola did far better as a courtesan. Her first liaison in Paris was conducted with the young editor and owner of *La Presse*, Alexandre Dujarier. He died after a duel with Guadeloupe-born Jean-Baptiste Rosemond de Beupin de Beauvallon in March 1845. He left seventeen shares in the Palais Royal Theatre to Lola, and his horses and furniture to Alexandre Dumas *père* (author of *The Three Musketeers*). Lola then embarked on an affair with Dumas from whom it was rumoured she contracted syphilis.[6] She fitted in well into the demimonde of Paris, befriending Alphonsine Plessis, upon whom Dumas' illegitimate son, Alexandre Dumas *fils*, modelled his tragic *Lady of the Camellias*.

Lola set her sights beyond Paris and travelled to the fashionable health resorts at Spa in Belgium and Baden-Baden in Germany. She returned to Paris for the trial of de Beauvallon, following the duel, who was acquitted. Lola made a wistful figure in black, a colour she adopted henceforth. After the proceedings, she left Paris with Robert Peel, the eldest son of the former British prime minister. Arriving in Munich on 5 October 1846 for the Oktoberfest, she was presented to King Ludwig of Bavaria, who was smitten immediately by her beauty and vivacity. Pretending she was a Spanish noblewoman, Lola henceforth conversed with Ludwig in Spanish. We can presume his Spanish skills were limited as she fooled him completely. After seeing her perform her Spider Dance – a fast-moving spinning performance – Ludwig took his passion to another level and installed her as his official mistress. His generosity was almost boundless – he provided his new favourite with a house that was lavishly renovated and furnished, horses, carriages, clothes, jewellery, servants and a substantial income. Within a few months he had lavished upon her millions of dollars in today's currency.[7]

Not only did Lola entertain the besotted elderly King in the bedroom, but she took to advising him on politics. These years in the late 1840s were intensely volatile across Western Europe, with challenges to traditional monarchies and demands for more representative government. Lola allied herself with the university students and members of the Munich middle class, thereby alienating herself to Ludwig's aristocratic court and advisers. Still, on 10 February 1847 he made her a Bavarian citizen and, six months later, on his birthday, Ludwig elevated her to a peerage. She became the Countess Marie von Landsfeld and signed her last will in New York under this name.[8] Immediately upon this elevation Lola became far more formal and distant to her benefactor.

On 7 February 1848 riots against her influence spread through Munich, endangering her safety. Three days later merchants and other prosperous citizens who had previously formed the nucleus of her supporters, marched in their thousands on the King's residence in protest against her extravagance and political influence. Ludwig was forced to concede when presented with incontrovertible evidence that his darling Lolitta, as he called her, was an impostor. Even more humiliating was the detailed evidence of her affairs with handsome young students conducted while she was the King's mistress. With her house ransacked and her life in peril, Lola fled to Berne in Switzerland and her Bavarian citizenship was revoked. There she learned that not only had King Louis Philippe abdicated after riots in Paris, but her devoted Ludwig had also abdicated on 10 March. And after everything he had learned about her, Ludwig was still convinced of her affection and hoped to join her in his long exile.

In April 1848 a satirical play entitled *Pas de Fascination or Catching a Governor, or a Farce in One Act ... performed under the title of Lola Montez, or a Countess for an Hour* was premiered at the Theatre Royal in London. Its author, J. Stirling Coyne, did not enjoy an extended career as a playwright or satirist, but the ribald comedy was a success. News of Lola's exploits and affairs had spread across the world, albeit slowly. The Australian colonial newspapers followed the now notorious Lola's career with avid attention. She had returned to London at this time though no doubt she avoided Coyne's scurrilous farce. Lola had lost her house in Munich but she retained her annual income from Ludwig, and she rented a grand house in Half Moon Street, near Green Park in Mayfair.

On 19 July 1849 Lola went through a form of marriage to a wealthy 21-year-old former Etonian and Second Life Guards officer George Trafford Heald. In fact she went through two wedding ceremonies, one in the French Roman Catholic chapel in King Street, Westminster, followed by another ceremony that same day at the fashionable St George's Church of England in Hanover Square. Neither of the couple were Catholic and Lola was still legally married, although she described herself as one 'Maria de los Delores de Landsfeld, widow'. Protestant by baptism and an ardent anti-Catholic, as her later lecture tours and writings revealed, she was nevertheless a supposed Spanish noblewoman and forced into this pretence. She gave her place of birth as Seville, though later she admitted in her autobiography that she was born in Limerick.

George Heald's aunt Susanna Heald, suspicious of the beautiful 'widow', made her own investigations and confirmed that her naïve nephew had indeed married bigamously.[9] In August 1849 a warrant for Lola's arrest on the charge of bigamy hung over her head. The court case,

Lola Montez – or the Countess of Landsfeld – in the blossom of her youth. Lithograph by Sarony & Major; Library of Congress LC-USZ62-3913.

commencing on 12 August 1849, was chronicled in *The Times*. Again reports spread across Europe and through the English-speaking world. At first she told the court she was divorced, and when this was proved incorrect, she pointed to the invalidity of the ceremonies because she had signed her declarations in a false name. Placed on bail at the enormous sum of £1000, which she didn't possess, Lola skipped bail for freedom in Paris, which was far more alluring than spending time in an English prison. She and Heald fled across the Channel, before going to Spain, their alliance soon descending into bickering, bitterness and separation. Heald bestowed on Lola an annual allowance of a mere £50, a pittance after the fortune lavished upon her by Ludwig.

Lola's response was to increase her demands on Ludwig for ever more money without the tediousness of cohabitation. Despite her new alliance, Lola had continued

to profess her undying devotion in letters to the exiled
Ludwig.[10]

Lola's relationship with Ludwig was now very useful.
She possessed his passionate letters and had no hesitation in
using them as a weapon for requesting further funds. Her
former life in Bavaria was also to provide source material
for future stage shows.

Lola's first autobiography appeared in the journal *Le
Pays* in 1851 and was also translated into German. Readers
would have been greatly disappointed, however, as it dealt
mostly with her reminiscences of her childhood in India.[11]
Attempts to reignite her career in Europe were haphazard
and, as it had for others before her, the New World
beckoned.

Lola arrived in New York City in late 1851 to a blaze
of publicity. The *New York Herald* of 30 December
1851 took up the promotion of the glamorous Countess.
Lola decided that rather than relying on her Spider
Dance, renamed 'Zapateado', she would lengthen her
performances with the addition of a *corps de ballet*.
Her shows were regarded as indecent; ladies not only
did not appear on stage, they did not attend theatrical
performances. Lola contributed to a benefit for the
Fireman's Welfare Fund on 16 January 1852. American
male audiences were fascinated by this supposed
aristocrat in her own right who became a *maîtresse du roi*.
Her beauty and fine figure were added attractions in this
Puritan society.

Lola embarked on an extensive theatrical tour of the east
coast of the United States, adding a new number entitled
'Lola Montez in Bavaria' in several sections – the *Danseuse*,

the Politician, the Countess, the Revolutionary, and the Fugitive. Unfortunately, no printed copy of the bill for the show survives.[12] Always a rebel and groundbreaker, Lola was photographed with the Native American Cheyenne chief Light in the Clouds in Philadelphia, and with a cigarette in her hand on another occasion in Boston – the earliest known extant photograph of a woman smoking to survive.[13] More material was added to her repertoire, including something on the life of Charlotte Corday, the killer of Marat in the French Revolution, and 'Maritana, or the Maid of Saragossa', set in the Napoleonic Wars. The *New York Times* of 6 September 1852 reported how fetching Lola looked in male attire in this now forgotten work.

In the United States occurrences of her erratic and often violent outbursts became apparent. She was arrested for assault in the theatre in New Orleans where she was performing and jumped bail. Such behaviour was the first outward evidence, along with increasingly painful headaches and eye problems, of secondary syphilis. Meanwhile, adverse publicity about her was appearing across the world with increasing frequency. None was worse than accounts by *London Times* senior reporter William Russell, made famous later by his despatches on the Crimean War. In his novel *Mrs. Seacole's Adventures* (1858), he portrayed a thinly disguised Lola on her arduous trip across the Isthmus of Panama as:

> A good-looking, bold woman with fine, bad eyes
> and collar turned down, determined bearing,
> dressed ostentatiously in perfect male attire ... she

carried in her hand a handsome riding whip, which
she could use as well in the streets of Cruces as the
towns of Europe; for an impertinent American,
presuming perhaps not unnaturally upon her
reputation, laid hold jestingly on the tails of her
long coat, and, as a lesson, received a cut across his
face that must have marked him for some days ...[14]

Lola was upset by Russell's report and devoted some space
in her second autobiography to his remarks.[15] She also
added into this strange little memoir, so full of errors and
reworkings of her past, that 'of Lola Montez's career in the
United States there is not much to be said'.[16] The global
press disagreed and her every move and performance was
avidly followed. The *Maitland Mercury and Hunter River
Advertiser*, for instance, had been keeping readers in its
small regional area up to date with her career, starting
around her time in Bavaria.

Arriving in San Francisco in May 1853, after an arduous
trip by mule, coach and then sea, Lola set about trying to
revive her allure on the stage. The gold towns of California
were ripe for the pickings, in her opinion. On the voyage
across she had met Patrick Purdy Hull, a young journalist
and owner of the *San Francisco Whig*, who also committed
himself to advancing her career. Within weeks of their
meeting, on 2 July 1853, Lola entered into a marriage with
Hull in a Roman Catholic ceremony. At this time, both
James and Heald were still alive, so this was her second
bigamous union.

Lola's acts on stage, supplemented with fare such as the
role of Lady Teazle in *School for Scandal*, were welcomed

by the culture- and leisure-starved miners. The price of admission at $5 a ticket was exorbitant compared to $1 in New York.[17] But the miners were far more discerning than she had anticipated and many appearances were marred by hissing and shouts of anger at her poor performances and lack of technical expertise. Lola countered this negativity by engaging in dialogue at the footlights with her detractors – something actors did not do – and managed to turn this into a form of theatre sport to which audiences flocked to see her ability to ad lib. By the standards of the day, Lola was a well-educated woman and her verbal dexterity was admired.

Lola Montez was clever in the way in which she capitalised on romantic notions of Spain, as noted by American writers Washington Irving and William H. Prescott. She appreciated the lengthy Spanish colonisation of California and the cultural heritage it bestowed. What was seemingly at variance with this admiration of *lo Español* was her increasingly frequent diatribes against the Jesuits; making claims they had tried to poison her with arsenic, that they shot at her on several occasions, and tried to kidnap her in Munich.[18] Such delusions may also have been caused by the spread of syphilis through her brain, with feelings of persecution and grandiose notions both appearing as the disease progressed.

Though seemingly isolated by distance from Europe, San Francisco was au fait with modern developments on the popular and traditional stage. Not only were *Hamlet* and *Romeo and Juliet* performed but also the farce *Lola Montez: or, Pas de Fascination*. Not to be outdone, local authors set about writing their own satires. One play, *Who's*

Got the Countess? Or, The Rival Houses, played to capacity crowds. At another theatre a series of scurrilous songs were enthusiastically received. Publicly, Lola laughed, seeing these attacks as generating more publicity for her.[19] In California, public morality was not as strict as in London, from where she had fled several scandals earlier.

Her tours of the Grass Valley and Nevada City regions were eagerly reported as far away as the Australian colonies. An indulgent spendthrift who frittered away her constantly renewed fortune, Lola purchased a mine in northern California. With her 'marriage' abandoned within three months, she settled in the unlikely spot of Grass Valley where she kept a bear cub along with a menagerie of more domesticated animals and birds. She stayed in this rural retreat until early 1855, when she decided on a two-year grand tour of India, China and the Australian colonies.

Lola and her new company departed from San Francisco on 6 June 1855. On advice from her manager, the proposals to tour India and China were abandoned as too ambitious. A handsome young actor named Noel Follin (stage name Frank Folland) soon caught her eye. With his estranged wife and family in Cincinnati, he was free to embark on a tempestuous professional and personal relationship with the world's most notorious woman. It was a hasty decision he came to regret, as Lola's demands, rudeness, arrogance and irrational delusions appeared with ever more frequency.

Lola decided to test the Australian colonies with her new entourage. After a two-month voyage the *Fanny Major* disembarked in Sydney. The *Sydney Morning Herald* of 17 August 1855 reported its arrival but refrained from announcing the presence of Lola and her troupe. In her first engagement at the Victoria Theatre in Pitt Street, she performed 'Lola Montez in Bavaria'. After a performance in Melbourne, the *Argus* of 31 August 1855 informed readers that:

> [H]er appearance is good; but her voice, if not bad, deficient altogether in flexibility, and sweetness, at least when raised to a pitch calculated for the stage. She is sometimes graceful for a moment or two, but coarseness and vulgarity is sure to follow hard upon such glimpses of a better spirit. Her grand effect is as a 'postures'.

If this was harsh criticism, the critic went on: 'The Piece she played in ... is about the greatest piece of trash and humbug introduced before an English audience ...' Sydney's leading broadsheet remained entirely silent on her performance and, indeed, her presence in their city.

In Sydney Lola continued to suffer from headaches and ill health, a sign the syphilis was progressing rapidly. Curiously, while in Sydney with engagements still to come in Melbourne she dismissed the American company. When she attempted to jump bail for breaking her theatrical contracts in a farce involving an officer of the court trying to serve writs on the vessel *Waratah* bound for Melbourne, the *Sydney Morning Herald* finally got interested and reported the incident on 11 September 1855.

In Melbourne Lola played in her show, based on her adventures in Bavaria at the Theatre Royal with a far smaller company. Seweryn Korzelinski, an educated Polish miner who left a record of his time in Victoria, reported that Lola largely danced her Spider Dance to '… sailors [who] were duly impressed'.[20] By this, he rightly inferred this was low culture for an undiscerning male audience. Today the performance would appear innocent enough; in the mid nineteenth century, however, the public display of a woman's legs and ankles was regarded as immoral and lascivious. Melbourne, though a new city, possessed a substantial degree of high culture, with the *Messiah* a popular production and the Melbourne Philharmonic Society running 200 performances a year in 1860. Opera was appreciated, with Madame Carandini and Irish soprano Catherine Hayes great favourites there and on the goldfields. George Coppin, the owner of the Olympic Theatre, put on *Lucia di Lammermoor*, *La Sonnambula*, *Norma* and *Il trovatore*. For the town's elite, particularly the ladies, *soirées musicales* at home were the order of the day.[21]

During her time in Victoria, Lola continued to be plagued by headaches and illness, which affected her performances. The critic for the *Argus* on 20 September 1855 denounced the spectacle as '… a nuisance and … utterly subversive to all ideas of public morality'.[22] The Reverend John Milton went so far as to demand her arrest. With the Methodist and Presbyterian churches strong in the new colony, his opinion held weight.[23] She was also attacked by theatrical types themselves. George Coppin produced a satire in which he mimicked Lola's addresses to the audience. Lola had to endure all these less than flattering attacks.

From Melbourne Lola went to Adelaide, where she found respectability not enjoyed at any other point in her career. A vice-regal performance and a benefit for the widows and orphans of the 'heroes of Sebastopol' by 'Lola Montez, Countess of Landsfeld, Princess of Bavaria' added a hitherto elusive lustre to her name.[24] How she suddenly became a princess is a mystery. The *South Australian Register* of 9 December 1855 praised this 'clever *danseuse*'.

Lola's tour of the goldfields of Victoria also met with controversy. Korzelinski recorded that her charms were fading and her expectations that the 'miners [would] kiss her hand' were unfulfilled.[25] Far worse from a public relations point of view, Lola horsewhipped Henry Seekamp, the editor of the *Ballarat Times*, in the public bar of the United States Hotel. He attempted to punch her and pull her hair in retaliation. *The Age* of 23 February 1856 reported the altercation with great relish. Frank Folland threatened the hero of the Eureka Stockade – who defended the miners' rights in the press – with a pistol. News spread internationally.[26] The *Melbourne Punch* of 28 February 1856 wrote a long amusing poem in honour of the 'Battle of Ballarat'. Moreover, unrest within Lola's small company over payments escalated. Lola was horsewhipped herself by Mrs Crosby, the wife of her manager. When the whip broke, she pummelled Lola with her fists and pulled her hair.[27]

Lola returned to Melbourne in early March 1856, where her performances were greeted with hisses and boos. Undeterred, she and her troupe returned to the goldfields and performed in Bendigo and Castlemaine, the tickets now priced at only ten shillings. The *Bendigo Courier* of 10 May 1856 reported Lola as now thanking her audience for their attendance.

The troupe left Australia on 22 May 1856 on the *James A. Falkenberg* bound for San Francisco. Her relations with Frank Folland, her manager, and the rest of the ensemble had reached the depths of distrust, enmity and loathing. Worse was to come when Folland fell overboard between Fiji and Honolulu. There were doubts about whether this was an accident or suicide. For a self-centred woman Lola behaved admirably, selling her jewellery to benefit his children.[28] She was genuinely distraught, and sought comfort in spiritualism and mysticism for the last five years of her life. She never regained her insouciance and rebelliousness from this point.

Lola's career as an actor and dancer faltered. As she had done previously, she reinvented herself as a public speaker on topics such as beauty, the evils of Catholicism, and the women and wits of Paris, which included her old lover Alexandre Dumas. These lectures appear in her slim second autobiography.[29] Lola was greatly assisted in these endeavours by the Reverend Charles Chauncey Burr, with whom she had developed an unlikely friendship. Her advice on beauty, hair, deportment, diet and exercise showed her to be ahead of her times in its sensible instruction. One sad incident occurred in late 1857 when Lola, the great sexual temptress and lover, was duped publicly by Prince Ludwig Sulkowski, whom she went to France to meet, hoping for another marriage.[30] He was a married man with a family and this hoax was mere sport.

In November 1858 Lola and the Burr family went to Ireland to promote her lectures, where Lola had not been since her marriage in 1839. *The Times* on 16 January 1859 gave a full coverage to her lectures on American values and society. Returning to London and attempting to re-establish herself, Lola fell into debt trying to maintain an extravagant lifestyle. Leaving creditors baying, she fled to New York City, where she became increasingly interested in the reformation of prostitutes. She began attending the Methodist Church, now a repentant sinner and public reformer. Her last two years were spent in poverty and reflection on sins of the flesh. After a series of strokes and paralysis, Lola died on 17 January 1861, leaving money to the Magdalene Society. Her tombstone reads 'Mrs. Eliza Gilbert, died 17 January 1861 aged 42'. In her inscription there was just that modicum of truth she had so effectively eluded in life.

Lola Montez is fondly remembered in Australia. The Sovereign Hill Museum in Ballarat, in its proud retelling of the history of the gold rushes, features posters of her performances. The Australian Elizabethan Theatre Trust in Sydney, established in the post-World War II era to promote Australian high culture firmly following American and British trends, debuted a locally written musical about Lola Montez on 22 October 1958. The national tour showed that Australian audiences were receptive to local material. Written by Alan Burke and Peter Benjamin with music by Peter Stannard, the musical sought to inspire Australian creative talents to engage with Australian culture.[31] Lola would no doubt have been amused to learn that a century after her sad, lonely death her life story was venerated as a vehicle of high culture.

CHAPTER 5

Ellen Tremaye (Edward De Lacy Evans)

(1838–1901)

Marion ('Bill') Edwards

(1874–1956)

The women who challenged the gender order and became men.

Colonial Australia was a repressive place for women. With little formal education and few opportunities to earn a living beyond domestic service, bartending, prostitution and, later, factory and retail work, women were mostly constrained within the bonds of marriage and motherhood. Without inherited money, they could hope for little independence and autonomy. Yet some women broke the mould completely, choosing to forsake the rigid and restrictive gender roles and live as men. In the late nineteenth and early years of the twentieth centuries, Victorians Marion (Bill) Edwards and Ellen Tremaye lived, worked and wed as men. As Edward De Lacy Evans, Ellen entered into formal marriages not just once, but on three occasions.

This was not a case of cross-dressing or transvestism, but an entire gender realignment. In the late 1870s, when her story became public, Evans was the most notorious woman-man in the Australian colonies. Regarded as a medical freak to be studied and pitied, she was the subject of extensive newspaper speculation. Presented as a type of vanilla pornography, with its coded messages and seemingly bizarre practices, her case encouraged a furtive curiosity in unconventional sexualities and identities. Her former workmates, neighbours, shipmates and casual acquaintances volunteered their stories for publication in the newspapers. A modern celebrity, as we now know it, was created through the colonial press.

Marion (Bill) Edwards, on the other hand, was a cheeky larrikin who never suffered Evans' humiliations. Funny and resourceful, Edwards negotiated gender identities at will, with flair and a keen eye for publicity.

There were notorious cases in the colony earlier in the nineteenth century of women dressing and working as men, for convenience rather than identity. Catherine Henrys (c.1805–55), commonly known as Jemmy the Rover, was an Irishwoman from Sligo, transported to Van Diemen's Land in 1835 for stealing and robbery with violence. Assigned to haberdasher John Swan in Hobart in 1836, after unruly and disruptive behaviour she was returned to the Female Factory where she was put on bread and water for six days. Her next assignments were in rural areas but they were no more successful. At one stage in 1837, Henrys was assigned to Aboriginal Protector George Augustus Robinson on Flinders Island Aboriginal Reserve. Absconding from various masters, Henrys took to the bush, where she lived and worked as a man. She joined several male fugitives, though it is not clear whether they were bushrangers (like Michael Howe and Mary Cockerill in the 1810s). Attempts to incarcerate her failed. On several occasions Henrys escaped from custody with great initiative and aplomb. The *Launceston Examiner* remarked that this 'notorious woman' had a reputation as a pugilist and 'her masculine appearance was quite in keeping with her character'.[1] Henrys was an aggressive, combative personality who enjoyed the freedom bestowed by men's occupations and attire. Unlike Tremaye, she did not consider herself a man trapped in a woman's body.

Kitty Gallagher was another convict who dressed and worked as a man, though again she did not consider herself one. Born in rural Ireland in 1770s, Gallagher was a rebel leader in the White Boys, a terrorist agrarian organisation with Roman Catholic members. Formed in 1759 to protest against the enclosure of common lands, these activists joined the wider insurrection in 1798 when the Irish, with the help of French revolutionaries, attempted to overthrow English rule in Ireland.[2] Kitty and her husband, Frank Gallagher, were transported to New South Wales for their part in the so-called Wexford Rebellion. They later established a small cattle farm at Scone where they were attacked by bushrangers in 1839. Using her military skills, Kitty fought them off with muskets. After Frank's death she worked on pastoralist Henry Dangar's station droving cattle. Dressed as a working man, and armed with pistols, she smoked a clay pipe. Local historian William Telfer recalled 'this Amazon when i [sic] was a little boy in the year 1844'.[3] Her rural skills were considerable, especially her use of the plough. She died at the age of ninety-six.[4]

Ellen Tremaye, or Tremayne as she was frequently called in newspaper accounts, represents an altogether different category of women dressing and working as men. This was not for convenience and comfort in the process of undertaking hard manual work; rather, the male attire, haircut, masculine deportment and modes of speech were manifestations of her preference to live as a man with all the privileges it bestowed. Her life was filled with excitement, joy, disappointment, humiliation and public exposure, for she was psychologically a man trapped in a woman's body.

We know little about her early life or what brought her to migrate to Victoria just after the gold rushes, but she was most likely born in Waterford in Ireland in 1838 and came to Victoria in 1856 as a domestic servant.[5] On board the *Ocean Monarch*, other passengers later recalled that she was a strange young woman, dressed every day in an outfit of a sealskin coat over a green calico dress and men's undergarments. This was quite a feat given that voyages took many weeks through hot equatorial regions to reach the Australian colonies. Her luggage was marked 'Edward De Lacy Evans'. This name and the persona it implies – male, well connected and fancy – shows that Ellen had already begun to turn herself into Edward. To the other passengers it meant something else. Perhaps the person, Edward De Lacy Evans, who owned the unescorted luggage was the fiancé or brother of Miss Tremaye.

Certainly, rural Ireland in the 1850s was hardly a tolerant society conducive to gender realignments and grandiose fantasies. Eccentricity was for grand urban people in London and Paris. Tremaye's desire to become a man was, however, strong and undisguised on the voyage out. Remarkably, Tremaye shared her bunk with two women at various times en route to Melbourne. Though it was common for steerage passengers to be housed in close and cramped sex-segregated quarters, it was highly improper for two women to share the intimacy of a bunk. On board, Tremaye publicly declared her intention of marrying fellow passenger Mary Delahunty, an older educated woman who initially recorded her occupation as governess. Most of the female immigrants were illiterate or barely literate domestic servants, making Delahunty stand out as an educated lady by comparison.[6] One account by Miss Wain, a fellow passenger, reported that before the vessel left Portsmouth, Tremaye was anxiously awaiting a companion, whom they assumed was a man.[7] This suggests Delahunty and Tremaye may have known each other before embarkation and intended to 'marry', safe in the knowledge that they were unknown in the colonies.

When Ellen/Edward was exposed in the newspapers in late 1879, the accounts were sympathetic to her situation, speculating on her decision to leave Ireland. As one account ventured to suggest, she was an unmarried mother who decided to 'face the world and adopted the masculine garb for her better protection and support'.[8] This is an unlikely scenario; most unmarried mothers did not pursue the option of male disguise to hide their shame and later marry three women.

On disembarkation, Tremaye went to work as a domestic servant, initially at Melton, before she returned to Melbourne following her reinvention as Edward De Lacy Evans. Perhaps she began to experiment with this total gender inversion in Melton, for there she often slept with the publican's wife 'for company' when the husband was away on business. The publican, however, took a horsewhip to this interloper in his marital bed.[9]

It was at this point that Ellen decided to entirely relinquish her feminine appearance, denoted by clothes, hairstyle and demeanour, to become her alter ego, Edward Evans. She had constructed a grand lineage: the nephew of General De Lacy Evans, and scion of a wealthy French family.[10] Assuming grand identities was not uncommon in the colonies, where people could easily reinvent themselves. Whether others believed them was another matter. That Evans had no money, did not speak French, and was an uncultured person would indicate the identity was somewhat questionable.

Evans married Delahunty in Melbourne at St Francis' Catholic Church, but the marriage was not a success. Clearly, Delahunty knew Evans' real identity and circumstances and yet went along with the marriage.

It is also intriguing to consider why Evans and Delahunty returned to the district where he had worked as a female domestic servant before the horsewhipping incident saw him flee. Clearly he was known and recognised when he returned with a 'bride'. Perhaps colonial Victorians were more tolerant than might be assumed. Often people had fled their home countries and cities to forge out new identities and make new lives. Even so, gender realignment was not on the conventional list of personal transformations.

Certainly there was local gossip and scandal. Mr Ready, who had worked with Evans in 1857, recalled that he used to tease Evans and say he was a 'girl', as he had no facial hair. Evans flew into a 'passion' when called Polly

Edward De Lacy Evans in 1879 dressed in both male and female attire. Photo Nicholas White; State Library of Victoria H96.160/147.

and chased his tormentor with a knife. Perhaps this man thought Polly was a young homosexual. The informant also said he called Evans 'Mollie' and 'Mary Anne', slang terms used to identify gay men, though these terms were usually employed within the gay community.[11] The term 'homosexual' had not yet been invented; 'sodomite' was the more usual name. Yet clearly Edward Evans was not at all interested sexually in his miner workmates. Thus they no doubt assumed he was an effeminate man.

The marriage to Delahunty failed and Delahunty embarked on an open affair with a mining surveyor, Lyman Oatman Hart, scandalising the local district in Blackwood, but laughing it off by stating her 'husband' was really a woman. We may speculate why no widespread scandal erupted at this time. The case of a woman marrying another woman, one who was living and working as a man, and the other a supposed married woman conducting an illicit affair, had all the elements of a good international scandal. In 1862 Delahunty took the bold step of marrying Lyman Hart and moved to Daylesford.[12]

In 1862 Evans married again, in Sandhurst, declaring he was a widower. Like him, Sarah Moore was an Irish domestic servant. When Evans ran into a woman he had known in Ireland he begged her not to reveal his secret. Thinking that this might be concerning his sex, this woman was surprised to find out that Evans feared exposure to his second wife as originally a Roman Catholic who had changed religion to the Protestant faith.[13] In a society where sectarianism was rife, this was a real fear. Exposure as a woman married twice to women would seem to us to be far more compelling in its gravity than embracing Protestantism.

When Mr Ready moved from Melton to Blackwood and encountered Evans with his second wife, he remarked in the press later that Evans '... got into a huge rage, and threatened to kill his wife' when his wife realised he was a woman in disguise. The likelihood that the second Mrs Evans, Sarah Moore, had not realised she was married to a woman in men's clothing is implausible, even accepting the naivety and innocence of many women in the late nineteenth century. Little is known of this relationship and Moore died in 1867.

In 1863, however, a year after his marriage to Sarah Moore, Evans undertook a third marriage. This time to a pretty Frenchwoman, Julia Marquand, a dressmaker who had been friends with Moore's sister. Evans told Marquand he was a French widower from a rich family, though why she did not reject him with this obvious deceit is hard to fathom.[14] Not only did she know he was not French, a widower or wealthy, let alone a man, she went along for over a decade with the masquerade. This third marriage was not amicable, with frequent arguments and separations. Evans often left in search of well-paid work as a miner. The State Library of Victoria in Melbourne contains a curious photograph of the young couple; Evans is a short man in a three-piece suit, one hand jauntily in his pocket and the other in the conventional pose of protection on his wife's shoulder. Marquand is a tiny woman in a day dress with a brooch at her throat. An opened book lies in her right hand, indicating symbolically she is a cultured and educated woman.

In 1872 the couple reconciled after a split. Then in 1877 Marquand gave birth to a baby whom she named Julia Mary, after her mother. Clearly Evans was not the father. In a spectacular court case in 1879, Marquand charged her brother-in-law with failure to provide maintenance for his illegitimate child. Marquand had lived with her sister and brother-in-law, Jean Baptiste Loridan. He had 'seduced her' while Evans was away working. The affair had apparently continued for several months until Marquand found she was pregnant. Loridan had pursued his sister-in-law since she was a child, Marquand told the court in December 1879. He held enormous power in Marquand and Evans' lives, as he owned the Great Southern Mine where Evans worked. Loridan had also given them money for the house in which they lived.[15]

Even stranger was Evans' confession in his declaration in court that 'I am hurted', and that he had watched the couple in bed on many occasions from a back window. This destructive emotional voyeurism damaged Evans for the rest of his life. The whole scenario was full of humiliation for Evans, for now he was forced to reappear as Tremaye dressed in women's attire. Worse, Marquand described herself as a 'single woman', while Tremaye– Evans said, 'I know Julia Marquand. I used to live with her. She was stopping in the house with me.'[16] This is a sad and pathetic declaration after so many years of marriage, however stormy and unstable.

Evans had endured a nervous breakdown and had been admitted as an insane patient to hospital a few months before the maintenance case. When he was 'outed' as a woman, the colonial press had a field day of titillating and racy revelations, dubbing the affair the case of the 'male personator'. The *Hobart Mercury* of 29 September 1879 kept Tasmanians up to date on revelations. Likewise

Edward De Lacy Evans with Julia Marquand in a very traditional pose, around 1871. Photo Aaron Flegeltaub; State Library of Victoria H29406.

the *West Australian* of 19 September 1879 regaled readers with this strange case in Sandhurst. They noted Evans was simply not physically capable of the hard manual work of a miner. He was constantly teased about his 'effeminate appearance' and lack of strength by fellow workers. Often he was seen 'ruminating' after the birth of the baby.[17] As an Adelaide journalist wrote on Evans' death in August 1901, 'From that time, Evans was not to speak the same man … no heart in her work'.[18]

In hospital, Evans refused to eat and was threatened with force-feeding by the matron of Bendigo Hospital, Mrs Holt. Given only women's clothing to wear, Evans refused to dress and was thus forced to stay immobilised in bed. Transferred to Kew Lunatic Asylum for refusal to resume his biological and cultural identity as a female, Evans supposedly suffered from 'cerebral mania'. The symptoms of this vague disease were apparently 'her' mistaken belief she could become a man and marry women. Doctors were confident that this was not a permanent condition and could be cured quite rapidly.[19]

The following year the *Australian Medical Journal* provided a report by Dr Penfold who conducted an examination of Evans. It makes painful reading, as the doctor described how he probed Evans' vagina, while he was 'weeping and sobbing the whole time, but making no determined resistance'.[20] His genitals were described as 'shrunken' and 'childlike'. The whole tone of the article demonstrates an intense psychological violence as well as physical pain inflicted upon the 'male personator'. As a physician in Melbourne, Penfold had come to the hospital specifically to examine the 'freak'.[21]

Evans, now forced to reassume his identity as Ellen Tremaye, attended the maintenance hearing where he declared how he felt 'hurted'. The rest of his life was filled with sadness. The colonial magazine *The Bulletin* on 25 September 1880 contained an article about the man-woman on display in the Egyptian Hall. Sitting on a packing case in a shapeless dress, this figure looked bored except when tormented by small boys. This was hardly the beginnings of an enhanced career. He also was an exhibit in the Living Waxwork display in Bourke Street, again with a lack of success. This is unsurprising. People wanted to see a hermaphrodite, a strange creature existing in the space between the sexes. But all they saw was a defeated, middle-aged, masculine-looking, depressed woman. In February 1881 Evans applied for re-admission to the Lunatic Asylum in Melbourne, unable to find work or sustenance. As he was not insane, he was admitted instead to the Melbourne Immigrants Home where he remained for the next twenty years. This operated like an English workhouse which only the most indigent would enter. Now living as a woman, she refused to use the name of Ellen Tremaye and preferred to be called Mrs De Lacy Evans.[22] In her numerous obituaries around Australia in 1901, she was called Mrs De Lacy Evans. An uneasy amalgam of her various identities. She assumed the persona of a married woman in the title 'Mrs', yet attached it to her male persona of De Lacy Evans.

Marion Edwards presents a different style of cross-dresser – flamboyant, jaunty and keen for publicity. Born in 1871 in

Marion 'Bill' Edwards, as pictured in *Lone Hand*, 1 January 1908. State Library of Victoria MC_--MC 0529; 84.

"-MARION-BILL" EDWARDS.

Murchison, Victoria, to a Welsh father, John Edwards, and a Scottish mother, Margaret McKay, Marion claimed Welsh birth. She spent a lot of her youth at her uncle's farm on the Goulburn River, where she acquired many of her bush skills. In her picaresque memoir, *Life and Adventures of Marion-Bill-Edwards* (1907), she claimed to have refused several offers of marriage, a sensible move given her predilection for making 'hot love' to as many women as she could. In the mid 1890s she decided to take on a male persona, and dress and work like a man. Marion became Bill.[23]

On New Year's Day 1900, William Ernest Edwards married widow Lucy Minihan at St Francis' Catholic Church in Melbourne, the same church where Edward De Lacy Evans had married Mary Delahunty. As a widow, Lucy must have been aware that her new spouse was not a biological man. Marion–Bill Edwards later asserted in the colourful memoir that this was a marriage of convenience. This assertion begs more questions than it answers. Lucy was a small businesswoman with a boarding house and therefore did not need someone else's income. As a widow she had a respectable status in society. Was the convenience for Marion to firmly establish her masculine credentials as a married man? Whatever their motive for marriage, it did not last, though the two were good and loyal friends.

Their friendship was severely tested on 30 April 1905 when Bill, now a racehorse trainer, was arrested on a charge of burglary at the Studley Arms Hotel in Collingwood. His friend 'Jigger' Pollock was also arrested. Bill waited a week in the cells before contacting Lucy, who arranged his bail; Bill was now described as her 'boarder'. The considerable sum of £50 was posted as bail. When Bill failed to appear for his hearing, Lucy served a term of one month's imprisonment.[24] Assuming the name of William McKay – his mother's surname at birth – Bill skipped bail and went to Queensland. There he worked at many casual occupations before a former acquaintance informed the police that, not only was William McKay a fugitive from justice, but he was a woman. A media frenzy ensued with much publicity generated from the subsequent arraignments and trials.

'Billarion' was a particular hit in Brisbane and remains part of its contemporary folk culture. On 5 October 1906, the *Brisbane Courier* featured an article on 'Little Willie: or Billie the Girl-Man'. To the journalist, Bill was a fascinating, vibrant character: 'Wealthy girl, horse owner, roughrider, masquerader, alleged burglar, painter, varnisher, fighter, barman, yardman, labourer, and ingenious lover – all these roles she is rightly or wrongly credited with having filled' were listed as Little Willie's accomplishments. Even more astounding, the journalist went on to declare that '… two things stand out – the affection she has everywhere inspired, and to-day remains loyal to her when behind gaol doors, and the successful endeavour she has made to earn an honest living'. Brisbane women showered 'Little Willie' with gifts, *billets doux*, notes of support and affection. She was a role model they distinctly approved of in this highly male-dominated society. Her send-off back to the south from the wharves in Brisbane was spectacular, with a large adoring crowd of mostly women and girls waving and cheering.

To confuse her critics, Edwards turned up in female attire at the burglary trial in Melbourne.[25] Both Bill and 'Jigger' were found not guilty. Bill then found instant fame as a waxwork exhibit as 'The Far-famed Male Impersonator'. One incident nearly stopped dead this career – literally. As part of the show, Bill demonstrated his skills as a sharpshooter, and a member of the audience was accidently shot, though not seriously. If there was a time to persecute him it was now. Yet the press, quite enamoured of the Australian Annie Oakley or Calamity Jane, dismissed the incident at the entertainment venue Cylorama as a mere accident.[26] Bill's public revelations of the number of sexual affairs conducted with women drew interest rather than censure. The *Brisbane Courier* on 5 October 1906 had already signalled the press reaction to these confessions: 'She liked her own sex – and they liked her. In fact the girls ran after her, for she was a loveable man with nice ways …'

Never was there a more damning indictment of Australian men's inadequacy in dealing with women's feelings and sexuality. On the other hand his former wife, now simply his boarding-house keeper, Lucy Minihan, told the *Truth* newspaper on 5 October 1906 that: 'As far as I know … EDWARDS IS A MAN. He has every appearance of a man and all the time I have known him I have taken him for a man.'[27] Supposedly to end confusion, Edwards granted an interview with the Melbourne *Herald*, published 18 October 1906, that simply created more speculation. When asked whether he preferred to be addressed as Bill or Marion, Edwards replied, 'Bill will do as well as Marion and Marion as well as Bill.' This gender play was taken as good fun, allowing the reader, then and now, to ponder the lines between identity, biology and cultural practices and conventions.

Edwards' autobiography has some correlations with Casanova's memoirs, though penned with far more delicacy, for it is largely an account of sexual conquests and affairs. There were stories of his days on the turf and of bar brawls, but largely it is a romantic and erotic journal. Cast often as flirtations, there is an ambiguity which requires the reader to add the details. The book garnered more attention for this folk hero. The nationalistic magazine *Lone Hand*, of 1 January 1908, featured a long article, 'Marion Edwards. A Modern de Maupin', portraying Bill as an enterprising hero with a fluid sexuality and identity. The journalist Beatrix Tracey was a sympathetic recorder and interpreter of Bill's life. At one revealing point she reports Bill saying: 'I don't think the world is much of a place for women. They have the same tiresome graft day after day; the same tucker (what the old man and the kids can't eat!) … And no amusements. That sort of thing would have killed me if I'd fallen in to it.' Clearly, as Marion she had a very astute understanding of the limited lives most women endured, tied to the house and rearing many children. Unlike most of them, though, Edwards had fashioned an independent adventurous life on her own terms.

In 1916 Edwards was again charged with a criminal offence, this time for selling sly grog. The case hit the newspapers, but the court proceedings were far more concerned with sleeping arrangements in the house where Edwards lived than in the matter at hand. There are some hilarious moments in the case when the judge told co-accused Annie McClelland that he found it hard to believe she did not know if Edwards was a man or a woman, despite sharing a bed together. McClelland rather evasively replied: 'I never asked her.'[28] McClelland was found guilty and sent to prison, though here it might be inferred her conviction was for sexual deviance while the nation was at war, rather than criminal activity.

Bill fell off the newspapers' list of sensational characters after this case. *Smith's Weekly* of 3 September 1927 referred to his career as a horse and pony trainer in Melbourne. In men's clothes, Bill continued to work in foundries and as a bookmaker in Melbourne, though by this time he was getting too old for hard manual labour. He continued to wear men's clothes until the indignity of being forced to don women's bedclothes on his admittance to the Mount Royal Geriatric Home.

Edwards died in March 1956, described incorrectly on his death certificate as an actress. Edwards would have been both furious and amused after all the masquerade, charm, good humour and irreverence with which she conducted her life both as a man and as a woman. The 1984 play *In Male Attire*, staged at the St Martin's Theatre, Melbourne,[29] would have appealed to her good sense of humour and her unrivalled achievement as one of Australia's most notorious women.

CHAPTER 6

'Madame Brussels' Caroline Hodgson

(1851–1908)

The wealthy madam of Melbourne who catered for only the best gentlemen.

In the late nineteenth century, Australia's leading citizens went sex mad. In 1878 the eccentric Melbourne evangelist Henry Varley began a personal campaign against prostitution and other sexual transgressions. He published a book, *On the Social Evil*, and followed this in 1891 with *The War Between Heaven and Hell in Melbourne*. Madame Brussels, the famous owner of elite brothels in Melbourne from 1874 to 1908, who catered for the upper end of the sex trade – her clients were cabinet ministers and the wealthy men of property and business – was his personal bête noir.

With a high ratio of men to women in the colonies, late marriage was common and sex was often a commercial transaction. Without adequate contraception married women did not usually view sex with their husbands as a pleasure, rather as a path to conceiving children. And for respectable unmarried women, sex was unthinkable. Many men found these restrictions too limiting for their libidos. Streetwalking and hotels catering for prostitutes and their clients, alongside the brothels, were regular features in every town and city. For many women with few skills, education and opportunities, prostitution offered higher wages, greater freedom and a modicum of economic independence. For some, like Caroline Hodgson, an exclusive form of prostitution offered a lucrative income and friends in high places in Victorian society.

Born Caroline Lohman in 1851 in Potsdam, Prussia, little is known of her early life. Potsdam, 25 kilometres south-west of Berlin, was a sophisticated centre of culture and scientific endeavour, and the administrative centre of Prussia before German unification under Bismarck in 1870. A city of magnificent buildings, ornamental gardens and lakes, it offered a vibrant and refined way of life.

It is not known when Caroline left Prussia, but in 1871 she married Studholme Hodgson, the son of a wealthy and well-connected Hampshire landowner, in the registry office at Hanover Square in London.[1] The couple went straight to Melbourne after their wedding, arriving in July 1871, suggesting the union did not have the blessing of the groom's family. The following year Studholme Hodgson joined the Victorian police force and was sent to the country station of Mansfield. Here he was appointed sergeant, a surprisingly low rank for a man of his background.[2]

A country posting was hardly the life for a well-educated, cosmopolitan young woman like Caroline. Horrified at the thought of living in a rural hamlet far away from cultural pursuits and talented people, Caroline did not accompany Studholme to Mansfield, and the marriage was over by 1873, although they remained on amicable terms until Studholme's death in 1893.

In 1874, Caroline began running her first exclusive brothel in the red-light district of central Melbourne, at 32–34 Lonsdale Street. The streets between Bourke and La Trobe, bordered by Spring and Stephen (now Exhibition) streets contained many types of venues for commercial sex, from hovels to the luxurious surroundings of the establishment of Madame Brussels, as Caroline Hodgson was known professionally.[3] At the lower end of the thriving market, conditions for both the workers and clients were dire, but at the exclusive end of the market Madame Brussels offered a heavenly retreat.

Caroline's establishment viewed from the outside was 'discrete rather than stately', an unpretentious villa screened by lattice enclosing a beautiful manicured garden.[4] A private entrance off Little Lonsdale Street allowed special clients with a key to keep their comings and goings quiet. The well connected and wealthy used this method in preference to the more public entrance.

The interior of Madame Brussels' establishment resembled a grand French bordello with marble bathrooms, carpets 'like meadow grass' and lavish furnishings in ebony, buhl and ormolu, alongside marble and alabaster statues of buxom women. Erotic though tasteful paintings adorned the walls. For particularly favoured and affluent clients, the grand boudoir boasted a large rococo bed 'canopied like an Imperial Throne', for services costing the extraordinary sum of £2000.[5]

There is no direct evidence that Caroline worked as a courtesan before she opened her brothel. It is, however, unusual for a madam not to have worked in the industry first before going into the organisational and managerial aspects of the business. As a young woman Caroline was breathtakingly beautiful and graceful, described as 'a magnificent pink, white and golden-maned animal'.[6] She did not accompany her husband to Mansfield yet, in those two intervening years, she gathered sufficient capital, cash flow and contacts to establish a successful 'gentlemen's club'. Some of the money came from parliamentarian and solicitor Sir Samuel Gillott, who financed her mortgage in 1877. He was also Caroline's solicitor and went surety for her mortgages on her first establishment.

How Caroline obtained the pseudonym 'Madame Brussels' is speculative. Cyril Pearl, in his *Wild Men of Sydney* (1958), proposed that she was originally married to a Belgian engineer who came to work in Melbourne.[7] This is not correct. Madame Brussels does have, however, a far more enticing Francophile ring to it than Madame Prussia or Madame Potsdam, and it suggests an exotic background, a synthesis between French and Belgian cultures.

With the huge land boom in the 1870s and '80s and a fluid population of literate, highly skilled men, there was money to be made in the sex industry. Not that Caroline would have employed such a crude and unvarnished term. Rather, her establishments offered affluent, often married gentlemen, whether in the pastoral, commerce, legal or parliamentary fraternities, a taste of high French frivolity with beautiful, well-mannered, well-educated young women in opulent surroundings. The best quality champagne and food was served in the evenings, and for those gentlemen who stayed overnight, a hearty breakfast of bacon, eggs and coffee was provided. Guests could stay for a week if they chose. One wealthy western districts pastoralist, after a large sale, spent a week there at a cost of £150, the equivalent of eighteen months' wage for a skilled workman.

By the end of the 1870s, Madame Brussels owned the finest, most exclusive establishment in Melbourne and perhaps the whole of Australia. She soon owned eight brothels, and two houses purchased for £1300. These businesses employed over thirty carefully chosen women, some of whom went on to be the mistress or, it was rumoured, the wife of a client.[8] Caroline took over her pre-eminent position from Sarah Fraser, who had entertained Prince Alfred, the Duke of Edinburgh, on his visit to Melbourne in 1867. Mother Fraser, as Sarah was known, had a brothel in Stephen Street that was luxurious and discrete. The Prince had been introduced to the brothel by none other than the Chief Commissioner of Police, Frederick Standish, thus allowing Fraser to capitalise on royal patronage. With the 1880–81 International Exhibition held in Melbourne, Stephen Street – adjacent to the exhibition buildings – was sanitised with a new name and the brothels relocated.[9] There were also other salubrious and well-appointed establishments operating in suburbs such as St Kilda.[10]

Unlike Madame Brussels' operation, other forms of prostitution were crude and highly visible. The investigative journalist John Stanley James, 'The Vagabond', wrote extensively of Melbourne's demimonde. He meticulously described the 'saddling paddock' in the Theatre Royal where '[t]heir startling dresses and painted faces, without reference to their manner, stamp them as lorettes … a positive nuisance and annoyance' during theatre performances as 'they flounce in and out of the stalls …'[11] In this bar, the prostitutes were watched over by their pimps or 'cads'. James noted that in Paris or Berlin by the 1880s a gentleman might take his wife or daughters to the theatre and 'sit next to a notorious member of the demimonde and not know it'. There, courtesans were refined and discrete, though well known to gentlemen. In Melbourne their behaviour was far more audacious. One writer to the *Herald* of 14 August 1882, using the *nom de plume* 'A Mother', stated that at a theatrical performance the prostitutes offered 'winks, nods, and sly glances … and speaking to every gentleman that passed, including those accompanied by ladies'.[12]

Madame Brussels' establishments stood out as the undisputed pinnacle of the vast network of the demimonde for over thirty years. Her clients came from the elite of Victorian society. The location of her central business in Lonsdale Street ensured easy availability to parliamentarians and cabinet ministers, able to meet in convivial surroundings. Caroline lived at the centre of political influence, albeit in a circumscribed and private way. No doubt her well-born first husband, now a member of the Victorian police force, was an entry card into police protection, but this did not stop her from being charged with brothel keeping in the 1890s, to which she was found not guilty.[13] In itself it was unusual for an elegant and well-connected madam to appear in court. The police usually hounded the older women and those on the street or in the 'saddling paddock'.[14] Her appearance may have been more a reaction to the public campaign against vice being mounted by the newspapers than about a conviction.

Associations with Madame Brussels sometimes proved dangerous for public figures. Solicitor David Gaunson, who acted for Caroline in addition to Samuel Gillott, was not the type you would expect to be taking care of a madam's legal affairs. His father, Francis Gaunson, was an elder in Dr John Dunmore Lang's Scots Church in Sydney. In 1869 Gaunson began practising as a solicitor in Victoria, entering parliament in 1875 as a progressive Liberal aligned with the Premier, Graham Berry. Engaged as defence counsel for Ned Kelly, he was a leading force behind the petition supporting clemency for Kelly. Yet his argumentative and combative personality, along with suggestions he accepted bribes, tarnished his reputation. His position as Madame Brussels' solicitor did little to improve his public image. Depicted as Garside in Frank Hardy's novel *Power Without Glory* (1950), the gambling baron John Wren's legal adviser, Gaunson's shady reputation endured.[15] He had wandered far from his stern Presbyterian upbringing into the dens of iniquity and sin.

Caroline's name had already been attached to a parliamentary scandal in October 1891. In newspaper reports it was revealed that the mace of the Victorian parliament was removed illegally and taken to a bordello where MPs satirised parliamentary procedures in a lewd and undignified parody. A parliamentary enquiry later suggested it was not in one of Madame Brussels' brothels but in her rival Annie Wilson's house of assignation – Boccaccio. However, the press continued to point the finger towards the infamous Madame Brussels' establishment.[16]

An astute businesswoman who ran her empire with Prussian efficiency, Caroline still found time to enjoy her private life. In 1894 she returned to Germany and met Jacob Pohl, whom she married in December 1895 at St Patrick's Cathedral in Melbourne. By this time, Caroline was matronly in appearance, wearing gold-rimmed spectacles, and described as 'looking like a benevolent midwife'.[17] Like her first marriage, this one did not last, and they were divorced in 1906.

She also had a long-term affair with the composer Alfred Plumpton. The music director of St Patrick's Cathedral in Melbourne, Plumpton was an unlikely choice for a brothel madam. His international music career involved co-producing Gilbert and Sullivan's *Trial by Jury* with Howard Vernon in Singapore in 1876, he was the music critic for *The Age*, and he composed the highly regarded Mass in G for the cathedral in 1881.[18] Apart from sacred music, he also composed popular tunes and light music. It was rumoured that together they had a daughter, Irene Hodgson, shortly before Plumpton's death in 1902 and while Caroline was married to Jacob Pohl. In a nasty exposé on 31 October 1903 *Truth* newspaper alleged that Madame Brussels kept Plumpton's photograph on her grand piano. 'When a female child was born the event was celebrated with a great orgie [sic]. All the "bloods" around town were invited and … the child was "christened" in champagne and named "Syphilia".'

No birth certificate for Irene has been discovered. Caroline frequently called Irene her 'adopted daughter', including in her will. Referring to illegitimate children as 'adopted' was a common stratagem, especially when the mother was engaged in nefarious activities. It also prevented the child suffering the label of bastard. Managing to avoid the usual pitfalls of illegitimacy, Irene was well looked after by Caroline. She lived in the expensive suburb of St Kilda and was educated at an exclusive private school.

But times were changing for Madame Brussels. At the turn of the twentieth century, the rise of sensational newspapers such as *Truth*, with its determined manifesto to uncover and denounce sin and scandal, meant that the topic of illicit sex dominated the newspapers. However veiled the terms, the astute reader could be assured of titillating revelations and salacious exposés. John Norton, the editor and owner of *Truth* since 1896, not only attacked wowsers – a term he claimed to have invented and popularised – but also the objects of the wowsers' ire. Thus he had it both ways in moral debates. A campaign with such headlines as 'The Central Cattle Pen' and 'Unhappy Women Herded in Stinking Sty' put brothel keepers of all levels on notice.[19] And it did not exclude those like Caroline who catered for the crème de la crème.

In 1904–06 Norton was a councillor in the Flinders ward of the Sydney Municipal Council, winning the seat of Surry Hills in the New South Wales Legislative Assembly. He had already exposed the operations of the Wind Club in George Street, Sydney, where worldly men met in a luxurious brothel, protected by police.[20] Not content with his Sydney domain, he set his eyes on a larger Victorian target for his next campaign. On 1 December 1906, *Truth*, under the headline 'Lechery and Lucre', directly addressed Sir Samuel Gillott, former Attorney General and Melbourne Lord Mayor, in the form of a letter accusing him of bankrolling brothels. A week later, more damaging allegations were printed concerning his professional alliance with Madame Brussels and her extensive empire of sin. To these allegations Gillott naively replied that he had been unaware of what sort of business she conducted on the various premises.[21] On 10 April 1907, *Truth* widened its concerns to include the relationship of brothel keepers and the police. Like Gaunson, Gillott had had dealings with John Wren, and in May 1906 was implicated in a gambling scandal and virulently attacked by the demagogue William Jenkins.[22] Deeply embarrassed, Gillott left the country soon afterwards.

The press offensive, along with these public outcries, resulted in the introduction of the *Police Offences Act* in 1907, whereby brothel keepers could be jailed and landlords who provided them with premises fined. This type of legislation had existed in the United Kingdom since 1885, but the colonial parliaments had been reluctant to take it on. By 1907 Caroline was seriously ill with diabetes and pancreatitis, and she closed everything. She died the following year and was buried next to her first husband, Studholme Hodgson, in St Kilda cemetery.

The era of the luxurious and decadent demimonde vanished with Madame Brussels' demise. In his autobiography, *The Pleasant Career of a Spendthrift* (1929), bohemian stockbroker George Meudell lamented the passing of the 'love palaces and their habitués. Where are they today? Gradually the Puritans annexed the money and power in the community ... and the joyousness of Melbourne night life was saliently squelched ...'[23]

CHAPTER 7

Helena Rubinstein
(1872–1965)

The poor Polish girl who established a global beauty empire in Melbourne and got ladies into make-up.

Helena Rubinstein, one of the most talented and successful businesswomen of the twentieth century, transformed women's appearance through her cosmetics and skin-care products. It would be fair to say that, along with fashion designer Gabrielle 'Coco' Chanel, she crafted the appearance of the modern Western woman. Her dictum that women needed to 'find themselves',[1] not just through the products and beauty regimes she developed, but as autonomous individuals, was revolutionary, and one that she practised herself.

The woman we know as Helena Rubinstein was born on Christmas Day in 1872, in Krakow, Poland, then part of the Austro-Hungarian Empire.[2] In her autobiography she describes her family as 'well to do', residing in the charming medieval section of Krakow near the university. She maintained that her grandfathers were wealthy mining magnates and that her father 'had a passion for bibelots, antiques and books', interests reminiscent of her cultivated and urbane first husband, Edward Titus, a dealer in rare books. The reality reveals an entirely different scenario.

Helena's birth name was Chaja, which she later anglicised to Helena. Her father, Hertzel Rubinstein, was a modest kerosene dealer with no business acumen. Her mother, Gitel Silberfeld, bore twelve children, four of whom died in infancy. Helena's parents were not legally married. They had undertaken the Jewish religious ceremony 'under the huppah', but had not legitimised their union in a civil service. They lived in the poor Jewish section of the ancient city.[3]

In her book, Helena states that she attended the local gymnasium, an elite secondary school, in preparation for entry into medical training at the University of Krakow – Copernicus' old university. Her assertion that she fainted on the first day of lessons in the operating theatre lacks credibility, as women were not admitted for medical courses to this university at this period, but it was a fabrication that established her claim to have been highly trained in modern science.

Some time in her teens, Chaja fell in love with a university student called Stanislaw, much to the horror of her parents who wished her to marry within the local Jewish community. With family tensions running high, Chaja left to live with her more sympathetic aunt, Rosalie Silberfeld Beckmann, never to return to her parents' home or secure their approval.[4] She later went to live with another aunt, Helena Silberfeld Splitter, in Austria. This Silberfeld sister had married well, her husband being a prosperous furrier. When the Splitters relocated to Belgium, Chaja decided to try her luck with another family who by this time had immigrated to Victoria.

Travelling as a 'tourist', 'Helena Juliet Rubinstein' left Genoa for Melbourne in 1896. 'I felt life in that part of the

world sounded much more promising than in Krakow,'
she declared in her autobiography. Already the romantic
version of her life story was being constructed in her mind,
with her Australian family branch described as wealthy,
cultured people. Again the reality was rather different.
Helena was headed for Coleraine, a small settlement some
300 kilometres west of Melbourne, where her uncle, Louis
Silberfeld, owned the local grocery store.[5] Life in rural
Victoria at the end of the nineteenth century would have
been challenging for young Helena, who had no interest in
rural pursuits, the weather and sheep prices – the usual topics
of conversation – but she settled in and learned English,
which she spoke forever with an exotic Polish accent.

Taking in her new surrounds, Helena was struck by
the women of Coleraine with their 'sun-scorched, wind-
burned cheeks'.[6] Helena abhorred the sun, which she
rightly believed destroyed a woman's fresh complexion. By
no means a beauty, she looked gorgeous compared to the
women around her, with her exquisite complexion of clear
white skin and her thick, glossy black hair. Petite, with a
high forehead and upright posture, she was an imposing
figure in her youth and later appeared fabulously gowned
and bedecked in exotic jewellery as she prospered.

Helena claimed she also brought twelve pots of face
cream from Europe with her, 'the cornerstone of my life',
and it is possible she obtained some from her family in
Poland to sell in Coleraine. Lindy Woodhead points out
in her account of Helena Rubinstein that it was quite usual
for Central European families to have their own recipes for
protective creams, which they would have made at home.[7]
Whether Helena could have obtained the ingredients in

Coleraine is not clear, but as a merino sheep-raising area Coleraine abounded in one ingredient she would later use with great success: lanolin.

Any business projects which Helena was conducting, however, were interrupted when she moved to Queensland around 1900. Why she left Coleraine we do not know, although she later confided to her secretary, the urbane Patrick O'Higgins, that her uncle 'took liberties' with her, prompting her to flee.[8]

It is possible Helena first worked with the well-connected Fairburn family at Meltham, near Geelong in Victoria, and that this was where she was invited by a friend who worked with Lord Lamington, the Governor of Queensland, to join his staff.[9] Accepting the position, she moved to Toowoomba where she supposedly acted as governess and language tutor in French and German to the Lamington children. As the children were infants and Helena had not learned French at this time, the story seems doubtful, but having lived in Vienna, she did have the rudiments of German.[10] It is more likely that she worked as a nurserymaid in Toowoomba, where the Lamington family often resided to escape the heat of the coast. Helena had assisted in the care of her numerous siblings and although later a stern mother to her own two sons, she had a good rapport with children all her life. She perhaps felt children did not judge her as more worldly, sophisticated adults might do. Whatever the case, within the Lamington household, Helena had the opportunity to observe the aristocracy in the colonies at close quarters and gather material on etiquette and manners which she later used purposefully.[11]

After leaving the Lamingtons' employment, following Lord Lamington's appointment as Governor of Bombay in late 1901, Helena went to Melbourne in 1902 where she first worked at the Café Doré, followed by the Winter Garden tea rooms, frequented by the city's bohemians. Her start in cosmetics in a big way came from John Thompson, the manager of the Robur Tea Company, whom she met at the Winter Garden, and a supposed shipboard acquaintance, a Miss MacDonald, who loaned her money.[12] They may have regretted later that they did not invest more heavily in her beauty salons and products! With the arrival of her sister Ceska in Melbourne, the stage was set to put the pieces into place.

With all the attention Helena had received for her skin, and given her presumable knowledge of family or folk recipes, it was perhaps natural for her to venture into beauty products, but establishing a commercial enterprise took real pluck. Helena was assisted substantially by John Thompson, whose eye for advertising and publicity was modern and aggressive. It is possible that they were lovers, although sexual liaisons were never a priority for Helena at any time in her life. She was also aided by the sponsor of her naturalisation application for British citizenship (as was the practice in Australia at that time), Frederick Sheppard Grimwade, the proprietor of a pharmaceutical manufacturing company. From his company she may have obtained distilled pycnogenol from Australian pine bark. Helena later claimed she had been given the original ingredients of her skin protector in Poland through the actress Modjeska, a patient of a supposedly famous Hungarian chemist, Dr Jacob Lykusky. Whatever their source, she adapted the basic ingredients of oil of almonds and pine bark extract with Australian products and the resulting Crème Valaze became the mainstay of her business.

Originally Crème Valaze was a versatile potion for both cleansing and moisturising the skin. With the addition of peroxide, the preparation was advertised as also assisting in the bleaching of freckles. Zinc oxide provided another agent to whiten women's skin.[13] There were already respected cosmetic products on the market, such as Theron Pond's Golden Treasure, launched in 1846 in upstate New York, followed later by his cold cream in 1905, alongside many products of dubious origin. But it was Crème Valaze that began the modern facial product business, luxuriously packaged and fragrant, replete with promises of transformation.

In 1903 Helena rented rooms in 138 Elizabeth Street in Melbourne, where she provided skin treatments and products. Originally she advertised her product as the work of 'Dr Lykusky, most celebrated European Skin Specialist …'[14] Protection of her product by patent, along with considerable press attention, resulted in the business taking off with extraordinary flair. However, a few mistruths were perpetrated in the advertisements. There were no rare herbs from the Carpathian Mountains, for example. Yet the product, in small glass bottles with tasteful labels, looked and smelt appealing and nourishing – just the luxury women needed to keep their faces fresh and smooth in the harsh Australian climate.[15] An early client, the famous actress Nellie Stewart, followed by the opera singer Dame Nellie Melba, lent endorsement to Valaze,[16] a marketing technique Helena perfected and used all her long career.

Helping to run the salon was her sister Ceska. Helena claimed in her autobiography that Ceska had studied chemistry with the famed Professor Joseph Kapp in Berlin, but Ceska had no more formal education than Helena, though she was an astute business manager and she ran the Melbourne salons for many decades.[17] Another of Helena's untrue claims was that Dr Lykusky himself came to Australia to assist her. Perhaps it was the chemists at Frederick Sheppard Grimwade's company who assisted in the scientific formulations of the product, but Helena was also an astute observer and practical researcher. She devised the system – now commonly used – of dividing women's skin into normal, oily and dry categories, each requiring different treatments. Later 'combination' and 'mature' formulations were added.

In early 1905 Helena left Melbourne and headed for Europe, where she briefly visited her mother in Krakow. Her mother may not have been pleased to see her 33-year-old daughter still unmarried and now embarked on a career in business. Whatever happened, the visit was cut short, with Helena claiming in her autobiography that she had to leave to undertake studies in dermatology in Paris with one Dr Berthalot and a Frau Dr Emmie List in Vienna.[18] She also visited a Dr Kapp at an exclusive spa at Wiesbaden, which proved to be a profitable relationship, for he kept her up to date for many years on various medical remedies for varicose veins and circulatory problems.[19] While in Europe surveying the various spa treatments available there, Helena also studied the new diet regimes that were fashionable and later adapted them for use in her clinics, along with a line of senna-based 'reducing' tablets, which were advertised as originating from King Edward VII's favourite spa at Marienbad.[20] An extensive section of her autobiography contains diet and nutrition schedules, but it is unlikely that she followed them herself. Helena's favourite foods were old Polish standards like crumbed chicken and fatty sausages.

Not content with surveying the latest European health and beauty treatments, Helena continued on to London where she sampled the treatments herself and visited Harrods and other department stores as possible vendors of her products. At this time such department stores did not sell cosmetics, which were still considered by respectable Englishwomen as paints for actresses and 'fallen women'. France was a little more advanced, with Guerlain producing lipstick as early as 1880, followed soon after by American Harriet Hubbard Ayer.[21] The Sears Roebuck catalogue of 1897 advertised 'lip rouge' but they did not sell well; in general they were too advanced for most women in the nineteenth century.[22]

Back in her expanded salon at 274 Collins Street in Melbourne's fashionable district, Helena proclaimed that with her two 'Viennese assistants', new equipment and face powders from Europe, she offered the most extensive treatments available in the country. The two Viennese attendants were her sister Ceska and cousin Lola. Helena called her clients 'patients' to emphasise the medical aspect of her business, and also offered massage treatments. Photographs of her dressed in a white laboratory coat reinforced the notion that her products were based on the latest scientific advances.[23]

Helena's business received considerable coverage in the fashionable Melbourne magazine *Table Talk*, established by fellow Jewish Pole Maurice Brodzky.[24] An exotic denizen of Melbourne at the time, Brodzky had served in the French army during the Franco-Prussian War in 1870–71; he was also language master at the exclusive Melbourne Church of England Grammar School. Brodzky later went to work for the Melbourne *Herald*, thus giving Helena access to influential journalists. The enthusiastic article about her new salon which appeared in *Table Talk* in December 1905 gushed at the beautiful carpets, ornate gilded chairs and modern equipment in her salon. Helena tactically offered the woman journalist who observed her premises a jar of her cream. In another article, Helena expanded on her scientific training, which now consisted of study with a Dr Pashki in Vienna, a Dr Lasaar in Berlin, a Dr Poitinoff in Paris and Dr Una in Hamburg, who had perfected the 'skin peeling' system for damaged complexions.[25]

Enthusiasm for Rubinstein skin products was not confined to Melbourne, or Sydney and Wellington in New Zealand where Helena had also opened salons. The provincial Hobart newspaper the *Mercury* regularly featured articles about her preparations. On 20 October 1909 an article entitled 'Beauty in the Making' advised readers they could purchase Mademoiselle Helena Rubinstein's book *Beauty in the Making*, translated from the original Russian, as well as purchase her Valaze Herbal Soap and Blackhead and Open Pore Cure. How a book was written in Russian when her native tongue was Polish with some Yiddish reveals a true show-woman in action.

By this time Helena had ventured into the field of cosmetics: an article in the *Sydney Morning Herald* of 25 September 1909 marvelled at her 'lip lustre' which coloured and protected lips. A widespread acceptance of lipsticks, or lip rouge as they were frequently termed, was set to revolutionise respectable women's appearance – cosmetics were moving from the brothel and the stage to the vanity case of the middle-class woman. In her autobiography, Helena maintained that it was Margot Asquith, the British Prime Minister's wife, who '… had the courage to use it [lip gloss] openly'.[26] In Australia Helena's and other cosmetics received support with the claim they protected the complexion from the harsh elements. As well, Helena's products were subtle in appearance, which made them attractive.[27] Other rival products were often brash-looking and far too medicinal for comfort. Baroness d'Orchamps, in her book *Tous les Secrets de la Femme*, published in 1908, advised women on the use of a pomade for the lips made from camphor.[28] No wonder Helena's products were popular.

It was in Sydney that Helena met her future husband, the American-born Edward Titus, who, like her, was of Jewish and Polish heritage. They married in July 1908. Initially Helena had employed him to promote her products and design packaging. Titus was urbane, well educated and sexually adventurous. As the journalist Grace Davidson observed, '[m]ost of all … [Edward Titus] adored beautiful, sexy women'.[29] Helena was neither and her autobiography contains a revealing incident concerning their honeymoon on the Côte d'Azur where Helena saw Titus – as she always called him – flirting with a beautiful young woman. Enraged, Helena stomped off to buy some expensive pearls and went immediately to Paris. She added, '[b]uying "quarrel jewelry" is one of my weaknesses. Some women buy hats, but I am more extravagant in anger, as I am in most things.'[30] Her vast collection of expensive jewellery attests to the stormy incompatibility of the marriage.

Their relationship always worked best at the professional level, and Titus was instrumental in launching Helena's European career. She acknowledged his valuable assistance when she made him an equal shareholder in Helena Rubinstein Ltd in 1909 (her sister Ceska also owned six per cent).[31] Moving to London, Titus convinced her to purchase a lease on a Georgian mansion at 24 Grafton Street, where she established a luxury beauty salon. This time the salon was launched not as her other salons in Australia and New Zealand had been, with extensive promotion and advertising, but with the offer of free patronage for wealthy, often titled, women. Enlisting the support of Argentinean Baroness Catherine d'Erlanger, a favourite of Helena (who rarely had time for friendship), Helena learned to cultivate, flatter and pamper rich women, the core of her new image.[32] Soon treatments were costing Helena's clients an expensive £200 per annum, but rather than paying for each service individually clients received annual accounts.

Not content with this success, on Titus' urging Helena invested in a salon at 255 Rue du Faubourg Saint-Honoré in Paris. This time Helena purchased an established business with a good clientele, as well as the formulas of the previous Russian proprietor's skin creams. Here Helena offered her Australian range and the renamed products of the new business. A new product named Liquidine spread over the world. Thousands of kilometres distant from the exclusive enclave of Parisian fashion, the Hobart *Mercury* of 2 October 1912 would feature an article entitled 'Is Your Complexion Safe?', recommending this new remedy for red and blotchy skin. Helena's excellent marketing skills, honed by Titus, allowed her to launch the first global brand of the twentieth century owned and promoted by a woman.

Back in London with her husband Helena gave birth to a baby, Roy, born in 1909. Helena was now getting about in much smarter clothes. In Paris, she had favoured the designer Paul Poiret. His Grecian-style robe was flattering in pregnancy and later his well-cut outfits with superb fabrics flattered her short and increasingly dumpy figure. She remarked in her autobiography that 'I caused a sensation when I returned [to London from Paris] with Poiret clothes in 1908.'[33] Like Helena herself, Poiret was a self-made innovator who became a major collector of modern art.

Though never a bohemian, Helena made many alliances in the Parisian demimonde. Another Pole, Russian-born Misia Natanson Sert, provided Helena's entrée into the artistic world of Paris. Years later Helena spoke cautiously of her friendship with the unpredictable and eccentric Sert, though she did not acknowledge how she benefited from her introductions.[34] Through Misia, Helena began to purchase modern art, including some valuable African masks that she kept all her life. Always a leader and initiator, Helena began also to use modern and avant-garde designs in her salons. She also introduced a massage regime that used vibrators as part of the treatment. The novelist Colette, then the lover of Misia, declared that after one of these massages she was ready for anything, including seeing her husband, Willy![35] In the years before World War I and the doctrines of Sigmund Freud, vibrators were regarded as acceptable therapy tools.

Never one to be idle for long, Helena commuted to Paris every month and ventured back to Australia again in 1911. In May 1912 at the age of forty, she gave birth to a second son, Horace, in England, where the family was living in a beautiful large house in semi-rural Richmond. In late 1912 the family moved to Paris, where Titus' business as a rare book dealer was more secure. Helena benefited as well, as she began her studies in dermatology at the St Louis Hospital. This gave some measure of veracity to the scientific claims of her products.[36] Her sister Pauline ran the salon in Paris while the London operation was left in the capable hands of a non-family member, Rosa Hollay. This was a strange move, for Helena usually entrusted the management of her salons largely to her sisters.

The outbreak of war made the beauty business appear frivolous. In October 1914 Helena decided to leave Europe and travelled alone to the United States, aided by Titus' American citizenship. No doubt the marriage was in trouble yet again, though she did not refer to any animosities at this time in her autobiography. Six months later Titus and their sons, accompanied by her impressive art collection, joined her in New York City. There the mood was far more carefree, as the United States would not join the Allies in war until April 1917.

Helena wisely travelled around the country, estimating where she could be most successful, before eventually opening a salon in May 1915 on 15 East 49th Street, New York, in the exclusive Upper East Side. Condé Nast's fashionable magazine *Vogue* covered the opening with undisguised enthusiasm. In a nod to the war effort in Europe, it announced that Helena's businesses in London and Paris were supplying much-needed products for the Red Cross. This would have heartened many wealthy women in Francophile New York who joined the war effort as ambulance drivers on the front and would later become her clients.[37]

Helena's new salon in New York was a masterpiece of design. With her collection of Nadelman sculptures, mahogany furniture covered in rose silk, and walls with dark blue silk wallpaper, the atmosphere was immediately impressive. But unlike with her operations in Australia and New Zealand, Helena had stiff competition in this vibrant city.[38] Her rival and adversary, Elizabeth Arden (born Florence Nightingale Graham in Canada) had already established her beauty business on Park Avenue in 1910. Decorated with a red door, Arden's trademark, the interior was a heaven of gold, white and pink, and her products were beautifully packaged and desirable. Both women were hard-nosed business operators who had no advantages of birth, culture or education. They were ambitious, driven and single-minded in pursuit of excellence and success. Like Queen Elizabeth I and Mary, Queen of Scots, these rivals never met, but kept their enmity alive for decades. They waged war in the press and through advertising campaigns.

Helena realised that she could not operate salons in every major city in the United States – she had a limited number of sisters and cousins willing to work under her stern directions for meagre salaries – so she established a salon in San Francisco under the direction of her sister Manka, then in 1916 she set on a plan that would revolutionise the entire beauty industry. Rather than purchasing cosmetics and face creams at her salons, by mail or in selected pharmacies – as she had pioneered in Australia – she determined to sell them in department stores. Thus her expensive treatments became available in exclusive stores such as the Texan store Neiman Marcus and Marshall Field's in Chicago. There they were displayed on special counters with staff dressed in pretty uniforms and well trained by Manka and Helena in both promotion and beauty techniques. Helena, Manka and several assistants toured the country, spying out suitable locations for the Rubinstein range. Helena personally oversaw the introduction into each store, arranging ahead of time for publicity in newspapers.[39]

In 1918 with her business flourishing, her home life spiralled to an all-time low. Titus had more than an eye for gorgeous women; he was a libertine who saw marriage as no bar to his sexual adventuring. There came a point when Helena could no longer keep turning a blind eye. She hired a private detective and found out more than she might have wanted to know about her husband's infidelities. Armed with the report detailing an affair, Helena declared war, and from then on often conducted her relations with Titus through lawyers, employees and relatives.[40] They maintained civil business dealings but avoided each other as much as possible. They were not divorced until 1937.

For those twenty years, Helena tormented Titus with her hold over money and his financial security. His business as a rare book dealer evolved slowly and his ventures into publishing, with the establishment of the Black Manikin Press in Paris, were expensive initiatives he could not afford. For someone unreflective of herself, Helena made a startling admission in her autobiography that she had become 'more difficult to work with' and was on 'the verge of a nervous breakdown'.[41] At nearly fifty, she was tired, angry and deeply lonely.

At the end of World War I, Helena left the boys with Titus, who was an exemplary father, and the business with Manka, and returned to Europe, where she consoled herself with massive expeditions to purchase art and jewellery. She purchased a beautiful apartment on the Quai de Béthune, which she filled with her expanding collection of art. She also acquired considerable commercial property in Montparnasse. Yet this reckless acquisition did not heal the pain of her estrangement from Titus. One of her hobbies, in her rare time off her work, was trawling through flea markets picking up bargains. This was a pastime she had enjoyed with Baroness d'Erlanger a decade earlier in London.

The post-war era launched a new approach to women's appearance and clothing. Influenced by Coco Chanel, clothes and hairstyles became streamlined and sleek, shown off best on thin, boyish figures. With the internationalisation of Hollywood films, new forms of cosmetics slowly became acceptable. Mae Murray and Clara Bow in the 1920s revelled in the new, coquettish modes for young women, with make-up, overt sexuality and fast lifestyles. Helena was always on top of new developments; indeed, she was ahead of them. She had earlier manufactured mascara for the silent star Theda Bara and devised a sophisticated silver eye shadow for her as well.[42]

Helena met this new challenge head-on with irrepressible energy and determination and new ranges of cosmetics. Her lipsticks, bright and long-wearing, were a far cry from the subtle dab of lip rouge of a generation ago. In some areas she remained steadfastly old-fashioned, though. She abhorred the new mode for sunbathing, made popular by Chanel. But with the boyish figure all the rage, Helena saw another opportunity for expansion. She added an exercise class in her new New York salon on 57th and Park Avenue; however, it was so exacting it failed. She also adopted the new styles, such as jersey pants, which hardly flattered her matronly figure. Always ahead of the game, Helena was an early client of designers Jeanne Lanvin and Elsa Schiaparelli.

Helena had an extraordinary eye for business. In December 1928 she sold out the US component of her business to Lehman Brothers, thereby avoiding the destructive forces of the Depression just a year ahead. She dissembled about this in her autobiography, claiming that she had wanted to be by Titus' side in Paris.[43] Part of her still wanted to be loved and cherished by her erring husband from whom she had been estranged for a decade, yet she did not tell him of her intending sale of the US business, or that she and their sons were going to Australia for a while. As she ventured from the United States, Helena was one of the wealthiest women in the country – and all by her own hands.

For a woman who was relentless in her pursuit of wealth and fame, this period in her life without her American business was depressing. She released a book, *The Art of Feminine Beauty.* It may have expanded on the first book she wrote in Australia in 1909, but it is now lost to researchers and we can only hazard a guess as to what was in it. Her relationship with Titus continued to obsess her. His affair with the writer of erotica Anaïs Nin so enraged Helena that she retaliated by removing Titus from their jointly held business dealings in Paris. She also bulldozed their property in Montparnasse, thereby destroying the famous Jockey Club.[44]

In 1934 Helena, who had taken on the persona simply of Madame, purchased back her US business at rock-bottom prices. She also ventured into the area of hormone rejuvenation, launching Hormone Twin Youthifiers, which did not pass the new Federal Drug Administration rules for cosmetics although her Ultrafeminine hormone crème was approved.[45] In response she expanded her cosmetics range. Her own rejuvenation came with marriage in June 1938 to forty-three-year-old Prince Artchil Gourielli-Tchkonia from Georgia, a year after her divorce from Titus. Both were pleased with the union – Madame was suddenly a princess, and he was connected to a wealthy woman who indulged his passions for gambling and an easy life. Living in a new apartment in New York, her business flourished – with the April 1939 *Vogue* cover featuring the Rubinstein Orchid Red lipstick. Her new waterproof mascara showed she was at the top of her game even as she approached seventy.

As the world entered World War II, avowed workaholic Helena began to find her husband's lifestyle a little too leisured, especially in wartime. Meanwhile, she had entered into the area of men's toiletries, opening the House of Gourielli in the St Regis Hotel lobby. This initiative simply sucked money out of her core business. With her extensive factories and supplies in the United States, Helena Rubinstein Inc. did not suffer unduly during the war years, but a shock to both Madame and her rival, Elizabeth Arden, hit suddenly in 1952 when Revlon launched the spectacularly successful Fire and Ice campaign. The following year Estée Lauder entered the skin-care market. The game had now clearly changed.

Yet Madame's greatest challenge at this time was personal. Gourielli died suddenly in 1955 while Helena was in Paris. His death was an event she could not have anticipated – he was so much younger than she was and never worked a hard day in his life. Too distraught to return to New York for the funeral, Helena was rich beyond her dreams, but now a lonely widow.

Taking two years to recover, in 1957 she embarked on an extensive trip which included Australia. There she was welcomed as a celebrity and continued her patronage of the arts. She established the Helena Rubinstein Art Prize in Sydney, and had her portrait painted by William Dobell and Graham Sutherland. These were more conventional portraits than earlier Surrealist-inspired ones by Dali and Dufy in the 1930s. What they captured was her imposing fortitude – she resembled an Easter Island stone monument in these renditions.

Towards the end of her life, though she was notoriously frugal with money (except on her art and jewellery), Helena invested heavily in philanthropy. The Helena Rubinstein Foundation was established in New York in 1953 and the Helena Rubinstein Pavilion for Contemporary Art in Tel Aviv was a generous gift to the new nation of Israel. In these last years, when work no longer consumed her, she travelled with an energy that belied her advanced years. When she did work, it was conducted from her lavish canopied bed, yet sadness and tragedy hit again when her son Horace died in April 1958.

In 1965, just before her death at the age of ninety-two, Helena published her autobiography, *My Life for Beauty*. Rather than setting the record straight, Helena codified her severely edited and fabricated version of her life, a story so extraordinary it needed no embellishments or fables. Instead she gave the fictionalised version of her family origins, her education, her training and expertise, making herself Madame Rubinstein, or simply Madame, a well-born Jewish woman from an educated and cultivated

Helena Rubinstein (undated) about to embark on one of her many voyages. Bain Collection, Library of Congress LC-B2-6558-1.

family, with scientific training, saviour of women's complexions worldwide. Helena was a notorious fabricator of her personal life, though never her substantial business achievements.

Helena Rubinstein died on 2 April 1965. In death she showed again her curious meanness. Faithful servants who had provided decades of service received pittances. For all those decades of striving and success, Chaja Rubinstein had never learned charity, kindness and generosity, thus diminishing the reputation of one of the world's finest business tycoons.

CHAPTER 8

Adela Pankhurst
(1885–1961)

*The rebel pacifist and socialist who became a fascist and
Japanese supporter in World War II.*

Adela Pankhurst was one of the most perplexing characters
in Australian history during the world wars. She was a
spirited suffragette and one of the founders of the Women's
Social and Political Union (WSPU) in England, a militant
socialist and pacifist during World War I and a founder of
the Communist Party of Australia (CPA) in 1920. In the
late 1920s, Adela switched to the right, and then to the
extreme right in the Depression years, only to find herself in
an internment camp during World War II as a supporter of
the Japanese. At all stages of her public career, she attracted,
in turns, notoriety, admiration and profound antagonism.
Deeply emotional to the point of irrational devotion to
various causes, Adela lived her life with passionate intensity.
She took the motto of her father, lawyer Dr Richard
Pankhurst, that 'life is nothing without enthusiasm' to
such extremes that her actions and fundamental changes in
beliefs were both bizarre and enigmatic.[1]

Adela's parents, Richard and Emmeline, were central
figures of the English secular reform movement intent
upon improving conditions in the mid Victorian age.

Unlike earlier radical movements in the very early nineteenth century, such as the abolition and emancipation campaigners at whose core lay evangelical religion, the newer movements from the 1830s were more secular and political. The Chartists sought to establish the legitimacy of the working-class labour movement, while electoral reformers sought parliamentary representation for the emerging middle class.[2] In some senses, Richard Pankhurst straddled both these eras of English radicalism. His parents were fierce Baptists and devoted to political liberalism, a common combination in areas such as Stoke-on-Trent where Richard was born in 1834. As a non-conformist Protestant, he was unable to study at Oxford or Cambridge, which only admitted Anglicans, and so was educated at Owens College (later Manchester University) and the University of London, established by the utilitarian philosopher Jeremy Bentham. Both these institutions were renowned for their radical emphasis. On his return home to Manchester in 1868, Richard devoted himself to republicanism, women's suffrage and the abolition of the House of Lords and the established Church. His attempts to enter parliament were unsuccessful; his blunt approach and self-righteousness did not attract voters. His third daughter, Adela, possessed much of her father's heavy-handed style and inability to compromise, or even to listen to others' points of view.[3]

Emmeline Goulden Pankhurst always claimed she was born on Bastille Day in 1858 although she was actually born on 15 July that year. The daughter of a wealthy cotton manufacturer, her early life was privileged and secure. This was new money and security, and the family was not far removed from industrial poverty in the previous generation.

Emmeline's mother, Sophia, had been an early feminist and supported Emmeline's education at an exclusive school in Neuilly, France. There her best friend was Noemie de Rochefort, whose father was banished for his activities in the Paris Commune in 1870–71.[4] When Emmeline returned to Manchester in 1878 she met Richard, a lawyer and fellow advocate of women's franchise rights. The pair married in 1879 and had five children: Christabel (1880–1958), Estelle Sylvia (1882–1960), Frank (1884–88), Adela Constantia Mary (1885–1961) and another Frank whom the family called Harry (1889–1910). Neither parent allowed their family to deter their intense political activities in the suffrage movement and the establishment of the Independent Labour Party (ILP). The children were left to the care of servants. Emmeline does not even mention Adela and Harry in her posthumously published autobiography, thereby writing her rebellious daughter out of her account of the suffrage movement. In any case, a sickly child with her legs in splints, Adela was rarely the object of her mother's affections.[5] An older father, Richard was often gruff and incomprehensible to his children, although he was more attentive than Emmeline.

In their new home in Russell Square in London in July 1889, a fortnight after Harry's birth, Emmeline, along with Richard, established the Women's Franchise League. Four years later the family returned to northern England where the girls were sent to the exclusive Manchester Girls High School. Much of their life education was spent watching their parents' involvement in radical social reforms, particularly for women and children. In 1898 Richard died at the age of sixty-three, leaving the family almost destitute. Adela was taken from Manchester Girls and sent to a local boarding school, then to the Disley Road School as an apprentice teacher.[6] Surprisingly, Emmeline was not entirely in favour of rigorous studies for girls, an attitude seemingly at odds with her militant feminism. However, Christabel was permitted to undertake law studies at Manchester University.

During the Boer War (1899–1902), Adela took her first independent steps towards political action. Both she and young Harry decided they were pacifists. Her deep hatred for British Imperialism stemmed from this period, as well as her distaste for financiers and Jews. With a mélange of views that were often contradictory, so began the pattern of Adela's political life: deeply held convictions, expressed with emotional vehemence, regardless of internal consistency and logic. Despite her secular upbringing, she also embraced a naïve, fervent fundamentalist Christianity. Adela's time as a pupil-teacher intensified both her incipient socialism and Christianity. Her pupils were desperately poor and ragged, even by the standards of industrial slums. Their poverty, malnutrition and poor health had a lasting impact on the young Adela. When she later moved to the far right during the Depression in Australia, she recalled the plight of these damaged children.

The WSPU was formed in October 1903 in the Pankhursts' front parlour, as a breakaway women's lobby group from the male-dominated ILP, but it was not Emmeline's efforts alone that established this new aggressive vehicle for political action. The movement crossed class boundaries, although most of its leaders were middle-class women with the time to devote to meetings, writing pamphlets and, soon, engaging in fierce demonstrations. Aged eighteen Adela was always more concerned with the rights of working-class women, especially those burdened with large families. Many of her talks were aimed at working-class women, whereas her mother and Christabel focused on middle-class women.[7]

In June 1906, Adela was arrested for disrupting a Liberal Party meeting and sentenced to seven days in prison. She had tasted the thrill of extreme defiance and now found herself hooked. The discipline required in teaching disadvantaged children taxed her emotionally, whereas the spotlight of public meetings, the camaraderie of a struggle, and the intoxication of fighting for a moral cause were far more seductive and appealing.

Adela moved to London in October 1906, where the feminist movement was larger and more active, and she threw herself headlong into militant advocacy. Along with others, she was arrested for being part of a demonstration in the House of Commons lobby, and spent time in Holloway Prison. This was a turning point in the WSPU campaign. From there on it escalated its confrontational tactics, causing much consternation within the ILP. By 1909, damage to 10 Downing Street, violent demonstrations in Trafalgar Square, London, Manchester and other northern centres, alongside hunger strikes by imprisoned suffragettes, marked the movement's transformation into a radical challenge to English democracy. Adela's capacity to understand the nature and limitations of working-class women's lives made her tours to provincial areas successful. The work was unrelenting and gruelling, and Christabel, in her memoir, generously praised Adela for her efforts in this area.[8]

In 1910 Harry died from poliomyelitis at the age of twenty. He had been Adela's confidant and comrade-in-arms throughout their childhood and adolescence and her health deteriorated due to exhaustion and stress in the wake of his death.[9] In many regards this was her breaking point with the suffragette cause. Along with her sister Sylvia, Adela had become increasingly devoted to socialist causes, and the split with Emmeline and Christabel, who were concerned with more conservative politics and were anti-socialist, was brutal and irrevocable. Surprisingly, Adela later said she thought the vote had been won by the more conservative methods of the National Union of Women's Suffrage Societies.[10] In a letter to former leading suffragette Helen Fraser Moyes, she wrote:

> I never regarded the militant tactics as more than
> a drum which attracts attention and brings up the
> crowd to hear the message. I had time to realize [in
> 1910] that militancy was out of control ...[11]

Her activities almost ceased when she undertook, at her mother's insistence, studies in agriculture in Warwickshire. Emmeline wanted to get Adela out of the spotlight, but this was hardly a suitable career move for a feisty young woman and she failed to complete her studies. She then worked as governess to Alec and Betty Archdale in Switzerland in 1912, and agreed to accompany them to Australia.

Adela was packed off to Australia with a meagre £20 in her purse, a letter of introduction to women's suffrage campaigner Vida Goldstein, and some knitted woollen clothes.[12] She arrived in Melbourne in March 1914 and was met by Vida Goldstein and the pacifist singer Cecilia John.[13] Vida was the first woman to run for parliament, after Australian women had won the right to vote in federal elections in 1902, twenty-six years before Britain. Adela's fame by association preceded her and she was no doubt less than pleased to be recognised as 'Miss Adela Pankhurst, daughter of the noted English suffragette'. Her play *Betrayed*, written in 1917, channels many of the emotional traumas she experienced through her mother's ruthless tunnel vision and favouritism towards Christabel.[14] It was reminiscent of a Victorian melodrama, with the black sheep of the family dispatched to the distant colonies, although its political themes – the dangers of a Chinese invasion and a military dictatorship if conscription was introduced – masked Adela's personal wounds.

In Australia, Adela the militant suffragette and passionate socialist was a star and did not have to compete for attention with her mother and sisters. She was famous as an orator and campaigner for working women's rights. Her first speech in May 1914 to an enthusiastic crowd in Melbourne, in a hall festooned with the purple, green and white colours of the WSPU, was highly praised in the socialist press. In July she gave an impassioned speech highlighting the plight of English women factory workers who earned one penny an hour,[15] yet the intense and uncritical adulation she received sowed the seeds of her eventual undoing. She loved the spotlight, the roar of the crowd, and the urgency of discussing radical issues in public. Her talks across south-east Australia were highly emotional and intense, as she castigated the British Liberal government under David Lloyd George for its inhumane treatment of women activists.[16]

These forays gave her the attention she desired but had a limited shelf life. In order to progress her reputation, Adela needed to find an Australian theme to interest her audience. The outbreak of war in August 1914 presented her with the opportunity to shine. Recalling her pacifism during the Boer War, which sat alongside a dangerous admiration for Germany, Adela revived her commitment to peace. Closely aligned with Vida Goldstein, who had visited England in 1911 to address the WSPU, Adela took on pacifism with an alarming fervour. With women split over the issue of Australia's participation in the war, the battle lines were drawn. Adela accepted the role of secretary of radical activist group the Women's Political Association in early 1915, while maintaining her membership of the Australian Peace Alliance. The war years were the highpoint of left-wing activism in Australia, with anarchists, socialists, Bolsheviks, anti-conscriptionists and various anti-war activists clamouring for attention to turn around militarism – although there were some Melbourne activists, such as Lizzie Ahern, who were militant socialists, not pacifists.[17] Adela's pamphlet 'Put up the Sword!' published in November 1915, sat firmly in the pacifist camp – at least for the moment.

In July 1915 Vida Goldstein and Cecilia John renamed the Women's Political Association the Women's Peace Army (WPA). This pre-emptory move alienated many progressive but mainstream feminists, as a militant pacifist and anti-conscription organisation ran counter to the beliefs of many supporters. Adela was among its first members. Her pronouncements often seem illogical. She pointedly asked a female audience to remember that 'Women! You have a duty to Humanity, to God', as she discussed the dangers to British womanhood of civilisation crumbled and women resorting to prostitution for survival.[18] At this Bijou Theatre performance in Melbourne her speech on 'The War and the White Slave Traffic' missed its mark, for the central concern of the audience was involvement in the war.[19] The origins of her move later to extreme right-wing politics and women's role in the family can be detected in these emotional pleas. Her activities were not always confined to polemic and public declaration, she had strong practical skills as well. Adela and Cecilia established a farm at Mordialloc to earn much-needed cash, as well as a women's employment bureau at 229 Collins Street, Melbourne. Adela also involved herself in the consumer issues of the day, as prices soared and wages fell.

The Socialist, a journal of the Victorian Socialist Party (VSP), proclaimed: 'Adela the star. Is she not the most popular woman in the world? And such a young thing too. Wherever did she pick up all that knowledge?'[20] This patronising praise only fuelled the beginnings of a desperate and ongoing need for public adulation. The referendum on conscription in 1916 gave her the perfect opportunity to expand her repertoire of activism. Labor Prime Minister Billy Hughes needed a positive vote in the referendum on the issue of compulsory military conscription for overseas service to overcome the *Defence Act* of 1909, which provided only for (male) conscription in the event of war on Australian soil. Deeply committed to the Imperial war effort, Hughes – knowing that the Allies were not doing well, especially after the Battle of the Somme in July 1916 – wanted to commit more troops. Adela exhausted herself with vehement anti-conscription protests as she toured Australia and New Zealand (where conscription was already a reality).

This arduous tour brought her into the orbit of Tom Walsh, a sympathiser of the anarcho-syndicalist organisation the Industrial Workers of the World (IWW). He had already clashed with former union leader Billy Hughes and aligned himself with the radicals. Walsh was elected New South Wales Secretary of the Federated Seamen's Union of Australasia in 1912.[21] There was trouble brewing; his union was anti-conscription but pro-war. This mirrored many allegiances in the labour movement in Australia. The Labor Party split everywhere except in Queensland, where the socialist government under T. J. Ryan was able to maintain unity. Adela undertook a tour of regional Queensland, New South Wales and then Adelaide in support of the 'No to Conscription' vote in July and August 1916. She showed herself to be tireless, charismatic and defiant.

Signs of later developments in Adela's thinking were on display at her performance at a rally in Melbourne on 27 September 1916. Criticising the Imperial tie, she demanded 'Australia for the Australians'. The gathering took on the atmosphere of a religious revival meeting.[22] In October 1916 Adela shared an open-air platform with later prime minister John Curtin and trade unionist Jennie Baines. With the arrest of the key members of the IWW on conspiracy charges that month, and increased state surveillance and intimidation of anti-war activists, Adela was on an emotional high. After a WPA meeting in Melbourne, she was carried on the shoulders of her supporters to much acclaim.[23]

On 28 October the 'No' vote to conscription prevailed all over the country, except in Victoria. Loyalties and old friendships were torn asunder by ideological rancour as the first conscription referendum was lost. Adela and Vida Goldstein too found they had less in common as Adela moved more towards radical politics with male colleagues. In early 1917 Adela resigned from the WPA and joined the VSP as an organiser, touring Western Australia with John Curtin to argue against Australia's commitment to the Allied war effort. To mark the occasion *The Socialist* advertised a 'plastic bust of Miss Pankhurst' on sale for three shillings and ninepence.[24] The government considered charging her with sedition but a wiser course was taken, although not one to Adela's liking: the press was forced to largely ignore her speeches through intense official censorship.

Adela lost the close ties of emotional warmth and support of her new maternal figure Vida and went to stay with Ethel and Robert Ross – generous socialists who had been caring for Tom Walsh's three daughters following his wife's death in 1914. Cut loose from Vida's more calming influence, Adela undertook a series of aggressive direct actions. With constant arrests, she spent a lot of time in court defending herself. The authorities tired of her almost hysterical harangues against the Prime Minister, and other federal parliamentarians decided to increase their pressure on her. She was sentenced to six months' imprisonment for leading a demonstration against rising food prices in September 1917, although she was released on appeal. Fed up with what he saw as her disruptive antics, Hughes called her a 'little devil' and considered her deportation. Earlier a series of IWW radicals had been deported, often illegally. Adela was a different category of rebel: she commanded too many supporters in England and Australia, and she was a woman.[25]

In late September 1917, dressed in her grandmother's remodelled silk petticoat, Adela suddenly married Tom Walsh. The service was conducted in Melbourne by reforming parson the Reverend Frederick Sinclair, with Tom's daughter Hannah Walsh as bridesmaid.[26] Adela sometimes claimed that she undertook this marriage to the much older Irish widower because she was threatened with deportation,[27] but their union was stable and happy, and the one enduring emotional calm in her life. No sooner were they wed than Adela was sent to prison for four months in November 1917 for leading a demonstration banned under national security regulations. This was not a good time for extreme antagonism towards the government. There had been a series of long, bitter strikes in 1917 in Australia, and a second conscription referendum had been lost. At the extended battle of Passchendaele in Belgium, lasting from June to November 1917, the Australian Imperial Forces lost many men to the savage brutality of trench warfare. But it was the success of the Bolsheviks in Russia that alarmed liberals and conservatives alike. The fear of communism was to dominate Australian politics for the next sixty years.[28]

On her release from prison, Adela resigned from her position in the VSP, largely in order to assist with editing the *Seamen's Journal*, from its base in Sydney to where she and Tom moved. In November 1918 she gave birth to Richard, the first of her five children. Like earlier feminists, Adela did not believe in contraception, seeing it as against nature. For a short time her life became more contained within the domestic sphere. However, with the seamen's strike in early 1919 and Tom in the spotlight, Adela again entered public life. This was a period of intense industrial and ideological struggle in Australia, with frequent clashes between ex-servicemen and radical workers, who were more and more inclined to Bolshevik doctrines. Adela took on the new ideology with her usual intense enthusiasm, but her activities were limited by the arrival of another baby, Sylvia, in late 1920. That year she and Tom had joined the new CPA as founding members. Her first article in the journal *Australian Communist* attempted to balance family and the revolution, a theme she would pursue more ardently as a fascist in the 1930s.

Adela was hardly a theoretical Marxist or doctrinaire in her approach; rather, her methods and loyalties were based on emotion. The new party, with its subservient devotion to the Comintern in Moscow, was scarcely aligned with the needs of a charismatic and iconoclastic woman like Adela, and she and her husband left the party within a few years. By this time they had three small children.

Adela and her family relocated to Melbourne for Tom to find work. Now the war was over, Adela found there were no longer the burning issues that had previously consumed her time. For someone who needed public attention, these were stultifying years. For Tom, too, they were hard years as he moved more to the right, antagonising many in his fiery union. He favoured arbitration, as well as tactics delaying ship departures, to secure his members better conditions. Employers successfully applied to deregister the seamen's union in June 1925, and the new conservative Prime Minister Stanley Bruce moved swiftly to introduce legislation banning certain radical organisations, with deportation provisions aimed at decimating the union leadership of its 'foreign' – non-British born – leaders like Irish-born Tom Walsh. Amendments to the *Crimes Act* provided the government with a powerful weapon to target radical unions. Tom and his deputy, Jacob Johnson, were arrested on charges of inciting workers to strike and sent to Garden Island in late 1925.[29] Adela, pregnant once again and with four children to look after, worried how they would cope if Tom was banished. For the Walshes there was personal tragedy when their new baby, Faith, died in January 1926. Adela retreated from public life to home and family to recover her spirits and strength.

Tom successfully appealed against his deportation, but his experience of the force of state power caused him to re-evaluate his position on industrial militancy. He lost the presidency of the union in 1928. That year, also, Adela made an extraordinary move to the right, founding the Australian Women's Guild of Empire, despite her earlier hostility towards the British Empire. She had made a cautious peace with her mother, who died in June 1928. For all her previous opposition to Emmeline's and Christabel's moves to more conservative positions, like supporting the Imperial war effort in World War I, she followed the same path from militancy to intractable conservatism.[30] She was a firm supporter of the conservative new Industrial Peace Union, and became now a determined enemy of communists and radical labour supporters. When Tom lost his earning capacity within the union movement, their resentments grew in wild profusion. Both of them supported themselves through casual journalism for magazines such as *Pioneers* and *Empire Gazette*, a considerable feat with seven children to support. Later the Guild provided a meagre wage on which the family survived.

Like earlier nineteenth-century feminists who preached the doctrine of domestic feminism to reinforce women's security in the home but worked tirelessly outside their own homes, Adela exhorted women to become better mothers. Yet she retained her interest in industrial peace and militancy, speaking frequently on these issues to often bewildered listeners who could not comprehend how her views had so dramatically turned around. She was not alone in such about-faces. Sir Oswald Mosley in England went from Labour MP in 1931 to founder and leader of the British Union of Fascists in 1932; and former suffragette Norah Dacre Fox also became a fascist.[31] The largest mass movements in Australia in the 1930s were organisations in Sydney such as the proto-fascist paramilitary New Guard. The worldwide Depression left parliamentarians, economists, trade unionists and citizens struggling with solutions to cope with this devastating dislocation so soon after the war. Communists may have been feared in Australia but they were few in number, unlike the extreme right-wing organisations.

The Guild's activities in the years 1933–34 were reminiscent of a Christian charity: supplying food to the needy, providing clothes and toys for children, and free entertainment for the families of unemployed workers. Expanding as the despair and poverty of the Depression escalated, the Guild attracted many well-connected women to its ranks, including architect Marion Mahoney Griffin. How Adela found her niche amid all this knitting and pouring of cups of tea in the streets is puzzling, as it was a domain far from suited to her adversarial nature. Her new doctrine was the destructiveness of industrial strikes and she pushed her views on former comrades-in-arms from the left, then she would dash off to a factory and preach to the entirely unconverted.

As the Guild's momentum slowed, in 1937 Adela expressed yet another developing passion – for Germany. Since the time of the Boer War she had despised British Imperialism and identified with the Boers (whom she had mistaken for Germans). She later sympathised with the Germans and lamented how harshly the Allies had treated a defeated Germany in the Versailles Treaty of 1919. By 1937 she took to arguing that the Nazis had been

Adela Pankhurst Walsh, standing on a chair in the street outside the Carrington Press Printers, Sydney, 28 January 1941. SMH News picture by Staff; Fairfax Media 2362105.

democratically elected and brought industrial peace to a troubled nation. With the maverick businessman William Miles funding the incendiary journal *The Publicist*, from July 1936, she was provided with a channel to convey her increasingly pro-German and pro-Japanese views.[32] That she reconciled these views with the presidency of the Women's Guild of Empire is remarkable.

Adela was ahead of her time in realising that Australia was not 'Britain in the Antipodes' but a nation in the Asia-Pacific region. Yet to support a brutal, militaristic regime like Japan in the late 1930s, especially given her earlier pacifist views, was almost incomprehensible. Her public denunciations against Jewish financiers, whom she believed 'caused' the Depression, constituted yet another instance of her extreme right-wing views. After war was declared in August 1939 but before Japan was yet involved, Adela struggled with poor mental health, ranting in public and crying in the Guild's offices. When deposed from its leadership, she was almost violent in her anger.[33] Even more worrying was her meeting with the Japanese Consul in Sydney. In late November the Walshes went to Japan as guests of the government. On their return Adela published 'Conditions in Japan' and 'What You Should Know about the Orient'.

In early 1940 Adela established the pro-Japanese People's Guild with a tiny membership. Its newsletter, *Voice of the People*, also attracted few readers. She stood for the Senate in the September 1940 federal elections, garnering few votes. Undeterred, she spent her Saturday afternoons proselytising in Sydney's Domain to bewildered and hostile onlookers. For someone so accustomed to adulation and support, this was a devastating blow. She seemed unable to realise this was not a popular cause, like opposing compulsory overseas conscription. When this new Guild failed, she joined forces with Percy Stephensen in the ultra-nationalist, anti-Imperialist Australia First Movement. Stephensen was a Rhodes Scholar from the University of Queensland who travelled from the far left to the far right in the inter-war years. This strange extreme nationalist group was also financed by the quirky businessman William Miles.[34] Violently anti-British hatred was hardly a view popular in World War II, when Australian troops were fighting in the Middle East.

When Japan entered the war on 7 December 1941, Adela's fate was sealed. After the Fall of Singapore in February 1942, Australia itself seemed at risk of a Japanese invasion. Security forces rounded up enemy aliens including Italians – most of whom were intensely anti-fascist – and groups such as the Australia First Movement, as potential fifth columnists. Adela was taken into custody on 20 March and interned in Liverpool camp. Tom was far too ill to warrant detention. Adela unsuccessfully demanded to appear in court in a public hearing, which was not permitted under the *National Security Act 1939–40*. Threatening to go on a hunger strike, she was released. Her military intelligence dossier makes sad reading, for Adela spoke warmly of her dying husband, her children at home and son Richard on active service, without any understanding of what had brought her to this final humiliation.[35] Tom died on 5 April 1943. Adela subsequently retired from public life altogether. Before her death in 1961, she converted to Roman Catholicism.

CHAPTER 9

Annette Kellermann

(1886–1975)

*The Sydney 'Million Dollar Mermaid' who got women out
of corsets and into the water in togs.*

Annette Kellermann was a rebel who revolutionised
women's dress at the commencement of the twentieth
century. Like Coco Chanel, Kellermann took a male
item of clothing, in her case the swimming costume, and
fashioned it into a practical garment that allowed women
freedom to swim and enjoy water sports. She also dared to
bare her legs in order to swim in public, and this act alone
tore down the restrictions of Victorian prudery that had
confined women within, through both psychologically and
physically restraining clothing.

Annette's notoriety made her an extremely wealthy
woman, and she carved out the life and career she wanted
on her terms. Her talents were manifold: she was Australia's
first international film star and the first star of any film
with a million-dollar budget in the United States; she was
the world's highest paid female theatre act for nearly two
decades, during which she performed dangerous diving
and swimming routines on stage to packed audiences; she
appeared on the New York stage imitating Pavlova, not in
a skit but as a credible dancer. Yet after all her success, she

died on the Gold Coast in 1975 in poverty and obscurity, a sad relic of an age that had forgotten those women who challenged and destroyed the boundaries of female restriction.

Australia produced several other women who boldly broke conventions. Isabel Letham (1899–1995) was the first Australian to ride a surfboard when she was chosen to ride in tandem with Duke Kahanamoku to show the Hawaiian surf riding technique in Sydney in 1915. At the young age of fifteen, Isabel, in that one ride, revolutionised women's participation in water sports. She went on to an international career in swimming instruction and was appointed director of swimming for the city of San Francisco.[1]

A contemporary and friend of Kellermann, Fanny Durack (1889–1956) was Australia's most notable woman swimmer for many decades. A New South Wales champion, she perfected the new stroke of Australian crawl or freestyle. Fanny's path to fame was not easy. Her father was a publican in Balmain, a rough area full of prostitutes and SP bookmakers, and as a working-class girl she had few opportunities for leisure.[2] Durack trained with Mina Wylie, whose father built and operated Wylie's Baths at Coogee, in Sydney, and who permitted the girls to train with leading male swimmers. In 1912 Durack represented Australia in the Olympics after much controversy about women's participation in the Games. She won the gold medal in the freestyle event, and Wylie took home a silver.[3]

Born in Sydney in 1886, Annette Kellermann came from a well-educated and cultured family. Her mother, Alice Charbonnet, was a concert pianist, trained by the illustrious Madame Paule Gayrard in Paris, before moving to the Paris Conservatoire to study with Cecile Chaminade. Alice was born in 1860 in Cincinnati, into a sophisticated and cosmopolitan family; her mother was American while her father, Amable Charbonnet, was the Chief Justice of the French Possessions and Colonies in the South Pacific.[4] Alice arrived in Australia in 1880 as part of the French government's contribution to the International Exhibition in Melbourne, where she demonstrated the Pleyel and Erard pianos.[5] She met Australian-born Frederick Kellermann, a talented violinist, though his background was not quite as illustrious as her own. His grandfather and father, also Frederick Kellermann, owned a shop in Sydney. They sometimes anglicised their name to Kellerman, though Annette was frequently called by both versions of her surname. Her book *How to Swim* (1918) uses the name Kellermann.

Alice and Frederick married in 1882 and established their own Conservatoire de Musique at 43 Phillip Street in Sydney, as well as the Sydney Orchestra Society.[6] They attracted talented students, among them Kellermann recalled a Helen Mitchell, later known as Nellie Melba, Australia's first internationally acclaimed opera singer. The young couple were the centre of musical excellence in Sydney, as well as popular hosts.[7] In recognition of her international career and training, Alice was known always as Madame Charbonnet.

The Kellermanns had four children: Maurice (1885), Annette (1886), Marcelle (1887) and Frederick (1891). Despite an affluent home life, young Annette contracted rickets, a disease often associated with poverty. Confined to a strict diet and with constant medical attention, her legs were encased in heavy calipers at the age of six.[8] She later recalled the humiliation of being thought of as a cripple.[9] One advanced medical practitioner, Dr David Cope, recommended that eleven-year-old Annette take up swimming to strengthen her weak legs.[10] In her later book *Fairy Tales of the South Seas* (1926), illustrated by her sister Marcelle Wooster, Annette explained that 'I was awfully scared of the water and did not learn to swim quickly, but Mr Percy Cavill, who was my teacher, never frightened me, so I lost all fear.'[11] Percy Cavill was largely responsible for developing the Australian crawl stroke.[12] Later Annette wrote: 'With strength came hope, and hope, reacting, gave more strength, and presently my legs began to take on normal shape.'[13] She had the good fortune to practise swimming with the future champions Snowy and Frank Baker. She swam at Farmer's Baths at Farm Cove aged fifteen where she learned 'overarm stroke'.[14] The water was not her only milieu; Annette took up other activities and became a proficient ballet dancer, as well as a champion tennis player.

Annette began competing in swimming carnivals in 1902 with the full support of her father, who, as her success grew, became her guide and manager. Fred Kellermann also began organising carnivals for women competitors at the St George Baths in Redfern. These were supplemented with displays of graceful underwater ballet routines. In March 1902 Annette competed against Mina Wylie and Fanny Durack, winning the 100 yards event in 1 minute and 26.5 seconds.[15] What made this competition unusual, apart from the women's events, was the presence of male spectators watching the girls. The display was considered an outrageous breach of public conventions on proper attire for a mixed audience.[16] Some of Annette's fiercest opposition in competitive swimming came from Rose Scott, the famous feminist and president of the New South Wales Ladies Amateur Swimming Association, who totally opposed 'mixed bathing' and went so far as to denounce male spectators at women's events. By the standards of today, the girls' heavy woollen costumes were cumbersome. Yet at the turn of the twentieth century, women often wore corsets, stockings and shoes in elaborate bathing ensembles. Indeed, Edwardian strictures even forced men to wear skirts over their bathing costumes at Manly Beach.[17]

In 1902 the Kellermanns made the decision to relocate to Melbourne, where Madame Charbonnet obtained a position as music mistress at Simpson's School, now Mentone Girls Grammar School. Annette and Marcelle attended the school, where Annette was an indifferent and uninterested student.[18] She began giving swimming lessons and public performances as a mermaid at the Princes Court entertainment centre and the Melbourne Aquarium. In 1903 she undertook a role in the play *The Breaking of the Drought*, at the Theatre Royal.[19] Her sister, Marcelle, later wrote that: 'She was being whirled around and towards the big [water] outlet, her arm already in a pipe, when a stage hand saw the danger and turned off the water ... Nothing daunted her if it was in the script.'[20] It was this daredevil courage that later caused Annette to be seriously injured and temporarily crippled with a long road to recovery during her film star years.

When her father, Frederick, suffered his first heart attack in Melbourne in 1903, Annette realised she had to earn a living to help support her family. Competing in marathon races up the Yarra was the start of her long-distance swimming career.[21] Today, long-distance competitions are often the preserve of men, but unusually in these early days of the sport, the conventions were more flexible. With her father as manager and chaperone, Annette transferred her career to London in 1905, after a tour of the Australian states. Within the dynamics of the Kellermann family, Fred sided with his athletic elder daughter, much to the dismay of the creative and refined Madame Charbonnet. By this time, however, Annette was a mature and confident nineteen-year-old. Her journey from colonial swimming star and aquatic performer to international star is a revelation in the construction of modern celebrity, albeit, in this case, one with immense drive and talent. Not that it was easy. Swimming was not as popular in England and promoters did not want the expense and trouble of erecting a pool on stage 'just to see a woman make a fish of herself'.[22]

Annette understood that fame meant a strong and active engagement with the mass media. For a cultured middle-class woman, her choice was both clever and surprising. She aligned her public career with the down-market *Daily Mirror*, the first newspaper to incorporate pictorials, thereby revolutionising newspapers and widening the readership. This newspaper, developed by the canny Lord Northcote, made sensation and deviance a core feature of its fare, although it also advocated a more liberal attitude to the place of women in society.[23]

In collaboration with this paper, her first feat was to swim 42 kilometres of the Thames River in 3 hours and

54 minutes. On 1 July 1905 the *Daily Mirror* reported on the immense crowd that watched Annette dive from Putney Bridge in her blue swimming costume, 'her youth and beauty alone have won all hearts; her pluck and skill require equal admiration'. She fitted very neatly into the racial and cultural construction of the lanky, robust Anglo-Australian – though in fact she was of European extraction – brimming with health, strength and vitality, the best of the British Empire. This swim in the Thames was hardly a doddle – it was cold, rainy and blustery that day. She arrived in the East End wharves covered in mud and debris from the dirty water to the acclaim of thousands of spectators cheering her exploits.

Her next stratagem, which is now mandatory for today's stars, was to endorse a product – Cadbury's Cocoa, promoted heavily through the pages of the *Daily Mirror*. Then she did something even more daunting. For the thirtieth anniversary of Captain Matthew Webb's Channel swim, Annette decided that she would be the first woman to successfully swim that body of water. Organised by the *Daily Mirror* and sponsored by Cadbury's, Annette, covered in porpoise fat to keep warm, attempted the crossing on 24 August 1905 but was unsuccessful. She tried again on 7 August 1906. Then *Paris Match* sponsored a swim in the Seine, passing by all twenty-four bridges. Scheduled for 10 September 1905, Annette came equal third with a male competitor.[24] What is most remarkable is that she made these attempts so close together. The *Daily Mirror*, dubbing her the 'Australian Mermaid', coined the term by which a considerable part of her future career depended – the half-woman, half-mythical creature with extraordinary powers, more at home in the sea and water than on land. Not only were her athletic accomplishments reported in the newspapers, but the *Daily Mirror* began to describe and show photographs of her in her swimsuit. This marked a fundamental shift in news coverage – a middle-class woman displaying her legs and torso was being scrutinised in public. Such notoriety breached all Victorian conventions of modesty and restraint – Annette was a lady by her birth and training, but she was a foretaste of the modern independent woman.

There was no scandal, however, for the Prince of Wales (later George V) attended a Royal Command Performance at the Bath Club. Annette also performed her aquatic act in front of Queen Alexandra.[25] In June 1906 she beat the first woman to attempt a Channel cross, Viennese Baroness Isa Cescu, in a 22 mile (36 kilometre) race down the Danube from Tulu to Vienna.[26] Annette was severely cut on rocks and bruised during this swim.[27]

Her attempts at cracking the music hall circuit in England with a season at the London Hippodrome were not so successful.[28] She also decided to pursue a theatrical career, but in consultation with her father, she decided to relocate to the United States, where vaudeville could incorporate her type of indoor performance. Her first engagement at Chicago's White City Amusement Park was hardly set among uplifting, genteel entertainment: she competed with a Filipino 'headhunter' for her audience. Called 'The Lady Dolphin' in the Chicago papers, the initial reaction was lukewarm. As crowds improved, the performance proved extremely well paid. For her fifty-five short shows a week, including eighteen on the weekends, Annette earned the extraordinary sum of £2000.[29] This was at a time when a working woman in Australia earned about £2 per week if she was fortunate.

In Chicago, Annette met a friend of her brother Maurice, Jimmie Sullivan, a former boxer who had become a successful theatrical entrepreneur. This was a business relationship fully endorsed by her father and Maurice. But in the meantime, her father, Frederick, was ailing, and unable to continue managing his daughter. He died in the USA in 1907.

In 1912 Annette and Jimmie married and remained together until Jimmie died in 1972. In their relationship, Annette was always the 'star' at home and in public, although she would not have attained her fame in the United States without his careful management of her career. But Jimmie was not a good business manager of her earnings. Rather than investing her considerable earnings in property, they were largely frittered away on extensive first-class travel, relocating across continents or half-hearted ventures that fizzled out.

The most famous incident relating to the early part of Kellermann's career, after she relocated to the Wonderland Park in Boston, concerned a banning for public indecency when she appeared in a man's swimming costume at Revere Beach, the first public beach in the United States. Most commentators on her life and career take her word, which is reiterated in her unpublished autobiography, that she caused a scandal and appeared in court, however, her talent for publicity and other research suggests she may have embellished the account. Marcelle's notes on her famous sister also maintain Annette was arrested 'for having bare legs in the water'. The incident forms a dramatic moment in her 1952 biofilm, *Million Dollar Mermaid*, starring Esther Williams, where the incongruously cast Victor Mature as Jimmie arranges a stunt to garner publicity.[30] The Australian biography *The Original Million Dollar Mermaid* (2005) reiterates this central image in the history of women's liberation and modernity.[31] Yet careful research by Jacqui Donegan in the court records and contemporary newspapers in the United States did not uncover the story.[32] The Boston papers sang her praises:

> No more Gibson bathing girl
> Shall Grace the Newport summer whirl
> Annette declares her garment's wrong
> At both ends too extremely long.[33]

Annette Kellermann in 1919, modelling her radical costume. Bain Collection, Library of Congress LC-B2-738-5.

Her fame spread further when, after examining the statistics of over 10,000 women, the eccentric Harvard professor Dudley Sargent, a former circus performer turned instructor in physical education, identified her as the 'perfect woman', in line with Venus de Milo.[34] Annette's athletic body heralded a change in standards of female beauty from the soft, curved Edwardian ideal to the modern, streamlined, trim and fit form. From Sargent's declaration onwards, Annette had the publicity tag for the rest of her career. Yet as she aged, it became a millstone around her neck.

The issue of how women should dress on the beach or when swimming advanced through Annette's advocacy of sensible, appropriate attire. In her autobiography she wrote: 'How could these women swim with shoes – stockings-bloomers-skirts-over-dresses with puffed sleeves in sailor collars – in some cases tightly fitted corsets? But then no one went swimming …'[35] Annette's ensemble – a man's costume plus leggings – were commonly referred to as 'Annette Kellermanns'. She often ripped her swimming costume with scissors on stage to demonstrate she was not wearing a corset. This was a sensational act for a respectable woman to perform in public. Her father would certainly not have approved and doubtless her mother suffered the indignities of her daughter's performances when she learned of them back home in Melbourne. By now, though, Annette was a rich woman, commanding the highest fees for any female performer in vaudeville.[36]

In her revised and more glamorous stage act entitled 'On the Beach at Boulogne', she wore a lighter costume. On 25 November 1908, she opened at B. F. Keith and

F. F. Proctor's Fifth Avenue Theatre, performing in a 25,000-gallon pool to huge crowds, including middle-class women, a new addition to audiences. This was despite reservations in some quarters about her attire and its lack of modesty. *Variety* assured potential patrons 'there is nothing shriekingly loud about her act …'[37] Annette also performed in the new Paradise Roof Garden Theatre, known also as Hammerstein's, built on top of a new invention, the skyscraper. Charlie Chaplin had also appeared there.[38] Annette widened her repertoire, adding a high-wire act, fencing and boomerang throwing, as well as diving from great heights. Her incorporation of ballet techniques underwater later gave rise to whole new genres of performance – water ballet and synchronised swimming.

Annette's reputation after her father's death was verging on unseemly. She was cited in a divorce case in March 1909, although she strenuously denied any wrongdoing. Her frequent arrests for speeding in her new white Buick she viewed as evidence of her modernity and carefree spirit; others saw it as dangerous behaviour, and some regarded her as a spoilt show performer who thought she was above the law. At the same time, Annette also made some serious errors in her career. When she went over to a new agency, William Morris, in 1909, Keith and Proctor immediately sued. Morris had challenged the Keith and Proctor monopoly two years before, and won the case. Stealing contracted artists was impudent, ambitious and illegal. The judge ruled that Keith and Proctor had developed Annette's new act and promoted her career, thereby making a landmark ruling in entertainment law.[39] Annette was forced to stay with

Keith, in a frosty relationship that endured for the next two decades.

The lengthy case did allow Annette to branch out into new fields of endeavour. She first tried to enter the world of opera with the help of her mother – who now lived in Paris – and Dame Nellie Melba, but nothing came of this late start. There was always an emotional tension between Annette's original training in the high arts of music and ballet and her commercial career based on athleticism, and motion pictures presented another challenge. She decided to launch into the new medium of cinema, then regarded as a rather low-class entertainment. Her first role, in 1909, was in *The Bride of Lammermoor*, followed by three other short films in the same year, all produced by the Vitagraph Company. In her first major film, *Neptune's Daughter*, Annette was billed as 'The Perfect Woman'. Directed by Herbert Brenon, the film was spectacular, with Annette performing her own stunts. She was severely injured at one stage and spent six weeks in hospital, and she carried the scar on her forehead for the rest of her life. Before filming started she suffered the loss of her mother in 1914. Filmed in the Caribbean under trying and primitive conditions, the film contained provocative scenes of Annette swimming naked. Strangely, this did not cause a scandal when it was released in 1915; presumably the audience understood mermaids did not have much reason to wear clothes.[40] A huge hit, the film ran for seven weeks in New York City.

Flushed with success, Annette made another extravaganza, *A Daughter of the Gods*, filmed in Jamaica in 1915, with producer William Fox and Brenon as director, although he was later replaced. Annette trained the 'mermaids' herself. This film was a cinematic landmark with its lavish sets, scenery and million-dollar budget. There was disharmony on the set, however, with rumours that Annette had more than a professional interest in her director. Jimmie baulked at his secondary role in her life, but it was beyond his control in the theatres of New York. The film opened to enthusiastic crowds in October 1916. With its expert tinting, photography and stunts, the film, now lost, was a rival to D. W. Griffith's and Cecil B. DeMille's great shows.[41] William Fox, who had founded the Fox Film Co., was a master of publicity. He realised that Annette was a commodity he could push to its limit, and arranged for a life-sized cut-out of Annette to be placed outside cinemas. Women could then use a tape measure to see how closely they resembled the 'perfect woman'.[42]

Annette was enjoying a busy professional period. Since 1909 she had endorsed a series of American products, just as she had done in London in 1905. They ranged from Buick cars and Du Pont raincoats to Black Jack Chewing Gum, which supposedly assisted with the prevention of coughs and colds.[43] She had also kept her stage career happening. In London in 1912, she appeared on stage in *Undine*, an 'idyll of forest and stream', followed later by a stint at the Winter Garden in New York, where Al Jolson also performed.

Her career stalled after a serious horseriding accident in 1918 when on location in Maine for her new film with Fox, *Queen of the Sea*. Paralysed and confined to bed, Annette showed true courage as she fought her injury. She began the slow process of recovery and learning

Frederic Shipman
Enterprises present Annette
Kellermann, 'The Perfect
Woman'. David Elliott
theatrical postcard collection,
National Library of Australia,
nla pic-an22948275.

to walk again. For someone who had been crippled as a child, this was a terrible nightmare to endure once again. It took a year for Annette to recover. Jimmie's steadfast support cemented their marriage, and from then on there were no rumours of infidelity. Later she pledged support to Sister Elizabeth Kenny's revolutionary methods of assisting patients with polio, and the principal's office at the Women's College at the University of Queensland is named in honour of Annette's support for the emerging profession of physiotherapy.[44]

In *Queen of the Sea* Annette swam and dived naked. The first director of the film, Lois Weber, was one of the pioneer women directors in the film industry, although she was replaced by G. Adolfi.[45] The critics and public were not so enthusiastic about this formula film. Critics found the film unconvincing and contrived, noting its weak plot and rehashing of previous efforts and stunts.[46] In Annette's following film, *What Women Love* (1920), she played a flapper; yet again it rested upon familiar, now hackneyed themes and scenes.[47] Her last major film, shot in New Zealand, *Venus of the South* (1924), directed by her husband, was also a flop.

Annette decided not to sign a five-year contract with William Fox, preferring instead to re-ignite her career in vaudeville and follow her aspirations for legitimate theatre as well. In her autobiography she revealed that in 1917 her performance of classical ballet, doing an impersonation of Anna Pavlova in Saint-Saëns' *Swan*, under the baton of Arturo Toscanini at the New York Metropolitan Opera House, was the 'biggest thrill of my whole career ...' On the same program Caruso sang arias from *Madama Butterfly*, and violinist and composer Fritz Kreisler also appeared. She later danced with Pavlova and military march composer John Philip Sousa in the Hippodrome. Annette was particularly proud that Pavlova's time was severely cut to allow more of her own performance on stage. She also revived her aquatic act, performing the diving scene from *A Daughter of the Gods*.[48]

With her stage career now a little passé, and despite spectacular stunts such as jumping out of a plane without a parachute and diving into the sea, Annette needed to reinvent herself yet again. With her brand as a marketable commodity, Annette Kellermann Inc., established in 1909, was launched in earnest with her book *How to Swim* in 1918. It is a curious book, with the first section focusing on her own life and its challenges, and the second an instructional manual. Capitalising on her depiction as the world's 'most perfect woman', Annette released another book in 1918 on health, beauty and fitness – *Physical Beauty: How to Keep It.* Having already patented her swimwear design in 1910, Annette began major production in New York with her own manufacturing company in 1920.[49] Her invention of a women's one-piece suit, made for comfort and speed, revolutionised women's apparel into a more streamlined design than men's. She capitalised on the mail order market, and from her Broadway office sold another book – now lost – *The Body Beautiful*, which also canvassed her struggles from disability and deformity as a child to 'the most perfect woman'. A firm believer in yoga and good breathing, Annette preached holistic routines of diet and exercise.[50] Articles by her that appeared in physical culturist Bernarr Macfadden's journal *Physical Culture* reached out to new audiences. Annette could be brutal in her advice to women. Her enemy was flab and fat. She advised lying on the floor naked with the legs rolled up to gauge fat deposits. This was surely a strike against Victorian prudery. How women responded to this test remains unknown.[51] Syndicated in the Hearst newspapers, her advice was widely read across the United States.

Annette was part of the revolution that saw the ideal of physical perfection and the use of health regimes directed from small coteries of believers to a mass audience, begun in earnest with Dr John Harvey Kellogg (1852–1943) and his strict food and exercise program at the Battle Creek Sanitarium in Michigan. A Seventh Day Adventist, Kellogg brought his religious principles into his medical practice in the hope of eliminating diseases caused by poor diet. Annette, like Kellogg, had been a long-term vegetarian and teetotaller. In 1909 she planned an 800-room health resort for women and children in Pennsylvania, but nothing came of it.[52] Her next attempt involved a ranch for women and children – the Kellermann Country Club, located north of Los Angeles, opened in 1925. The club was far in advance of then current practice, with facilities for disabled children, pools and gymnasiums. It was based on Kellogg's idea but vastly expanded.[53] This venture did not last long and went out of business. Later, in the 1950s, Annette opened a health food store in Los Angeles, which also proved to be too far ahead of its time to be profitable.

In some ways Annette managed her stardom well, but by branching out into so many areas she dissipated her core vision. She possessed the energy and foresightedness to understand what might work, but the constant juggling act between various parts of her commercial empire made them all, at times, precarious. Resuscitating her vaudeville career, just as that whole institution was at the point of decline, was not sensible. In 1921 she toured Australia and New Zealand, staying for two years. Adept at languages, she learned Danish and Dutch in order to be able to tour to Denmark and Holland and speak with the locals. She also knew some Swedish.[54] In London in 1925 she introduced a new high-wire act at the Coliseum, where she had moving dolls of Mary Pickford, Buster Keaton and Charlie Chaplin dance on the wire with her. A serious fall on stage did not stop her run.[55] How she could hope to manage her country club and sanitarium in California at the same time showed a confidence and energy that was sometimes out of step with reality.

Always apolitical, Annette went to Germany in the mid 1930s to preach her brand of athleticism. This showed a curious lack of judgment on her and Jimmie's part. But her views on bodily perfection and discipline resonated with Aryan ideology. She was also very proud of her German and French heritage. Nothing much is known about the three years she spent in Germany.

In 1937 Annette returned to the United States, where she met President Franklin Roosevelt and advised him on diet and exercise to assist with his polio. Returning to Australia in 1939, she lived on Newry Island, off Mackay, where she took an interest in the Great Barrier Reef. By this time, her sister, Marcelle, and Marcelle's husband had joined Jimmie and Annette permanently. During World War II, Annette engaged in a considerable degree of war work for the Red Cross and created a show called *We're All In It*, performed with 200 swimmers at the North Sydney Olympic Pool to raise money for the organisation.

Her performing career was virtually over by 1945. On her return to the United States, she continued working for the Red Cross, often visiting rehabilitating soldiers to whom she played the piano accordion and reminisced. Her parents would have been mortified to see their daughter perform on a folk instrument in public.[56] Suddenly, in 1951, plans were afoot for a film biography of her cinematic career, but Annette was aghast that an uneducated American from humble circumstances – Esther Williams – was to portray her. Even at the age of sixty-five she felt she could do the role much better,[57] and if not her, she requested the role be filled by a fellow Australian. The film, *Million Dollar Mermaid*, was panned by critics who found the story line unconvincing and thought Busby Berkeley's choreography was merely an echo of his great days in the 1930s. Yet the image of a heavily made-up Esther Williams smiling underwater made a lasting impression on many baby boomers. Williams also starred in a remake of *Neptune's Daughter*.

However, the public no longer remembered Annette Kellermann, who was now referred to as the 'Esther Williams of her day'. This was the woman celebrated in F. Scott Fitzgerald's *This Side of Paradise* (1920) as the essential modern woman and exemplar of the jazz age, but by the end of her life, Annette had become conservative. Her contributions to public debate, such as her criticisms of the bikini in the 1950s, seemed old-fashioned and prudish. She took the position of: 'My goodness, things have changed since my day,' without recognising the irony that she was the very person who successfully challenged Victorian strictures of dress for women.[58] Relocated to a poor area of the Gold Coast and living in a fibro shack, Annette became a relic of an earlier time, swimming every day in gaudy costumes and doing high kicks in public. The house she lived in was owned by her Brisbane relatives Mervyn and Ede Clarke. She kept much of her memorabilia in the tiny dwelling, a poignant and constant reminder that once she had been the highest paid woman in American theatre. Signed photographs of Lucille Ball, Grace Kelly and John Wayne adorned her walls.[59]

With Jimmie in declining health, she spent her days caring for him, until he died in April 1972. An arresting item appeared in the *Sydney Morning Herald* in March 1975: 'Movie Star, Retired to Gold Coast, No Longer

Had Need of Mink Coat',[60] describing how Annette's coat, sold to a woman for $600, was worn to the opening of the Sydney Opera House.

Annette was thrilled to be inducted into the International Swimming Hall of Fame in Florida in 1975, but she was too feeble to attend the ceremony.[61] Admitted to a Gold Coast nursing home, where she exercised every day, including doing high kicks, she died on 6 November 1975. Funeral rites were conducted in the Catholic faith of her childhood. Her sister, Marcelle, her faithful companion through all the heights of success and lows of her travails, undertook Annette's last wish that her ashes be scattered over the Great Barrier Reef waters that she loved so much. Annette's papers, costumes and memorabilia were initially donated to the archive of the Sydney Opera House, though they were later dispersed and some sold at public auction. Annette would be both amused and delighted to learn that her name and image are the central features on a series of murals painted by Wendy Sharpe, adorning the Cook and Phillip Park Aquatic Centre in Sydney.

CHAPTER 10

Lady Maie Casey
(1891–1983)

*The bohemian artist, writer and chatelaine of Yarralumla
who met the who's who of the world.*

Maie Casey was a most unlikely bohemian. Born into the Australian upper class in 1891, she was a talented artist and writer whose work was constrained by the demanding career of her husband, Lord Richard Casey. Appointed the inaugural Australian Ambassador to the United States, Governor of Bengal, a cabinet minister in Australia, member of the British House of Lords as Baron Casey of Berwick and Westminster, and, lastly, Governor-General, the demands of Richard Casey's public life always came first in this close but puzzling relationship. Despite that, Maie maintained several intense, long-term romantic relationships with women and in some ways she resembled the character of Princess Margaret or Lady Edwina Mountbatten – bohemian, adventurous and unconventional at one level, but deeply status conscious, snobbish and demanding of reverence on another. She moved in the highest international circles, a confidante of Gandhi, Churchill, Noël Coward, Dame Judith Anderson and Eleanor Roosevelt. Her book, *Tides and Eddies* (1966), reads like a rollcall of the rich, famous and powerful of the mid-twentieth century.[1] Maie also had much in common with the effervescent Dame Zara Holt (1909–89) who mixed in similar circles. Unlike Maie, who was cool and often cutting in conversation, Dame Zara possessed a warm personality, good business intelligence and sincerity that made her a popular international and national figure.[2]

Both sides of Maie's family quickly rose up the newly established hierarchy in Victoria in the 1850s. Her maternal grandfather, a Protestant Irishman named Theodotus Sumner, was a merchant, who entered into partnership with businessman Richard Grice in Melbourne in 1855.[3] The business owned a shipping line, well-appointed pastoral properties in several colonies and a guano plantation on Malden Island in the Central Pacific.[4] A public-minded philanthropist, Sumner was on the board of the Royal Women's Hospital in Melbourne from 1856 to 1870, a member of the Victorian Legislative Council and also of the Melbourne Club.[5] Theodotus purchased the family home, Stony Park, at Brunswick for his bride, Sarah Peers, the daughter of a Welsh builder who had made his fortune first in Van Diemen's Land in the 1830s and later in Melbourne from 1838.[6]

Maie's mother, Alice Elfrida, was, by Maie's account, a self-absorbed beauty who made her feel anxious as a child. She realised at the young age of seven or eight that '[my mother] … had a tall beautiful body that moved with grace …'[7] For the rest of her life Maie was haunted by her own dissatisfactions with her appearance, teased by her aunt Maud Nash that 'Maie is stumpy, like the Ryans [her father's side of the family]!'[8] As Maie herself remarked, 'I did not admire myself at all: a depression settled on me every time afterward that I saw myself in a mirror.' Certainly she was no beauty – her face was broad and square with a strong chin. Her forceful character and her talent were, she would come to realise, far more important.

Her father, Sir Charles Snodgrass Ryan (1853–1926), was a charismatic, handsome man of adventure. His Protestant father, Charles Ryan, arrived from Ireland in 1840, marrying Marian Cotton. The Cottons in London were a wealthy family connected with Sir Joshua Reynolds.[9] Born on Killeen Station in Victoria, Charles was educated in medicine at the University of Melbourne. He undertook postgraduate studies at Bonn and Vienna before working as a military surgeon in the Turkish army during the Turko-Serbian and Turko-Russian Wars in 1876–78. Charles later wrote an interesting account of these years in his book, *Under the Red Crescent* (1897). Returning to Melbourne in 1878, he set up as a surgeon with a large commitment to poor patients.[10] Charles was a well-connected young man about town before his marriage, and Maie recalled in her book on Nellie Melba that as a child she visited a society dressmaker who asked about 'Charlie'. She recalled thinking this was 'a strange way not to say your papa'.[11]

The Ryans were a cultured family. Charles' sister, Ellis Rowan (1848–1922), was a distinguished botanical artist.[12] Another sister, Ada, married Lord Charles Scott, the younger brother of the sixth Duke of Buccleuch and eighth Duke of Queensbury. In her family memoir, Maie recalled discussing this marriage with Queen Mary, who joked about the dangers of marrying Australians in the nineteenth century.[13] The story reveals that Maie mixed in the highest circles of the British aristocracy and that

Australians were formerly perceived as descendants of convicts.

In July 1883 Alice Sumner married Charles Ryan at Christ Church, Brunswick. Maie wrote in her memoir that she was born at home at 37 Collins Street, Melbourne, 'opposite the Melbourne Club'.[14] She was actually born in her Grandmother Sumner's house, Stony Park. Her birth names, Ethel Marion Sumner, display the mark of family lineage. Yet from early childhood she became 'Maie', an altogether more charming name than Ethel. Like many privileged children, Maie was not reared primarily by her parents but by a Swiss nurse, Berthe Tissot, whom she later wrote was the 'real pivot of my life'.[15] Although Berthe was Swiss and spoke French, Maie's mother insisted she take 'proper' French lessons from 'Madame Princep who exhaled Eau de Cologne; Mlle Maillard, a poor sad disarming woman with chilblained fingers like bunches of bananas; the beautiful goggle-eyed Madame Hossendoff'.[16] From these descriptions, which breathe life into her teachers in a short phrase, Maie's creative talent can be appreciated.

Along with Grandmother Sumner, her mother and Berthe, Maie went to England at the age of five. She was privately educated with the daughters of the Australian barrister Sir Edward Mitchell, KC, before attending St George's School at Ascot in England at the age of sixteen. This had been Winston Churchill's old prep school.[17] During her holidays she spent time with her aunt, Lady Scott, in Northamptonshire, and with her brother, Rupert, who had been sent to the exclusive Harrow School.[18] Maie completed her education at a 'finishing school' in Paris. She did not attend university, despite her ability and intelligence, on advice from a family friend, Sir Richard Stawell.

Maie returned to Melbourne in 1910 to the life of a privileged young woman but was back in England in 1914 to be presented at court to King George V and Queen Mary, the epitome of acceptance for a young Australian hoping to scale the social heights. That same year both Rupert and Charles volunteered for war service and Maie began work for the war effort as a housemaid at the Home for Wounded Officers in Park Lane, an unusual choice for such a well-placed young woman. In 1915 she joined the Australian Wounded and Missing Enquiry Bureau established by Vera Deakin, daughter of the former Australian prime minister.[19] Maie recalled the trauma of the war: 'we were afraid to read the casualty lists in the morning newspapers'.[20]

On her return to Melbourne, Maie and her friend Joan Weigall (later Joan Lindsay, and now better remembered as the author of *Picnic at Hanging Rock* [1967]) set about studying art. In 1921 she accompanied Rupert to Coblenz, Germany, where he worked for the Inter-Allied Rhineland High Commission. Some of his colleagues, including Josslyn Hay, son of the High Commissioner, Lord Kilmarnock, were distinctly bohemian in their attitudes. Later, as the Earl of Erroll, Hay was murdered in mysterious circumstances in Kenya in 1941, a central figure in the sexually promiscuous and drug-taking 'Happy Valley' set. Along with Hay's sister, Rosemary, Maie experimented with opium in Germany.[21] At this time cocaine was also a popular drug among the fast-living and privileged.[22] By some accounts Maie was seriously attracted to the vivacious young Rosemary and encouraged her far more sedate brother to pursue Rosemary, and indeed in 1924 they were married.[23]

In October 1923 Alice died. Maie's account of her mother's death is brutal: '[she] … dropped dead while staying with Rupert …'[24] but what resentments she harboured towards her mother were never fully explained in her published works. In early 1924, Maie relocated to London, sharing a flat with journalist Lady Kitty Ogilvie Vincent, later the eccentric author of *Two on a Trip: With Sledge Dogs in Canada* (1930). At a wedding that year, Maie met Richard Casey, a man she had vaguely known in Melbourne.[25] Born in Brisbane in 1890, Richard studied engineering at Trinity College, Cambridge, before serving in World War I. He was part of the first landing at Gallipoli in 1915. Awarded the Distinguished Service Order in 1918, Richard worked in Melbourne first before going to London as Australia's liaison officer. His close relationship with conservative Prime Minister Stanley Bruce (later Lord Bruce), opened many doors for Richard, then and in the years to come.[26]

Maie and Richard were married on 24 June 1926 in St James' Church in Piccadilly. At the age of thirty-five, Maie was an older bride for the time. She had intended wearing black taffeta before her friends convinced her that ivory was a more suitable bridal colour.[27] They returned to Melbourne the following year, briefly, before settling in London. Their daughter Jane was born in October 1928, much to Maie's horror, as she had wanted a son.[28] Their son, Donn, was born in 1931, yet she was equally as cold and demanding towards him. This set the tenor of her relations with both her children for the rest of her life.

Maie and her family returned to Melbourne that year as Richard intended to stand for federal parliament. He won the seat of Corio in late 1931 for the conservative United Australia Party.[29] Living in the tiny capital of Canberra after her sophisticated life in London was a challenge for Maie, made more palatable by horseriding and gardening. In 1932 she took on the responsibility for her nephew Patrick, Rupert's son. This was hardly a good move for Patrick, abandoned by one mother and placed into the care of a frosty aunt. In 1934 Maie's Aunt Winifred died, leaving Maie and Rupert – along with two relatives who were bought out – her beautiful house and estate, Edrington, at Berwick in the Dandenongs. There was some suspicion in the family that Maie had induced this bequest while tending to her dying aunt.[30] This was unlikely; but undoubtedly it shows that even her family regarded Maie as ruthless and manipulative. The property proved to be a bolt-hole for Maie.

In 1933 Richard was appointed deputy federal treasurer, although Maie did not see it as incumbent upon her to be the dutiful public wife engaging in political networking and entertaining. This was a surprisingly independent stand; Maie was devoted to Richard, not to his career. She decided to learn art properly, enrolling with George Bell, a former official war artist. Bell had a sound lineage, as he studied with Fred McCubbin and also in Paris.[31] A decided Modernist, he was just the mentor that Maie needed, as her work was highly individual, frequently focusing on Aboriginal themes.[32] Through the school, Maie later met Sali Herman and Russell Drysdale.

In 1937 Maie ventured out of the bohemian art world to attend the coronation of King George VI. Among other duties, Richard accompanied the king when he went trout fishing with Neville Chamberlain, whose career was soon to be discredited with his unfortunate 'peace in our time' pronouncement. And Maie purchased a Picasso painting, *Le Repos*.[33] This was the first Picasso to arrive in Australia. Another passion was also indulged. Since World War I Maie had been fascinated by aircraft. She purchased a Miles Whitney Straight, commencing lessons for her licence when she returned home.[34] Soon she could fly from Edrington to Canberra to be with Richard. The children were left totally in the care of nannies and governesses.

Maie kept up her passion for painting, meeting Cynthia Reed (later Nolan) for whom she developed a passion, if an unrequited one. Cynthia reported to her sister-in-law, Sunday Reed: 'Maie is over and has brought a Picasso painting. I was having a mild flirtation until it made me sick and I got out.'[35] This behaviour, perhaps acceptable in the bohemian world, was at odds with Maie's position as the wife of a potential prime minister. When Prime Minister Joseph Lyons died suddenly in April 1939, Maie thought Richard might step up to the role. She flew immediately to Canberra to discuss Richard's chances against his rival, Robert Menzies, who described her as a 'Lady Macbeth'. This was not to be, as Richard was not a capable networker, and favoured the return of Stanley Bruce from London. Richard's decision displayed a considerable lack of political judgment, as Bruce had lost his seat while prime minister in the 1928 election and now sat in the House of Lords.[36]

As a consolation prize, Casey was appointed as the inaugural Ambassador to the United States. At the time

Australian foreign policy was totally reliant upon that of the United Kindom, so this was a highly audacious move. But it was a role far more suited to his skills and personality. On the way to Washington, Maie met a woman who was to become significant in her life for many years. Pat Jarrett was a champion swimmer and journalist, assigned to sports writing, then an unusual role for a woman.[37] The two found themselves travelling by ship to the United States together, where Pat taught the children to swim and Maie to dive. Maie asked Pat to act as her secretary but this was not quite what Pat had hoped for in her journalism career in America, so she declined. Capitalising on her connections with Pat's employer, Keith Murdoch, Maie arranged for Pat to come to Washington for a trial run of two months. Pat realised even then how cold and manipulative Maie could be, a warning she should have kept in mind for their future dealings.[38] The pair became increasingly close after a trip to Connecticut in July 1940, Maie happy to throw off the restrictions of marriage and her role as an ambassador's wife. Pat later recalled these were some of the happiest days of her life.[39] Reading between the lines suggests that they were lovers and that Richard was aware of the affair.[40]

Maie was a talented hostess in diplomatic circles, although frustrated by the strict protocols and boring people she had to endure. Her life had always been much freer. There was some compensation though: she met Noël Coward, already a friend of Richard's, and they became firm, enduring friends. Richard invited him to visit Australia in 1940.[41]

At this time the United States was not yet involved in World War II. Richard undertook the role of selling the

Allied cause to the Americans.[42] Maie also took on the role as advocate of the Allied war effort. She travelled a lot in this endeavour, sometimes flying. One of her chief delights during her time in the States was her association with the exclusive Ninety-Nines, the original women's pilots' association that counted Amelia Earhart and Amy Johnson among its members. When the States entered the war in December 1941, Maie continued her intense war work.

Her life changed abruptly again when Winston Churchill appointed Richard as the British minister in Cairo in March 1942. This was a sensitive appointment, with northern Africa and Lebanon under the Vichy French, Libya under the Italians, Spanish Morocco under neutral Spain, and Egypt and Palestine under strong British influence. With the desert campaigns in progress this appointment was an enormous task.[43]

For Maie again, life became highly restricted. She was guarded by Gurkhas, who took their duties seriously, and she was not permitted any idle tourist activities. Maie busied herself by contributing to the war effort, working with blind servicemen at St Dunstain's Hospital and travelling with the Hadfield–Spears Mobile Hospital. Visitors provided some distractions. Maie met Cecil Beaton, who later revelled in a story that when Maie was presented to Queen Farida, she ignored the strict protocol and showed her mosquito bites to an astonished royal party.[44] Fortunately Queen Farida was a fellow artist and an ardent feminist, so she took this enormous breach calmly.

Other guests included Noël Coward, who was then engaged in troop entertainment. More importantly, Churchill stayed with the Caseys in December 1943 as part of the Allied heads' meeting with President Roosevelt and General Chiang Kai-shek. Richard did not entirely enjoy the confidence of the British government, as senior minister Harold Macmillan regarded him as 'weak' and 'not … very clever. Mrs Casey is, however'.[45] Richard was clever in his own profession of engineering, but he lacked cunning and guile as a diplomat.

At the same time as this important event, the children arrived from America, where they had been left in the care of the Squire family. This was hardly an auspicious arrival for Maie. Not only had she not seen the children for some time, but they were both seriously ill, and her attention was taken away from her important guests.

When Richard was appointed as Governor of Bengal in November 1943, Maie was again presented with new challenges. Richard went without a title, after turning down the offer of a British peerage, as this would not go over well in Australia, where he still maintained political ambitions for the future. Pat Jarrett was once again released from her duties with the Murdoch press in the United States to act as Maie's personal secretary.[46]

Maie arrived in Calcutta in early 1944, fully aware that her knowledge of India was negligible. Her informality caused distinct tensions in the rigidly run Government House. The snooty staff were accustomed to British lords and ladies in the vice-regal role. Initially Maie was left to cope with her new role alone, as Richard contracted dysentery. Worse for the status-conscious staff was Maie's decision to have Cecil Beaton as an extended house guest. His effete ways were never a hit with them, or with Richard. When Pat arrived on 4 March, Maie's life was made far easier and more pleasant, especially when the children were sent to Hallett, a boarding school for British children in India. They were now distinctly Americanised, much to their mother's disapproval. Fortunately for Donn and Jane, Pat proved to be a wise friend and supporter for the rest of her life, providing a bulwark against their parents' aloofness.[47]

Maie was not entirely self-absorbed, however. She worked remarkably hard for Indian Red Cross efforts to gather supplies for the terrible famine that had earlier ravaged Bengal. She and Richard were surpassingly egalitarian in Bengal, at least in comparison to the British. Both were strong advocates of Indian independence after the war.[48] Their relative informality found warm acceptance among the Bengalis. Maie's work to enhance the status of women and to encourage education was particularly appreciated. The Australian press made much of her diligent reform activities on her return to Melbourne.[49] In further recognition Maie was appointed a Commander (Dame) of the Order of St John of Jerusalem. This was an ancient order; in its modern mode it was fiercely religious and anti-communist. She was also awarded the Imperial Gold Kaisar-i-Hind medal for her work in India.

Maie and the family returned to Australia in early 1946, fully expecting that the Liberal Party would fall at Richard's feet. This did not occur overnight; he waited until the next year before he became party president, and then entered federal parliament by winning the seat of La Trobe in 1949. By then Maie was active as a speaker and as an artist, lending many of her own paintings – including her Picasso – to an exhibition at the National Gallery of

Victoria. She was the patron of luminaries such as Sidney Nolan, purchasing a painting of his in 1949 and writing the introduction to the catalogue of a Sydney exhibition. She also used her formidable international network to promote his work.

In 1951 Maie again met Frances Burke, another artist with whom she developed a long and passionate relationship. They had originally been students together in George Bell's school in the 1930s, but their lives had taken different trajectories. Like Florence Broadhurst, Frances was an important innovator in arts and design in Australia.[50] She established the first major screen-printing business as early as 1937. Taking orders from Frances Burke Fabrics, Maie displayed these innovative designs in Washington and in Calcutta. Unlike Maie, Frances was open about her sexual relationships with women, and was called 'our resident lesbian' when they were students together.[51] Pat had returned from New York in March 1947, and by this time she was working on, of all things, the women's pages of the Melbourne *Sun News-Pictorial*. From the early 1950s she lived in Berwick near Maie, for several decades on part of Edrington Maie had given to her, though this was hardly convenient for her work as a journalist.[52] Given Maie's public reticence and the gaps in her papers, we do not know for certain how her relationship with Pat evolved after Frances became Maie's great source of womanly affection. Very soon Maie and Frances went away for weekends together at Anglesea, with Richard's approval. They dined frequently at the Lyceum Club in Melbourne.

Maie found a new enthusiasm for her career when she collaborated with leading artists such as Daryl Lindsay, the husband of her old friend Joan Weigall, on a project named *Early Melbourne Architecture, 1840–1888* (1953). Acting as editor and compiler, Maie worked tirelessly on an innovative assessment of buildings that included the grand and humble.[53] She was passionate about preserving Australia's colonial heritage and was far ahead of her time in this. In 1953 she also took part in the inaugural all-women air race.[54] Her life was also filled with overseas travel as she accompanied Richard in his role as Australia's External (now Foreign) Affairs Minister. Maie continued her own career, researching and writing her family history, *An Australian Story, 1837–1907* (1962), which she illustrated beautifully. Her gifts in portraiture and landscape were fully realised in this charming memoir. The following year she introduced the exhibition of her aunt Ellis Rowan's botanical illustrations in London.

Her life changed dramatically in 1960 when Richard was appointed a life peer, the second Australian after Stanley Bruce to accept this Imperial honour. This appointment was entirely in keeping with the Caseys' world view, but it was totally out of touch with modern Australia. His title, Baron Casey of Berwick and Westminster, attempted to reconcile his dual loyalties. From now on Maie was known as 'the Lady Casey', and the title was not lost on her assertive public interactions with women. She made a play for a young woman in the Lyceum Club in 1962, until told by a friend, 'Lay off, Maie, she's married.'[55] This is an interesting observation; what if the object of her desire had been single and unattached?

Maie's literary career continued. Her self-published book of poems, illustrated by Frances Burke, was a far more personal undertaking.[56] Yet she allowed Margaret Sutherland to set some of the poems to music in 1964. She and the distinguished composer further collaborated in 1965 on the opera *The Young Kabbarli*, about the life of Daisy Bates, whom Maie had met in 1934. A limited edition of this rare work was published in 1972. Maie was fascinated by this strange relic of the Edwardian era who had lived in the desert like a prophet for so many decades. Far more competent was her memoir of her public life, *Tides and Eddies* (1966), which was necessarily tactful about many eminent personages still alive. The opium and other drug-taking in Germany in the 1920s with the future Earl of Erroll was discreetly omitted.

In 1965 Richard was appointed Governor-General. Maie was perhaps the most eccentric and fascinating of all the spouses of this high office. As highly decorous but reserved conversation bored her, her dinner *bons mots* could be provocative and racy. She made new friends, including the waspish Patrick White. Her invitation list to Yarralumla included many artists and creative people, and never before were so many gays and lesbians entertained by the governor-general. After four years Richard retired from this office, pleased to be recognised as a Knight of the Order of the Garter. In 1970 he was named Australian of the Year, a somewhat surprising honour given his deep commitment to the United Kingdom. Life for both the Caseys in retirement was an anti-climax after decades of fascinating public service. During this period both Richard and Maie relied upon Pat Jarrett's support and practical skills.[57]

When Richard died in 1976, Maie was inconsolable and deeply depressed with grief. One of the strangest manifestations of Maie's self-centredness occurred at Richard's funeral. After decades of loyalty, service and affection from Pat, Maie decided she was not welcome at the funeral. What Pat did to deserve such shabby and insensitive treatment remains unclear, since Maie destroyed most of the correspondence between them. Yet it demonstrates Maie at her most selfish and manipulative. Pat left Berwick and settled in Mount Eliza.[58] Maie's treatment of her children had always contained these elements of disapproval and ruthlessness. She was hard, self-serving and callous beneath the superficial charm and humour.

When Maie died in 1983 her tributes were fulsome, especially from the Australian Women's Pilots' Association. Her beloved Edrington was sold by her daughter, Jane. Previously Maie proposed leaving the property to four grandchildren.

CHAPTER 11

Florence Broadhurst
(1899–1977)

The girl who came from poverty in Mount Perry in Queensland and conquered the worlds of haute couture and wallpaper design.

Florence Broadhurst was a highly accomplished woman as well as an extraordinarily bold, determined liar, and notorious self-promoter and mythmaker. Born into humble circumstances at Mount Perry, a tiny hamlet inland from Bundaberg in Queensland in 1899, she later purported to be an English aristocrat, invited to Princess Elizabeth's wedding in 1947. A good seamstress who learned needlework from her mother, in the 1930s Florence adopted the persona of Madame Pellier, trained in Paris, and established a *maison de couture* and was appointed a court dressmaker in Mayfair. With a lot of courage and cheek she carried it off successfully. Although she had left school at thirteen, Florence declared she had studied to a high level at the Trinity College of Music and the Slade School of Fine Arts in London, as well as studying art for ten years in Paris.[1] Yet later in life she had a brilliant career as a wallpaper designer and manufacturer that required no dissembling and fudging of the truth. Unable to celebrate her own rise from rural hardship at the beginning of the twentieth century to international recognition, she presented an incongruous figure, full of bravado, talent and deep insecurities. Her brutal murder in 1977 ended the life of one of Australia's most fascinating and talented women.

Florence Maud Broadhurst was born on Mungy Station near Mount Perry, population 250. Her father, William, was a drover, promoted to team leader before he purchased a modest property of his own, 'The Oakes', in 1902. Bill later became a favourite publican when the population of Mount Perry grew to 3675 after the copper smelter brought wealth to the community. Her mother, Margaret Crawford, was a quiet homemaker, fond of needlework and the arts. Florence attended the local state school where she obtained a basic education. As a young teenager she had penned her ambitions to '... do great things', a document she kept for the rest of her life.[2] She was to take the ambition and drive inherited from her father, and her mother's craft skills, to forge several illustrious careers as an adult.[3]

Under Margaret's influence, Florence studied singing and dancing in Bundaberg, necessitating a long 95-kilometre drive on unsealed dirt roads from their small hamlet. Bundaberg was a wealthy sugar town with beautiful wooden Queenslander homes owned by the sugar planters, such as the Crann Brothers and Angus Gibson. Later renowned for Bundaberg Rum, the town was a thriving provincial centre. Gladys Moncrieff was born there in 1892. Her mother, Amy Wall Moncrieff, had been a professional singer in Melbourne before her marriage and encouraged the musical development of the town, as well as of her young daughter. Gladys went on the stage at the age of six, touring around north Queensland, before her spectacular rise to an international career in musical comedy and light operetta. By the time Florence began her lessons in Bundaberg, Moncrieff had already paved the way for a girl from Bundaberg to sing professionally.

Florence's career took another path: she began with the local music festivals, most notably the well-regarded Queensland eisteddfod. In August 1918, after success at the eisteddfods, Florence performed at the Princess Theatre in Toowoomba for a patriotic concert. She had joined a group called the Smart Set Diggers, known for their renditions of popular patriotic songs and sang 'Beyond the Dawn'. Florence befriended the female impersonator Ralph Sawyer, a key performer in the Smart Set Diggers. Through his invitation, she joined the troupe. At this time a female impersonator was more like the Barry Humphries' character Dame Edna Everage, rather than code for a transvestite and the genre of the male-as-female revue was popular among troops in World War I. Two months later at a fundraiser, Florence gained attention when she sang the well-known 'Still as the Night'.[4]

The highlight of her amateur career came when she sang with Dame Clara Butt, in 1921, at St John the Evangelist Anglican Cathedral in Brisbane.[5] Dame Clara had studied at the Royal College of Music in London, and Queen Victoria had paid for her training in Paris. A woman of great presence and stature – at 6 feet 2 inches (189 cm) – she is now remembered for the 'Sea Pictures', composed for her by Sir Edward Elgar.[6] To be chosen to accompany such an internationally renowned singer was high praise for the young woman from Mount Perry. But a career in the classical and operatic repertoire did not appeal to

Florence, who was far more modern and racy in attitudes than the redoubtable Dame Clara.

In 1922 the Smart Set Diggers were renamed the Globetrotters and embarked on a fifteen-month tour of South-East Asia and India.[7] For Florence this was the opportunity to leave the bush forever and embark on the first chapter of her international careers. From this point until the end of her life, she would rewrite the areas she felt ashamed of and wished to ignore. Mount Perry was eliminated firmly from her biography. In this regard she was unlike Gladys Moncrieff, who never pretended she came from anywhere but Bundaberg. Such honesty was no hindrance to long runs on the West End stage in London.

The Globetrotters consisted of Ralph and Charles Holt, both female impersonators; Richard Norton and Dick Crichton, the comedians; and Wallington Tate as pianist. In line with this ensemble, Florence became the 'boy' of the group and was renamed Miss Bobby Broadhurst. A flapper in full flight and costume, Florence left Brisbane on the *Montoro* bound for Singapore in December 1922.[8] Though not a typically beautiful woman, she had dazzle and vivacity aplenty – a sharp wit and a predilection for wisecracks, abundant energy, an open mind and plenty of talent equipped her first steps to success. At her age many young women in rural Australia had already married, their ambitions hemmed in by narrow expectations and opportunities. This was not for Florence – ever.

The tour was a successful undertaking, ambitious in its scope as it ventured through Singapore, Bangkok, Kuala Lumpur, Penang, Delhi, Karachi, Hong Kong, Shanghai, Tientsin (now Tianjin) and Peking (now Beijing).

The nearly all-boy review. Florence is the one dressed in the top hat. Mitchell Library, State Library of NSW PXE 937_no8.

Modern, flippant and very gay in its approach, the ensemble entertained local elites and expatriate colonials in these distant outposts of Imperial influence. Somerset Maugham, international bestselling author and spy, travelled through China and Hong Kong in 1920 gathering material for his book of short stories *On a Chinese Screen* (1922). His version of colonial life was not the frivolous light-hearted world of the Globetrotters, but in some way their worlds did intersect with their gay subtexts. This was a world recovering from the devastation of the Great War, and for many, the years of suffering and anxiety had not ended with the war. For young people who never went into combat or lost family in the global conflicts, the new jazz age, as F. Scott Fitzgerald dubbed it, was fast, exhilarating and dangerous. They were tired of sorrow, grief and tearful

melancholic renditions of 'Abide with Me'. Fast cars, fast
lives throwing off Victorian and Edwardian prudery, new
sexual mores, and even drugs made for a dramatic change
in the 1920s. Even in the early novels of Agatha Christie,
such as *The Murder of Roger Ackroyd* (1926) and *Death in
the Clouds* (1935) 'Bright Young Things' snorted the odd
line of cocaine.

For Bobby Broadhurst, it was a heady taste of the high
life, in which she was courted by rich and powerful men.
In 1924, Florence and the troupe went to India. The
Maharajah Amer Kashif fell desperately in love with her
after seeing her performance and shot a tiger in her honour.[9]
The troupe went to Shanghai, the most sophisticated,
decadent city in Asia, which had been divided up into
Western European sectors under American, French and
British control. Shanghai grew in the 1920s when White
Russians, loyal to the tsar – or at least opposed to the new
Bolshevik government – fled to this cosmopolitan city.
Many Russian Jews, often highly educated and formerly
wealthy, were a part of this wider European community.
The exotic and dangerous atmosphere of Shanghai was
captured in the film *Shanghai Express* (1932), directed by
Josef von Sternberg and starring Anna May Wong and
Marlene Dietrich.

Florence entered into this heady world at full throttle.
Performing at the ritzy Carlton Club, the Globetrotters
was a popular act. Florence – or Bobby – also performed
with other groups such as the Broadcasters, Carlton Follies
and Carlton Sparklers, leading to extensive press coverage
of her singing and Charleston dancing.[10] When the original
troupe disbanded, Florence decided to capitalise on her

popularity and establish her own business. In February 1926 she opened the Broadhurst Academy Incorporated School of the Arts, which gave instruction in violin, piano, singing, banjolele, modern ballroom dancing, ballet, musical culture and journalism.[11] She employed experienced tutors such as Madame Boulueva who studied at the Dresden Conservatorium in pianoforte and Boulueva's daughter, a classical dancer from the Imperial Russian theatre.[12] With extensive publicity in the local and English-speaking press, the academy got off to a good start.

Unfortunately, though, this was not a particularly stable or secure time to be in Shanghai. With civil war raging between the communists and the Kuomintang forces, the city was a target for both combatants who opposed Western influence and control of Chinese territory. On 12 February 1927 a general strike erupted. A fierce conservative and Anglophile, Florence defied the fearful atmosphere of the city, and hosted a fundraiser for the British troops stationed there two weeks later. On 12 April 1927 the Kuomintang forces entered the city, looted property and massacred residents, particularly those suspected of being communists. Six weeks later, Florence brazenly and publicly celebrated Empire Day.[13]

With civil war at her very doorstep, Florence had no alternative but to abandon her business and return to Australia. She visited her family in Mount Perry, having not seen them for nearly five years. She had left as a local country girl with high ambitions and returned a glamorous international celebrity, a worldly, sophisticated and confident woman. In July she was involved in a car accident in her father's Studebaker and sustained injuries to her back, destroying any possibility of her returning to the stage.[14] After recuperating, Florence decided to try her luck in London. Clearly the confines of her childhood were far too narrow, and even Sydney seemed small and tame after glamorous, menacing and decadent Shanghai.

Florence left Australia in October 1927 and arrived in London little more than a year after the horrors of the General Strike. Florence was not deterred by the continued calls for class warfare and the tense atmosphere. Hit hard by the enormous casualties of World War I, with men destroyed forever by combat, and massive war loans crippling the economy, London contained elements of deep poverty and depression. This was not a world in which Florence had any intention of inhabiting. Her aspirations were far more concerned with conquering the world of the supposedly carefree upper class, so wittily satirised by Evelyn Waugh in his debut novel *Decline and Fall* (1928). It was upon the world of gay, quick repartee and graceful living that Florence set her ambitions.

With her formidable skills in dressmaking and embroidery, she went to work for the couturier Madame Corot at 33 Old Bond Street, London. At this time women couturiers such as Madeleine Vionnet, Coco Chanel and Elsa Schiaparelli extended the tradition set by the design houses Callot Soeurs and Jeanne Lanvin. Madame Paquin opened a couture house at 39 Dover Street in London in 1902, while Scots-Canadian Lucile (Lady Duff Gordon) was another successful society dressmaker in London in the early years of the twentieth century.[15] These women maintained a leading role in a profession that was later transformed after World War II by such men as Christian

Dior, Hardy Amies, Hubert de Givenchy and Cristóbal Balenciaga.

Florence then went to work for W. W. Reville-Terry, the prestigious Grosvenor Square couture house which, like Norman Hartnell, was among a number of other establishments that made court presentation clothes.[16] Florence's experience in the finest haute couture establishments in London gave her invaluable skills for her subsequent careers. While there she also designed film and theatre costumes.[17]

In June 1929 Florence married stockbroker Percy Kann at Brompton Oratory, an exclusive Roman Catholic church, in South Kensington. They set up house in St John's Wood, a charming, leafy suburb not far from the London Zoo. In 1933 Florence, with Percy as a director of the company, established Madame Pellier Ltd Modes et

Florence Broadhurst on her wedding day. Mitchell Library, State Library of NSW PXE 937_no1.

Robes at 65 New Bond Street in Mayfair. There was already a Madame Pellier in the St James Building in George Street in Sydney, who brought Parisian sophistication and chic to women in Australia.[18] To use the name of a well-established identity, albeit one in Sydney, was a daring move.

But in her new venture Florence was first intent upon taking away business from her former employers. From 1935 to 1937 her *maison de couture* was listed as a court dressmaker. The salon was expensively outfitted in silvery grey and adorned with fresh flowers daily. At this end of the market, the clientele may not have felt the cold winds of the protracted Depression.[19] Even riskier was Florence's decision to pretend she was a French woman who had trained in Paris. Here was a young woman with little formal education from a bush school in Queensland, now inventing herself as a French *grande dame*. Other contemporary London couturiers, such as Captain Edward Molyneux, had couture houses in both France and England, but he didn't assume a French identity, although he was fluent in the language and familiar with the customs. Yet with pluck and steely nerves she pulled off this persona. No doubt many of her clientele were aware of the charade, but she made damn fine clothes!

The Kann marriage did not endure Florence's commercial and creative success. In 1937 Florence, now aged thirty-eight, met 23-year-old Leonard Lloyd Lewis who later went under the surname of Lloyd-Lewis. A diesel engineer by trade, Leonard was Florence's partner in life and business for decades to come. They never formally married, yet, after Leonard left her in 1961 Florence presented herself as a divorced woman.[20] Her only child,

Robin (Robert) Lloyd-Lewis, was born on 3 April 1938. Suddenly Madame Pellier disappeared entirely, as the new 'Mrs Lewis' went to live in the stockbroker belt suburb of Banstead in Surrey. (Banstead is now remembered for its location in H.G. Wells' 1895 novel *The Time Machine*.) This undertaking was an extraordinary move for an ambitious, successful woman to contemplate, let alone execute; to abandon her hard-won independence, financial security and prestige to become a housewife of sorts. Evidence did not suggest Florence was particularly maternal – as later her son was sent to boarding school in Australia when his parents lived in London. In the summer holidays Robert was sent to various camps.[21]

During World War II, the family had a safe haven in semi-rural Barnstock, as it was not a target for the Luftwaffe. Never one to sit still, Florence joined the Australian Women's Voluntary Services which provided amenities and entertainment for Australian soldiers on leave.[22] After the war, the family moved to Worthing in Sussex. Perhaps Florence had gone there as an entertainer in the war, as this seaside town accommodated and trained several Allied divisions preparing for the D-Day landing in 1944. Near Chichester, Worthing is famed for its sailing. Florence, always alert to acquiring new skills, obtained her fishing and professional passenger boat licences.[23] A resolute anti-Labour stalwart, Florence joined the Art Women's Movement Against Socialism.

Post-war England was a sad and deprived society, and full rationing remained in force until 1954. Florence and her family decided to move to Sydney. They arrived in 1949 and Florence set about reinventing herself. Having triumphed

Florence Broadhurst with her husband Percy Kann. Mitchell Library, State Library of NSW PXE 937_no6.

in her theatrical career and as a couturier, she decided that conquering the art world would be her next challenge. The Lewises settled near the seaside again, in Manly. Florence visited her family, whom she had not seen since 1927 when she left Australia for London. After Florence's return from Mount Perry, she decided to undertake an extensive tour of the continent to get inspiration for her new career. In two years she produced some 114 paintings. In 1954 she held an exhibition in Sydney at David Jones department store gallery, followed in 1955 by a show at Finney's department store in Brisbane.[24] Other venues were more down-market, such as her showing in Bathurst.[25] Her declarations in the press about her aristocratic heritage, her training at the Slade and in Paris were distressing for her family in Queensland to endure.[26]

Leonard also had to be recast and glorified in this process of self-aggrandisement. But far from being a 'financier', as Florence had claimed he was in the press,[27] Leonard opened a car and truck yard, where Florence also worked, in Crows Nest, Sydney. But some of her public representations were correct: she *had* been a court couturier and an international performer.

Florence saw an opportunity to engage in high-level charitable activities as the means by which her aspirations could be attained. She joined the Royal Arts Society, a rather old-fashioned organisation even in the 1950s. What the society did have were connections with Sydney's elite. She was invited to a reception at Government House in January 1958 and was associated with Nola Dekyvere, the president of Sydney's elite Black and White Charity Committee, and the Countess d'Espiniary.[28] Florence was a superb networker, even if she was too pushy and aggressive in her manner. With a flair for publicity and good organisational skills, she got things done and she was noticed; not something these genteel institutions were known for.

Her big chance came in early 1958 when the Queen Mother undertook a tour of Australia. Invited to Government House and to several other regal functions, Florence unexpectedly landed her indisputable entrée into Sydney high society. The Queen Mother came forward to Florence at a gathering and asked how she was doing in Australia. Florence had previously told various ladies in Sydney that she had attended Princess Elizabeth's wedding in 1947, and now the Queen Mother recognised her in public![29] This act corroborated her fanciful stories. More likely, Florence and Robert were spectators along the road to Westminster Abbey to see the bridal party in the royal coach. Yet the royal family may have patronised Madame Pellier in its brief existence in the 1930s. No matter why the Queen Mother recognised her, from then onward, Florence was set up for the rest of her career in Sydney.[30]

Florence carefully mounted her campaign to be a Sydney society *grande dame*. She lacked a title, her husband lacked a knighthood and she was neither new nor old money. In essence Florence was a pushy, outrageous parvenue who had conquered other worlds seemingly more impenetrable than the eastern suburbs of Sydney. With determination, skill and single-mindedness Florence began her new offensive by making herself indispensable on the Australian Red Cross Fundraising Committee. Her most influential coup occurred when she assumed the mantle

A theatrical costume designed by Madame Pellier. Mitchell Library, State Library of NSW PXE 937_no37.

of president of the Black and White Ball Committee. This charity work, however, had many uses apart from the contacts she made. Florence was placed in charge of assembling the decorations for the 1964 *Die Fledermaus* Opera House Ball.[31] Alongside the role of organiser for the United Nations Association of Australia International Ball Committee in 1966, Florence was a member of the Sydney Opera House Appeal and a foundation member of the Art Gallery of NSW.[32] Her interest in opera and music was genuine, and she brought an extraordinary range of skills to her roles in these prestigious organisations.

The reality was that Florence worked with Leonard in the truck and car business until it was sold to TNT. Their relationship finally faltered in Sydney; her insistence on a lifestyle far above their means and his different expectations of cultural fulfilment made for constant conflict. Their lives were for a long time joined by the business and its obligations. In October 1958 Robert married and this was the first step in Florence and Leonard's final separation. But more devastating for Florence was Leonard's affair with a young woman whom he later married. There was nothing she could do about it. They never legally married so there were no messy divorce proceedings.[33] No doubt Leonard was tired of playing second fiddle to Florence, whose fantasy world of privilege and titles was hard to sustain both emotionally and financially.

Before the permanent rift with Leonard, her companion since 1937, Florence began tentative moves towards the career that secured her international fame. Like the couturier Paul Poiret, who had established a successful wallpaper enterprise in 1912 with a store at 15 Baker Street in London,[34] Florence moved into interior décor. In 1959 she established a small wallpaper business called Australian (Hand Printed) Wallpapers Pty Ltd at the rear of the trucking business shed. This brought together a series of elements in her life: first her tours through Asia in the 1920s, where she was inspired by delicate Chinese and Japanese drawings, especially of birds and flowers and second, her artistic talents in composition which had floundered in the 1950s. She was never destined to become a famous artist such as Sidney Nolan, Joy Hester, Judy Cassab or Margaret Olley, as painting was not the right medium for her expansive talents. The production of high class wallpaper allowed her skills in craft, construction and design to come together. There is controversy about what role Florence played in the designs that she claimed as her work.[35] A more accurate assessment suggests that Florence had the ability to choose highly competent, loyal designers who could execute her vision. As a couturier in London in the 1930s she hardly cut out and sewed every garment she sold; yet they were her designs, and her talent brought her clientele to her *maison de couture*. Again, with her increasingly poor eyesight, she needed artisans with perfect sight to undertake the complex task of making luxury wallpaper.[36] She secured a loan of £5000 to finance the business in August 1960.[37]

Certainly Florence learned to screen print from Phyllis Sholto and relied on artists John Long, Peter Leis and David Bond. The production of finely crafted wallpapers required a series of skills far beyond the design. The patterns had to match exactly, not an easy task with intricate designs, especially those of her geometric forms. Like Poiret, who pioneered modern bold patterns, Florence was also innovative, steering away from the Sanderson English floral chintz tradition so beloved in Mayfair and more conservative homes in Australia. Her patterns contained vibrant colours, textures and production innovations like printing onto metallic surfaces and vinyl finishings. The latter were particularly useful in hotter subtropical climates where mould presented innumerable problems with traditional paper.[38] The magazines *Australian House and Garden* in April 1965 and *Australian Home Journal* in February 1968 both featured flattering and informative stories of the achievements of this new endeavour. *Vogue Living*, in 1972, prominently assessed Florence's contribution to Australian design.[39]

In 1969 the expanding firm changed its name to Florence Broadhurst Wallpapers Pty Ltd, with the slogan 'the only studio of its kind in the world'. This referred to the airy and spacious new premises in Paddington that were a far cry from the hot, cramped operation in the car yard in Crows Nest. Florence sold her wallpapers to the top interior decorators in Sydney, such as Leslie Walford, Barry Little and Yvan Méthot. Walford was a crucial advocate of her products; a well-educated Englishman with wide cultural and intellectual interests, he catered to the crème de la crème of Sydney society. Far from a stuffy traditionalist, Walford was a promoter of new talents and creative expressions, but also had a formidable knowledge of more traditional modes. This was the beginning of international interior decoration conducted by highly trained professionals. Australia never produced an Elsie de Wolfe, although decorators like Marion Best conducted successful businesses from the 1930s in Sydney.[40]

Florence's business expanded after the move to trendy Paddington. She secured contracts in Kuwait, Los Angeles, Peru, Norway, Paris and the United Kingdom. The refurbishment of the Raffles Hotel in Singapore was a particularly prized assignment. And her career as a singer and dancer was launched in Singapore in 1922, so she had fond memories of the place.

Florence's appearance became more stylised as she grew older. She was one of the first recipients of a facelift in Sydney and in 1973 she underwent cell therapy in England in the hope of rejuvenation.[41] Her brightly hennaed hair, strikingly bold clothes and large items of chunky, antique jewellery made her a memorable figure in Sydney society. Rather than settling for one partner, she conducted many affairs and sexual adventures of varying durations. For a woman in her seventies such behaviour was risqué and confronting.[42]

Florence's life came to an end in the most brutal of circumstances when she was murdered in October 1977. The person may have known the premises; the police were convinced the building had not been forcibly entered. She suffered two massive head wounds, as well as the indignity of being placed head first in a toilet bowl after death. Her funeral was held at St Mark's Church at Darling Point on 20 October 1977.

In death Florence's reputation grew, albeit slowly. Robert attempted to run the business, but in the end sold the collection of patterns and designs to Wilson Fabrics, later owned by James Hardie Industries. In 1999 David and Helen Lennie purchased Florence's library of over 530 designs when they assumed control of Signature

Prints, the artistic arm of Wilson Fabrics. Celebrities such as Carly Simon, Marc Jacobs and Stella McCartney have all adorned their homes with Florence's designs. The Japanese-trained designer Akira Isogawa used her prints when he undertook a commission for the Sydney Dance Company in 1999. The following year he used her designs for his Chelsea and Nagoya clothing range. Karen Walker and Nicole Zimmermann employed Broadhurst designs for their women's clothing lines, Funkis used her motifs for homeware, while Customwear Carpets and Rugs produced carpets à la Broadhurst.[43] The Powerhouse Museum in Sydney owns a substantial collection of Broadhurst's oeuvre.

Few Australian women born at the end of the Victorian era had the opportunity, tenacity and flair to have three substantial international careers, all of which she directed with aplomb and an often cavalier disregard for the truth. As Leslie Walford remarked after her death in 1977: '[Florence Broadhurst] was a red-hot character; a red-hot manner, bright-eyed and flame-haired. She was fierce and determined with sassy sex appeal, still having affairs into her seventies.'[44] Talented, notorious and quixotic, Florence Broadhurst was a remarkable achiever and innovator.

CHAPTER 12

Pamela Travers
(1899–1996)

*The creator of Mary Poppins who hid her Queensland
origins but delighted the children of the world.*

The celebrated author of the *Mary Poppins* series, P. L.
Travers, spent her life reconstructing her identity. The
trauma of her father's death when she was only eight years
old left her forever determined but emotionally vulnerable.
Born Helen Lyndon Goff in Maryborough in coastal
Queensland, she became a famed literary *grande dame*, more
English than the English as she evolved into her persona,
Pamela Lyndon Travers. In the *Dictionary of Literary
Biography* her nationality is still listed as 'English'.[1] During
her lifetime she was sometimes called a New Zealander,[2] and
one encyclopedia entry lists her as an Irishwoman.[3] In 1966
she simply said that she was born in 1907 in the 'British
Commonwealth'.[4] She later remarked: 'I grew up and was
nurtured on the Celtic Twilight, Yeats and all. Therefore
Australia never seemed to be the place I really wanted to be.
My body ran around in the southern sunlight but my inner
world had subtler colours …'[5] Even more revealing was
her contention that '… sorrow lies like a heartbeat behind
everything I write …'[6] This flight from her origins made her
a notorious dissembler throughout her adult life.

Travers Goff in the late 1880s. Mitchell Library, State Library of NSW PX*D 334/no20.

Pamela was related to the wealthy Queensland pastoralist and parliamentarian Boyd Dunlop Morehead. Like many children who are thrown down the class system through family financial disasters, Pamela never lost her resentment that her entitlements had been stolen from her. When she died in April 1996, her obituary in the *Guardian* incorrectly stated that her grandfather was the founder of the Colonial Sugar Refining company.[7] All her life she confounded the truth, weaving stories of lost glories and distinguished lineage, maintaining a false privacy that deterred too ardent an interrogation of her origins and tribulations. Yet, as with many of the women in this book, her achievements as the creator of one of the most enduring characters in literature, the redoubtable Mary Poppins, belied any need for fabrication and dissembling.

In many ways it was her charming, but less than truthful, father, Travers Lyndon Goff, who made the mould of how she was to live her life. Pamela maintained her father was a younger son of the Irish gentry from Wexford, but in fact he was born in Deptford, London, to a ship's agent and chandler. This working area on the south bank of the Thames was renowned for the Royal Docks established under Henry VIII. There were no grand houses with gravel drives in Deptford. Goff initially went tea planting in Ceylon before arriving in Queensland in 1891. This was hardly a propitious time to establish a career; the sugar industry had gone bankrupt in 1889 and the colony was in the grip of a depression with class wars erupting in the pastoral industry.[8] Travers went into bank management. His first major post in 1898 was in the beautiful subtropical city of Maryborough as manager of the Australian Joint Stock Bank, with a salary and allowances of £300 per annum.

Pamela's mother, Margaret Morehead, came from far more exalted stock. She was a niece of Boyd Dunlop Morehead, a wealthy pastoralist and former inspector for the Scottish Australian Investment Company. His Scottish father, Robert Morehead, had established and managed this large enterprise alongside an impressive portfolio of other industries. A fervent laissez-faire Liberal, Boyd Morehead was a parliamentarian in Queensland from 1871–96, and served as premier in 1888–90.[9] The family residence in O'Connell Street, Sydney, was opulent. Margaret's father, Robert, died early from tuberculosis, and when her mother, Maria, remarried in 1870, Margaret went to live with her grandfather and unmarried Aunt Helen, later known as Aunt Ellie. Margaret received an inheritance from her father, which was left under the control of her uncle Boyd, however, the tangle of wills and legacies left a lasting impression on her, and was later transferred to her daughter. In the *Mary Poppins* series the drive for prosperity at 17 Cherry Tree Lane, London, and the mysterious world of the father, Mr Banks, reflects much of the anxieties in the Morehead and Goff households.

Margaret met Travers Lyndon Goff in Sydney and married him in the Anglo-Catholic church All Saints in Brisbane in August 1898. This was, in itself, unusual, for the Moreheads were socially prominent in Sydney. Possibly the young bride wished to signal her connections in the Queensland ruling class by this choice. Her Uncle Boyd gave her away. Little did she suspect he had also frittered away her inheritance in dubious investments. Nine months after the wedding, Helen Lyndon Goff was born, named after her mother's guardian – Aunt Helen – and her father. In childhood she called herself 'Lindy' or 'Ginty'. These were Gaelic words for water and stone.[10]

Though Goff was an amiable and congenial companion, who told tales of mystical Ireland, he was also an alcoholic. When Margaret realised this is uncertain, but she spent part of her early marriage back home with Aunt Ellie in the comfort of an ordered home with servants. Thus, young Lyndon (or Lindy) was initially reared in comfortable luxury, which later fed her aspirations and sense of dissatisfaction as an adult. Often absorbed in daydreams, in which she imagined she was a hen sitting on a nest, she was developing her creativity.[11] Back in Maryborough life was far sparser, but for Lyndon there was the delight of her father's company and his tales of long ago in Ireland.

While Goff drifted into the ethereal world of Gaelic spirits and spiritualism, Margaret was practical, replete with maxims for every occasion. Later, these were given to Mary Poppins in her attempts to bring order to the Banks' household. Margaret needed this steadfastness; in 1905 Travers was moved to another office, no longer the manager. His salary was cut and his pride shattered. In July Lyndon was sent to live with Aunt Ellie again, as Margaret coped with two new arrivals, Moya and Barbara. Later, Lyndon re-created those days in her book *Aunt Sass* (1941). When Goff was moved to the bank at Allora, young Lyndon returned to her family. This was Goff's chance for reformation, but unfortunately he was demoted again in early 1907. He died of pneumonia on 8 February 1908. The following week Margaret and the children went to live in the security of Aunt Ellie's world, before relocating to Bowral to reside with Great-aunt Christina Saraset.[12]

For the times, Lyndon was well educated, attending the Sydney Church of England Girls Grammar School in Bowral and later a private school in northern Sydney when she moved back to Aunt Ellie's. Some of the characters she later developed were based on local identities in Bowral, which now claims to be the home of Mary Poppins.[13] Lyndon faced indignity as a poor relation, and after completing her schooling at Normanhurst Aunt Ellie insisted she begin work as a secretary at the Australian Gas Lighting Company in 1916.[14] She later recalled that, as the eldest daughter, she felt the burden to support her mother.[15] Without money, she would need to marry well or pursue a career. So, in 1920, with financial security in mind, Lyndon took to the stage, to the horror of the Morehead ladies.[16] Her first performance was in a pantomime, *Sleeping Beauty*, as a dancer. Her next role, in *The Merry Wives of Windsor* with Allan Wilkie's Shakespearean Company, was met with greater approval in the Morehead household, thanks to the Shakespearean element. For Lyndon, this new career, however tentative, heralded a change in her persona and she became known as Pamela Travers. Her new identity didn't meet with immediate success and she toured the regional circuit with a small troupe from the company. Pamela's first major role was as Titania in *A Midsummer Night's Dream* in April 1922 in Sydney.[17] She performed in *Othello* the following year, where press notices called her 'the budding poetess'.[18] With her fair hair, beautiful skin and piercing eyes, she was a gorgeous ingénue.

In 1923, touring New Zealand, Pamela again transformed herself. She fell in love with a journalist and began writing slightly erotic poetry to express these new feelings. Emboldened by her newfound creativity, she submitted them for publication and they appeared in *The Triad* and the *Christchurch Sun*. For a new author to publish in the leading arts journal *The Triad* was a coup.[19] Launched in Sydney in 1915 after a successful period in New Zealand, the journal published leading writers such as Katharine Susannah Prichard, Vance Palmer, Dorothea Mackellar, Eleanor Dark and Dymphna Cusack.[20] Pamela's poetry was also accepted by *The Bulletin*. But it was Frank Morton, the editor of *The Triad*, who guided and nurtured her early career. He introduced Pamela to theosophy and mysticism, which she took up more consistently in the next decade. She began working in the journal's Sydney office as a columnist in May 1923, just months before Morton's death.[21] Her columns were often witty, with the wry sense of humour that she later developed in her Poppins novels.

With Morton's death, Pamela felt little tied her to Sydney. Despite some reservations, Aunt Ellie paid for her passage to Southampton and she departed in February 1924. Pamela listed her occupation as 'actress' for the ship's records, rather than journalist or writer. Unlike most Australian writers who sought recognition overseas, Pamela was emotionally located in Ireland, set to rediscover her father's legacy of enchantment and fantasy. London culture had moved on considerably since her father's adoration of William Butler Yeats and the Irish Revival. Poetry was sharp and modern – with Americans Ezra Pound and T. S. Eliot in vogue – and sat alongside the varied artforms of the Ballets Russes, Michael Arlen, Virginia Woolf, Edith Sitwell, Noël Coward, and jazz. There were few sweet longings for old Eire here. That dreamy world had been shattered by the horrors of World War I. The most prominent Irish writer was the exile James Joyce, whose gritty narratives hardly accorded to the tenets of Yeats' 'Sailing to Byzantium'. Still, Pamela managed to keep herself financially afloat by continuing her contributions to Australian and New Zealand publications.

Determined to make her name, she sought a mentor and patron. George Russell, or 'AE' – from the Greek word for distant time as well as the mystic notion of power from the Divine Being – an Irish writer and painter, had been involved with the Irish Revival with Yeats and theosophy. Born in 1867 he was, like Frank Morton, another father figure. Certainly there was no sexual attraction: in his late fifties, AE was corpulent, with dark, discoloured teeth from his pipe smoking, and badly dressed. He was, however, generous, charismatic and charming. As the editor of the *Irish Statesman*, he was an influential figure in literature and the politics of authorship.[22] His reputation now is overshadowed by that of Yeats, although a character in Samuel Beckett's 1938 novel *Murphy*, reads from Russell's *The Candle of Vision* (1919).

Pamela first made contact with Russell through writing letters of devotion. The standard praise he issued to aspiring authors beckoned her to Dublin, where she was not disappointed with his welcome. Promises of publication added to her joy. Her discovery of her Wexford relatives, however, was far less jubilant, as they were nothing like the mystic Irish her father had portrayed. After the flurry of letters, AE came to visit Pamela in her London flat, assuring

Pamela Travers as a professional actor, Sydney, 1922. Mitchell Library, State Library of NSW PX*D 334.

Pamela Travers on stage
in Sydney, 1922. Mitchell
Library, State Library of NSW
PX*D 334_folio26.

her he had met her in a previous life.[23] On this visit he gave
her a gift, an inscribed copy of one of his books, which was
exhilarating.[24] Her papers in the Mitchell Library reveal
her lifelong devotion to him. By 1926 she was publishing
her lyrical, old-fashioned poems in the *Irish Statesman*. Yet
she maintained her contributions to the *Christchurch Sun*,
detailing much of her day-to-day life in London, such as
her move to 14 Old Square in Lincoln's Inn.[25]

This year, 1926, also saw the burgeoning of the
character of Mary Poppins. Although Pamela later claimed
that the characters and story suddenly appeared to her in
1934, there had been hints of the dreamy world of children
and their hopes and fears at least a decade previously in
The Triad of December 1924.[26] She later also refuted
the notion that she wrote for children.[27] Like other great
writers of children's books, such as A. A. Milne and Frances
Hodgson Burnett, her stories can be read at different levels
by young and old. A story published in the *Christchurch*

Sun on 13 November 1926, 'Mary Poppins and the Match Man', introduced the Banks family, Mary with her parrot-headed umbrella and white gloves, and Bert the pavement artist and match seller.[28] Pamela was later horrified when the Walt Disney film production of *Mary Poppins* suggested a romance between Mary and Bert with the song 'It's a Jolly Holiday with Mary'. Julie Andrews was also far too saccharine and pretty for the plain but mysterious and sharp-tongued Mary.[29]

Pamela's emotional and creative life was caught up with AE. She went on holidays with him to Donegal in north-western Ireland. The cold, wet and boggy country was still not the mystical Ireland of her childhood imagination.[30] Surveying AE's beautiful paintings, such as *Carrying Driftwood*, *Girls Playing in a Forest* and *Mystical Figures*, it is clear that Pamela, with her halo of fair hair and dreamy eyes, must have seemed like an apparition straight out of these works. Set in verdant soft landscapes, the young, chaste women figures in these paintings glide through the air in a manner reminiscent of the English Pre-Raphaelites decades earlier.

In 1927 AE travelled to New York where he was regarded as a prophet of the new independent Ireland.[31] His absence left a vast emptiness in Pamela's life. Even more pressing was the urgency of rent. Her income from journalism was meagre. Though she liked privacy, Pamela took on a flatmate, Madge Burnand, the daughter of Sir Francis Burnand, a prolific playwright and editor of *Punch*.[32] Born in Ireland, Madge maintained many literary friendships with Irish writers, which was an important attraction for Pamela. The exact nature of the relationship remains in contention. In the 2009 Sydney play *The Knowing of Mary Poppins* Madge and Pamela are lovers.[33] A photograph of Pamela bare-breasted taken by Madge suggests an intimate relationship, but Pamela's papers in the Mitchell Library contain little about her. Certainly there seemed to be no young men in Pamela's life. All her close male associates and friends were older men with whom she maintained a platonic relationship more in keeping with acolyte and master.

By the late 1920s Pamela began travelling, on some occasions to improve her health. She always complained she suffered poor health, although she lived for nearly a century. Holidays in 1928 with Madge to Spain and Italy were for leisure; others, like her visit to the USSR, were for professional reasons.[34] To afford to travel more, Pamela and Madge moved to a smaller flat in Woburn Square near Euston Station, an area on the fringe of Bloomsbury. They moved again before eventually relocating in 1930 to the rural peace of Pound Cottage near Mayfield in Sussex, with Tunbridge Wells the largest town in the vicinity. The house was old and charming, but lacked modern conveniences. Not that that concerned Pamela too much, for she left the cooking and all practical daily matters to Madge. However, the location was vastly inconvenient, being fifteen minutes or so by car to Mayfield. This move to the country was brought about by several events in Pamela's life. Her mother had died in November 1924, leaving her with only a modest estate. Pamela continued to fret about her health and feared she would be struck down with tuberculosis like her grandfather – a real concern in the '20s and '30s, before the advent of penicillin in 1944.

She had several prolonged stays in sanitariums due to lung problems.[35]

In the early 1930s AE moved into his mystical stage of life, selling his possessions after his wife's death. He left Ireland, satisfied that his contribution to the Irish Revival was complete, and settled in Sussex Gardens near Paddington Station in London, often visiting Pamela and Madge in the country. AE introduced his protégée to Alfred Orage, the influential Yorkshire editor of the *New English Weekly*. Pamela and Orage were colleagues and friends for only a year before Orage's death in 1934.[36] His biography was reviewed in Melbourne in 1937 with no mention of his connection to a distinguished Australian author.[37] Orage's influence on Pamela's development was substantial, however, for he introduced her to the thoughts and teachings of Armenian-born George Ivanovich Gurdjieff. These were a mixture of Indian mysticism and the works of Madame Helena Blavatsky, the founder of theosophy. With the challenge of Darwin's ideas to conventional Christianity in the mid-nineteenth century, various forms of mysticism became popular. Spiritualism and Eastern religions, without their emphasis on Judeo-Christian monotheism, alongside the post-Freudian notion of self-improvement and self-development through an inner spiritual quest, attracted many followers. The charismatic cult leader Gurdjieff required obedience and subservience from his followers, in whom he induced self-doubt.[38] He claimed to have studied Tibetan mysteries and Indian wisdom. His acolytes were often rich and well connected, but despite this he lived on meagre rations.

Pamela at Pound Cottage with her mentor 'AE' George Russell. Mitchell Library, State Library of NSW MLMSS5341_ ITEM6_.

When AE was ailing in 1934 and Orage had died, Pamela was left without a creative master to worship. Gurdjieff filled the need to devote herself again to a dominant older man.[39] Yet this was Pamela's most creative period, for in 1934 she published her first novel in the Mary Poppins series, dedicated to the memory of her mother, which was strange, given her devotion to her father. The book is set in Edwardian London before the destruction of that orderly society by the Great War. Like Agatha Christie's great creation Hercule Poirot, Mary and all the other inhabitants of Cherry Tree Lane never age. The five children – Michael, Jane, Barbara, John and Annabel – and Mr and Mrs Banks along with the rest of the household, the maid Ellen, the cook Mrs Brill and the handyman Robertson Ay, live in chaos before the arrival of the tart-tongued Mary Poppins. She brings order and magic into their closed little world. Published by Gerald Howe in London and complemented by the wonderful illustrations of Mary Shepard, the book was an instant hit.

Pamela's relationship with her illustrator does not show her in a positive light.[40] Mary came from a distinguished line of illustrators. Her father, Ernest Shepard, illustrated A. A. Milne's *When We Were Very Young* (1924) and *Now We Are Six* (1927), as well as the series beginning with *Winnie-the-Pooh* (1926); her mother, Florence Shepard, was also an artist. Pamela had wanted to collaborate with Ernest but he was unavailable. Madge knew Mary Shepard and recommended Pamela take a chance with her. Pamela had seen a Christmas card drawn by Mary, who at twenty-three was fresh out of art school, and reluctantly she took on Ernest's daughter as her illustrator. Mary always knew she was second choice, a situation hardly conducive to a good working relationship. An equal relationship had never been Pamela's intention, for the books were always *her* work in her mind. She did not understand that great partnerships derive from mutual respect.

Though AE was seriously ill in early 1935, he was able to help Pamela with suggestions to market her book. While in the United States, he had given a copy of *Mary Poppins* to the head buyer of Marshall Field's, a Chicago department store. Published through Reynal and Hitchcock, it was initially advertised in the Chicago press and soon became an American bestseller.[41] AE returned to London terminally ill. He died in July 1935 with his friends around him. His body was returned to Ireland where he was accorded a state funeral attended by President Eamon de Valera and Yeats. For Pamela, this was a period of deep grief and introspection, compounded by the death of her Aunt Ellie, also in 1935.

The year did not end badly, however. Pamela completed *Mary Poppins Comes Back*, which was also published in the States. Aunt Ellie had left her a handsome share portfolio and real estate in Sydney, which supplemented her journalism and book royalties to provide a period of financial security. With this assurance she purchased Pound Cottage and hired a maid, Doris Vockins. The power balance between Pamela and Madge shifted with her newfound independence. After a romantic disappointment in 1935 with the Irish poet Francis Macnamara, Pamela began another deep emotional attachment with Jessie Orage, her mentor's widow, staying with her and her children when in London. In early 1936 Jessie and Pamela went on holidays to Switzerland. They became friends with American Jane Heap, the editor of *The Little Review* and a devotee of Gurdjieff, and her lover Margaret Anderson, who had founded the magazine. Indeed with Jessie, Pamela met the master, Gurdjieff, at the Café de la Paix in Paris in March 1936.[42] The alarm bell should have rung, for he demanded money from all his disciples. They were always an exclusive, talented group, numbering among them T. S. Eliot – despite his attachment to Anglo-Catholicism – Katherine Mansfield and Georgia O'Keeffe. Timothy Leary was a later devotee.

By the following year, Pamela's relationship with Madge reached breaking point. Madge went to the United States and never returned to live at Pound Cottage. Then Pamela took the extraordinary step of enquiring whether she could adopt her young maid, Doris, one of seven children. When Doris' parents refused, Pamela sacked Doris on the spot. She had observed how Jessie adored her children and fixed on the idea that a child would be her perfect love object. In 1939 she adopted John Camillus Hone, one of twin boys, from a distinguished Irish literary family and a cousin of Francis Macnamara. Ironically, it was Madge who knew the Hone family and their impoverished circumstances. The family urged Pamela to take both boys, but on her initial visit to Dublin she went away empty-handed. She obtained a horoscope for the twins which decided her upon Camillus. Pamela took to wearing a wedding ring, for it was unusual for a single, middle-aged woman to adopt a child in 1939.[43] This decision to separate the twins so carelessly was to have long-term repercussions. Young Camillus did not know he was a twin until he was seventeen.

With the Blitz starting, Pamela and Camillus evacuated to Canada. Her task was even more daunting, for she chaperoned otherwise unaccompanied children from Tunbridge Wells. For a self-absorbed, neurotic woman, always a hypochondriac and fussy, the sudden responsibility of a baby and strange children was terrifying. Fortunately, Pamela met the sculptor and wood engraver Gertrude Hermes on the boat, who not only assisted with the children, but formed a strong bond with Pamela. Little is known about this intense relationship, as references to Gertrude were excised from Pamela's papers. Moving to East 52nd Street in New York in 1940, Pamela resumed her writing career. She published *I Go By Sea, I Go By Land* and *Aunt Sass* in 1941, followed by *Ah Wong* in 1943. That same year *Mary Poppins Opens the Door* was released in the United States and published in London the following year.

In 1944 Pamela was offered a trip to New Mexico by the Commissioner of Indian Affairs, John Collier. Like

D. H. Lawrence, US arts patron Mabel Dodge Luhan and artist Georgia O'Keeffe before her, Pamela fell in love with the stark, pink beauty of the desert landscape. She had already travelled there the previous year with Camillus to visit Jessie Orage, who had moved to Santa Fe after their relationship ended. From Jessie's diaries, it appears that Pamela was full of despair about her deteriorating relationship with Gertrude.[44] Pamela took to wearing a version of the south-western costume with floral shirts and turquoise jewellery, reminiscent of Frida Kahlo.

In March 1945 Pamela and Camillus returned to England, buying a Georgian house in Smith Street in Chelsea. When Camillus went away to board at Dane Court preparatory school in Pyford, Surrey, Pamela was lonely and dissatisfied. She resumed contact with the London Gurdjieff group and visited the master in Paris in 1948. He died the following year, having survived the war, supported by his many disciples. Pamela joined the vigil over Gurdjieff's body. He was buried with a Russian Orthodox service at Alexandre Nevski Cathedral in Paris. Pamela was emotionally distraught and physically ill from grief. The next few years passed in a blur for her. In 1952 *Mary Poppins in the Park* was published, perhaps the most mystical of all the series, and reflects some of her beliefs garnered from Gurdjieff's teachings.

Through a chance meeting in a pub, Camillus met his twin in 1956. His confusion and anger were explosive and he never forgave Pamela her deception and separation from his 'other half'. For several years Pamela carried the legacy of her deceit, suffering depression. This lifted in 1959 when she was asked to sell her rights to the *Mary Poppins* series to Walt Disney Productions. What seemed delivery from eking out a modest but comfortable living, however, had its pitfalls, as the American company could and would develop the story in its own way.

Pamela travelled to Los Angeles, staying at Disney's expense at the Beverly Hills Hotel. She met Walt Disney at his studio in South Buena Vista Street, Burbank, where they discussed the *Mary Poppins* project. The new script by Bill Walsh and Don DaGradi substantially revised her script, which had been an adaptation of seventeen episodes from the first three books. The Disney script concentrated on three stories only, 'East Wind', 'The Day Out' and 'Laughing Gas', with new material and different interpretations to the original themes. Pamela was horrified by the incorporation of American slang into her Edwardian England setting and chirpy songs by Richard M. Sherman and Robert B. Sherman, although during the filming of *Mary Poppins* Pamela corresponded with the lead actress Julie Andrews.

To accompany her professional anxieties along came the news that Camillus had been sent to jail for drink driving in 1960. After his release in 1961, Pamela decided to sell her home in Smith Street and purchase a new home in Shawfield Street, Chelsea.

In 1963 Pamela made a short trip back to Australia where she was less than forthcoming in interviews, and then went to Japan to study Zen Buddhism. She travelled to Los Angeles for the 27 August 1964 premiere of Disney's *Mary Poppins* at Grauman's Chinese Theatre on Hollywood Boulevard. Walt Disney ignored her and concentrated on the lead actress Julie Andrews. In a further

Pamela in later years. Mitchell
Library, State Library of NSW
PX*D 334_ folio28.

insult, she was acknowledged in the credits as merely a
'consultant'. In small type it read, 'Based on the stories of
P. L. Travers'. At the London premiere on 17 December
1964, Pamela was presented to Princess Margaret and
Lord Snowdon, standing in line with cast members Julie
Andrews, Hermione Baddeley and David Tomlinson. The
film went on to win five Oscars in 1965.

After her less than perfect experience with the Disney
film, Pamela decided to take up a writer-in-residence
sojourn at Radcliffe College in Boston in 1965–66, but
this was not a success.[45] Pamela was distressed that she
was now known only for the Disney film and not, as she
believed, for her own creativity. Searching for another guru
to follow, she became devoted to Krishnamurti, the Indian
mystic who claimed many rich followers in Hollywood.[46]

In 1975 she wrote to her Swedish translator and the
author of a book on her work, Staffan Bergsten, that
she declined to write an autobiography or consider an
authorised biography as 'All that matters to me is the story

of a soul and I am not going to wear that on my sleeve for the general public. And one little life – what is that?'[47] A notorious dissembler and chameleon all her life, Helen Lyndon Goff, who became Pamela Lyndon Travers, always hoped she could find true peace and security in the mystical fairytale world her father bequeathed to her.

Pamela spent the last decades of her life largely as a recluse in her Chelsea home. She was delighted to receive an OBE in 1977, but from this point on her life revolved increasingly around mysticism and meditation. She did, however, prepare a version of her own obituary which mentioned little of her life and nothing of her origins. She died at her Shawfield Street home in April 1996, and no dates or details were included on her tombstone in St Mary the Virgin Church in Twickenham.[48]

CHAPTER 13

Enid, Countess of Kenmare
(1892–1973)

The daughter of the winemaking family who married into the aristocracy and took many lovers but never forgot her Australian beginnings.

Over the last century, several Australian women notably married into the higher echelons of European aristocracy. 'A high society beauty', Sheila Chisholm from Woollahra, Sydney, in 1915 married the son of the fifth Earl of Rosslyn, known as 'the man who broke the bank at Monte Carlo', then in 1928 Sir John Peniston Milbanke, and lastly Prince Dimitri Romanoff in 1954. A member of Edward, Prince of Wales' fast London set in the 1920s, Sheila was a cultured woman who was great friends with novelist Evelyn Waugh.[1] Born in Melbourne in 1948, fashion journalist Dale Harper married Lord Tryon in 1973 and was a favoured mistress of Charles, Prince of Wales before he met Camilla Parker-Bowles. Even more spectacularly, Tasmanian Mary Donaldson married Crown Prince Frederik of Denmark in 2004.

Perhaps the most notorious among those select few who married so well was Enid Lindeman from Sydney, who ended her days as the Countess of Kenmare, but was viciously dubbed 'Lady Killmore' after she was widowed four times. When she was depicted by author Dominick Dunne as a cruel, drug-addicted social climber in *Vanity Fair* in March 1991, Enid's reputation was shredded. In 2004 the autobiography of her daughter Pat Cavendish O'Neill, *A Lion in the Bedroom*, shed further light on Enid's life by presenting a frank account of an extraordinarily sexually promiscuous woman. Yet Enid's kindness to her three children and stepson reveals a complex woman who charted the dangerous waters of the upper echelons of British society for much of the twentieth century.

Enid was born into the distinguished Lindeman family, which established the wine industry at Cawarra near Gresford in the Hunter Valley in New South Wales. Dr Henry Lindeman studied viticulture in France and Germany after finishing his medical degree at St Bartholomew's Hospital in London. Lindeman claret won prizes in Bordeaux in 1882.[2] His son Charles assumed control of the business in the late 1870s and established a family. Daughter Enid was born in 1892, preceded by three brothers from whom she learned to ride horses, shoot and fish. This stood her in good stead later when she participated as an equal with her lovers and husbands in such sports. Rather than sit on the sidelines, Enid was accomplished and determined to win.[3]

As with many well-born girls of her day, Enid's education was to prepare her for marriage and domestic life rather than a career or an active role in the family business. At the age of nineteen, Enid met the shipping magnate Roderick Cameron in Sydney. He was twenty-four years older than she. His father, Canadian-born Sir Roderick

Cameron, established the Australian Pioneer Line in 1852, carrying supplies from the United States to the Australian goldfields. (Lola Montez and her troupe arrived in Sydney in 1855 on one of his vessels.) Sir Roderick owned a magnificent estate, Clifton Berley, on Staten Island in New York, as well as a sixteen-storey skyscraper in Manhattan.[4] Like his father, Roderick Jr was a good judge of horse flesh and perhaps this is how young sports-mad Enid first met him. Enid and Roderick married in 1913 and went to live at Clifton Berley. Tragedy struck when Roderick died of cancer the following year, leaving Enid with a baby son, Roderick, always known as Rory.

Not one to mourn for long, Enid started an affair with financier Bernard Baruch, thereby scandalising New York society – not so much by the speed of the liaison but by Bernard's being Jewish. Dominick Dunne alleged that Enid had an affair with Bernard before her marriage when she was sixteen. Like so many other issues in his coverage this is incorrect; at that time Enid was a schoolgirl in Sydney.[5] Bernard and Enid remained lifelong friends.[6] Enid showed few of the prejudices of her times; she was later criticised for mingling with all sorts of guests, from royalty to jockeys, at her magnificent home, La Fiorentina on the Côte d'Azur. One notable socialite from that era, Elvira de la Fuente, claimed Enid was just as happy sitting next to a prince or a waiter. At her lunch parties at La Fiorentina, the Duke of Veduna and Greta Garbo might sit with 'people no one had ever heard of'. Thus, an unusual democracy prevailed at her gatherings.

Leaving for London in 1915, Enid took on a role as a *grande horizontale*, having affairs with such powerful men as Group Captain Walter Wilson and the Minister for War, the Earl of Derby, before marrying the impoverished, handsome aristocrat Brigadier General Frederick 'Caviar' Cavendish, the second son of the fifth Baron Waterpark in Paris in June 1917. In the early twentieth century the social code for a wealthy young widow was to marry and then pursue whatever life she wished. The Cavendishes are one of England and Ireland's most distinguished aristocratic families. They are related to the Dukes of Devonshire, Dukes of Marlborough and the Spencer family, thereby making 'Caviar' a relative of Diana, Princess of Wales, and Sir Winston Churchill. Georgiana Cavendish, Duchess of Devonshire in the late eighteenth century, the renowned beauty painted by Gainsborough, was a notorious ancestor who gambled away a large fortune. Frederick's relative Richard Cavendish married Kathleen ('Kick') Kennedy, daughter of the US Ambassador to the Court of St James, Joseph Kennedy, and sister of President John F. Kennedy. This was also a scandalous marriage, as the Kennedys were Irish-American Catholics who gained their fortune in dubious circumstances.

All this was a far cry from Enid's family of solid professional and business entrepreneurs in Australia. Her grandfather and her brother, Grant Lindeman, were respected physicians and wine makers, and she was never allowed to forget her origins as she moved into the aristocracy. At one time the famed beauty Daisy Fellowes, daughter of the third Duc Decazes et Glücksbierg and Isabelle-Blanche Singer, heir of the Singer sewing machine fortune and niece of Princess Edmond de Polignac, described Enid as 'an Australian with a vague pedigree'.

When Enid remarked in conversation 'people of our class', Fellowes raised her hand and stopped her midsentence: 'Just a moment, Enid. Your class or mine?'[7] Enid's retaliation to this snobbery was to tell elaborate yarns about her family's convict origins, embellishing sordid details as she went along. Unlike many Australian women who did well in England and hid their origins, such as Pamela Travers, Enid was fiercely proud of her Australian identity and her family's wine business in which she later invested heavily.[8] Her intended humour and attempts to deflate the pomposity and snobbery of many of her European acquaintances later rebounded on her. She often joked she had murdered all her husbands. An Australian audience would understand this as an immensely dark jest, a form of the tall tale in dubious taste. The British did not.

Enid was a firm supporter of the Allied war effort and her ability to drive a car, a rare feat for a woman in those days, was put to good use. She served on the front line of the battlefields as an ambulance driver. This was a particularly dangerous operation. Her son, Rory, recalled in his memoirs that his mother, when not in uniform, wore fabulous dresses by the couture house of Worth. All the officers fell madly in love with her.[9] Her splendid war work counted for not much against the story that on a bet she supposedly bedded all the officers in her new husband's regiment. With a taste for the high life and his polo ponies, Frederick was dependent on her capital from Cameron's will to maintain his lifestyle and in no position to complain. Her whole style was outrageous and confronting. When Frederick was transferred to Egypt, Enid dressed as a man and played in a band in the officers' mess, thereby challenging both the gender and class codes of the time. Frederick had received the French Legion of Honour, a rare honour for an Englishman, and served on Marshal Foch's staff, so Enid's public behaviour dented his heroic reputation.

Enid was never mercenary in her dealings with rich men, though decidedly high-handed to those without a fortune, as Frederick could attest. When another admirer, Group Captain Walter Wilson, died, he bequeathed to her the fortune he had accumulated from his investments in the White City Stadium in London. Enid generously gave half to the woman with whom he lived for many years. Her daughter, Pat, joked that her mother spent much time with lawyers going over the wills of various lovers and admirers who left her fortunes.[10] Not that Enid needed money. She was, after all, remarkably wealthy from her first marriage. Her life in Mayfair, London, was luxurious in the extreme; her freshly ironed sheets matched her negligee each night. Her bedroom was sprayed with Patou's expensive perfume 'Joy' every evening. Yet Enid was not entirely self-absorbed. She often visited poor and injured ex-servicemen to take them and their families food and money, in her chauffeured car. This highlights two aspects of her character: she thought of others who were not as fortunate as herself, yet she never compromised her standards or patronised anyone under any circumstances.

The Cavendishes were not well suited, but then Enid needed only the façade of a marriage in order to pursue her chosen lifestyle of pleasure, sport and sex. They had two children: Patricia ('Pat'), born in June 1925, and Frederick Caryll, born fifteen months later. Both parents were devoted to their children. Pat fondly remembers her father teaching her to ride in steeplechases and picking her up from her ballet classes. Frederick died in December 1931 when Enid and the younger children were at Biarritz. The injuries he sustained on the front in World War I shortened his life.

By this time Enid had assumed the character that fascinated many and repelled others. No one denied that she was a striking beauty with a perfect oval face. Her fair hair went sleek silver at age twenty-eight in 1920 after a bout of illness. With her green eyes and perfect complexion her appearance was distinctive. One unnamed person from her days in Kenya in the 1930s thought she had 'cold cold, cruel eyes'.[11] Her acutely snobbish first sister-in-law, Anne Cameron Tiffany, remarked that Enid's beauty made the 'cars [in New York City] come to a halt the better to view this vision of perfection'.[12] Pat claimed incorrectly that at least five men committed suicide over her mother, including the distinguished scientist Franz Meissner and Peter Coats, the talented garden designer.[13] And this was only during the time she was married to Viscount Marmaduke Furness.

Enid was not widowed for long. She met Marmaduke 'Duke' Furness and married him in August 1933 without introducing him to her children. Duke hated children including his own, Richard (Dick), Averill and William – known as 'Tony the bastard', hinting that the Prince of Wales was his biological father. His first wife, Daisy, died at sea on board his yacht in 1921 and rumours followed that he had murdered her. Unlike the Cavendish family, the Furness fortune and title was extremely recent. His second wife, Thelma Morgan Converse, whom he married five years after Daisy's death, remarked in the autobiography she wrote with her twin, Gloria Morgan Vanderbilt, that Duke had a strong north Yorkshire accent and was a well-tailored plain man with red hair. His mother was an old-fashioned Yorkshire woman who longed for life to go back to the certainties of the Victorian age when, she imagined, life was stable and good.[14] Later Thelma experienced his vile temper, excessive drinking and jealousy. Enid discovered his less desirable character traits all too soon during their marriage.

Duke Furness was one of England's richest men. His family had originally owned collieries then went into shipbuilding. His father, Sir Christopher Furness, was an astute but hard-nosed, aggressive magnate with no pretensions to good manners or culture. His only concession to cultivated society was his decision to name his son Marmaduke. He did not think much of his son or his abilities. Duke did not originally inherit the business, which went to his cousin, Stephen. When he acquired the business empire after Stephen's sudden death in 1914, Duke showed a rare acumen for all sorts of dealings and improvements. He was elevated to the peerage for his substantial contribution to the war effort. In 1926 when he married the actress and socialite Thelma Converse, who had been reared in Europe where her father was a distinguished diplomat, he was a much-feared and disliked man. Thelma recorded that she mixed with people in the Prince of Wales' set at the Embassy Club, among them Australian-born Sheila Milbanke (née Chisholm) and the Duke and Duchess of Westminster.[15] This may have been a warning sign of incompatibility, for it was Thelma who had the introductions into royal circles not the nouveau riche businessman Duke Furness. The marriage broke down when Thelma began an affair with the Aly Khan and was the acknowledged mistress of Prince Edward before he married Wallis Simpson. Thelma and Duke were divorced in 1933; Thelma retained the title of Thelma, Viscountess Furness. They were eventually on good terms after an early period of intense acrimony.

Duke married Enid soon after his divorce. He was already a troubled and deeply suspicious man, embarrassed by being a public cuckold. His background from the upper middle class of northern England did not encompass the aristocratic amorality allowing affairs for married women. Rather than take pride in Thelma's royal liaison he was hurt and angry. A man like Frederick Cavendish would have been proud to be the husband of the mistress of the future monarch. Enid's daughter, Pat, reported that Furness was very cold and distant to Enid's children and housed them in separate quarters with their own staff at his home, Burrough Court, near Melton Mowbray in Leicestershire. His son, Dick, a cavalry officer, was charming to both Pat and Caryll, in contrast to his father's behaviour. Dick was disinherited by Furness in one of his tyrannical outbursts; he later died a hero at Dunkirk, trying to save the men under him. In turn, Enid was solicitous for the welfare and emotional state of her stepson, little Tony, whom she regarded as abandoned and neglected. Her treatment of the various children in her life showed Enid at her best – warm, solicitous and amusing.[16]

At first the marriage went well. Each morning Duke and Enid went out riding with a pack of hounds when

they were resident in Burrough Court. Enid, attired in a
top hat and veils, rode side-saddle with speed and accuracy.
A warning should have been signalled when Duke always
went out with a silver hip flask. His vile language at even
the slightest annoyance also indicated a nasty temperament.
His second wife, Thelma, had found these outbursts
worrying and tiresome.

By the time of her third marriage, Enid had acquired,
among her domestic animals like her pet hyraxes – always
called Tikki – and fifty poodles, two silver foxes, several
porcupines and a cheetah. This glorious animal had long
featured as the ultimate status symbol. Charlemagne had
a pet cheetah and the Mughal Emperor Akbar the Great
kept over a thousand of these extraordinary animals. In the
twentieth century, avant-garde aristocrats such as Nancy
Cunard and the Marchesa Casati each appeared in public
with a cheetah on a lead in an elaborate jewelled collar.
Usually Enid was accompanied by a pet crow and the
current Tikki, including at the dinner table.

With the Furness fortune, Enid travelled better than
royalty on ships, aeroplanes and in the best cars. When she
moved to one of her favourite spots such as Le Toquet or
Biarritz, her maids and valets had the unenviable task of
assembling the entire luggage and menageries of wild and
domestic animals ready for travel. Enid, meanwhile, was
oblivious of the chaos and stress this manoeuvre entailed.
Often sixty trunks were included in her personal luggage,
not counting that of the children, their governesses, nurses
and servants.[17] In Kenya, where she spent the winter
months, Enid kept a leopard named Chui. While all this
sounds pretentious, Enid always had a deep respect and

love of animals. In later life when all the husbands and lovers were put aside, she devoted herself to animals.

Their winter months in Kenya were luxurious in the extreme. Duke was dubbed 'Champagny Lordy' for his display of wealth, which included Lord Allenby's Rolls Royces from World War I and maintaining a retinue of local and English servants dressed in the Furness livery. Life among the 'Happy Valley' aristocratic set in Kenya in the 1930s was decadent and opulent. Enid and Duke stayed with Lady Idina Sackville, the famed 'bolter' who abandoned her children and husband, Charles Gordon, when she ran off with Josslyn Hay – later the Earl of Erroll – in 1923. The spoilt rich aristocrats Danish Baron Bror Blixen and American Alice de Janzé led lives of promiscuous abandon, in which cocaine and sometimes morphine were the party drugs of choice. In his *Vanity Fair* article Dominick Dunne alleged that Enid was a drug addict who enticed others into abusive behaviour. While she certainly took prolonged prescribed medication for a serious back injury sustained when she fell from a horse at Burrough Court – this kept her in hospital for months on end – she was not part of the inner circle of the sex- and drug-addicted coteries within the Happy Valley set. For one thing, she was closely watched by Duke who took to setting private detectives on her tail to report her every move.

Tensions between Duke and Enid reached a crescendo when he suspected she was having an affair with the Duke of Westminster, England's richest man and a senior royal. He threatened that he would not attend the coronation of King George VI with her in 1937; she retaliated by threatening to attend with Westminster. They had one last trip to Kenya in 1938. Then Enid took the younger children to meet her former relatives, the Camerons, in New York. On board the *Queen Mary* they met Gary Cooper who was charming to the children, unlike many celebrities who put on the charm only for adults. Later they met William Randolph Hearst and his mistress Marion Davies in California and attended the 1939 World's Fair in New York. While she was away Enid decided she would have a facelift. She chose the New Zealand-born surgeon Sir Archibald McIndoe, who was shocked when he entered her recovery room to find a cheetah happily ensconced there.

Enid left for France soon after her operation. She had made friends with P. G. Wodehouse, the author of the Bertie Wooster and Jeeves stories, and his wife at Le Toquet. Duke was jealous even of this innocent friendship. As war approached, Enid went to her villa on the Bay of Beaulieu on the Côte d'Azur, La Fiorentina. When war was declared and shortages were felt even among the rich in France, the ever-resourceful Enid got a herd of goats from which the villa residents obtained both cheese and milk. Other guests, including an unnamed Belgian countess, brought other less welcome habits like severe drug addiction. Enid dealt with this situation quickly, sending the poor woman to the local asylum.[18] She also apparently hid Allied airmen on the run in her home, dressing them as maids but the Germans were not in the South of France so this may have been a fanciful contribution to the war effort.

Back in England Enid decided to assist the war effort by working in a factory to which she ventured in her Chanel and Schiaparelli gowns. She learned how to weld and practised in her London residence until she reached an admirable proficiency. Burrough Court was taken over by Allied airmen, who carelessly burned it down. Duke, by this time, was terminally ill from decades of heavy drinking. Enid nursed him at La Fiorentina but he died on 5 October 1940. Enid was devastated despite the eruptions in their marriage. In her autobiography, Thelma Furness hints that it was she who nursed her former husband.[19] She tried unsuccessfully to have Enid charged with murder. This was nonsense; had Enid wished to she could easily have divorced Duke – there was no need to resort to murder. The Australian press followed developments between the two Ladies Furness with some glee, clearly on side with the local girl done well.[20] Enid's career and fabulous lifestyle were avidly reported, though curiously in the Sydney press she was usually termed 'sister of Dr Grant Lindeman'.[21] Somerset Maugham's quip that Enid was 'Lady Killmore' was cruel, especially given her kindness to this crusty and difficult man. She hid Maugham's valuable art collection in her home and spent many hours playing bridge with him.[22]

Enid married Valentine Castlerosse, the Irish Earl of Kenmare, in February 1943. He was a direct descendant of Mary Tudor, Henry VIII's sister. They made a strange pair. Born in 1891, Castlerosse was enormously fat by the 1920s. He served in the Irish Guards without much distinction during World War I; he was a man hardly suited to the discomfort and athleticism required to endure war. He was, however, proud to have served and worshipped the men and officers of his old regiment with a strange devotion all his life. Though his mother was a Baring of the banking fortune, Valentine was virtually penniless. Well educated at Cambridge, he was a bon vivant and aesthete without the income to finance his lifestyle, and after the war he went to Paris to live as a dandy. He took the extraordinary measure of writing a gossip column in the *Sunday Express*, one of Lord Beaverbrook's popular newspapers. This was a remarkable move in 1926 for an aristocrat, albeit an impoverished one. He was successful in his new career: witty, erudite and far less catty than gossip columnist Godfrey Winn. Divorced from actor Doris Delavigne in 1938, he married Enid at Brompton Oratory Church in Kensington, London. This too was a strange move for a devout Catholic; divorce was hardly condoned by the Church. Enid and Valentine went to live in her house in Lees Place, just behind Park Lane and Marble Arch.

They moved to a suite in Claridge's Hotel when bombing intruded into their home. The Earl died suddenly of a heart attack on his estate in Killarney some six months after his marriage. Enid was then in London.[23] Over 7000 people attended his funeral in Ireland, from the poorest tenant farmer and worker to the grandest in the land. At this time Enid was fifty-one but she claimed she was pregnant with his child. Her daughter Pat maintains that Enid, in consultation with her mother-in-law, the Dowager Countess of Kenmare, decided that an abortion was necessary. This seems implausible as women of fifty-one can rarely conceive and the Dowager Countess was a devout Roman Catholic who would hardly countenance abortion, a mortal sin. Rather, it appears to have been a strange delaying tactic. Kenmare's bachelor brother Gerald inherited the title and the estate.[24]

By this time Enid's son Rory Cameron had joined the newly formed American Office of Strategic Services, the forerunner to the CIA, and was engaged in high-level operations. With his proficiency in languages and his contacts among the wealthy and well connected in both Europe and the United States, he could pretend to be an idle man of leisure while conducting espionage. He worked often in England with the distinguished historian Hugh Trevor-Roper. Pat was now a young woman, rather shy and reticent despite her beauty and kind temperament. From this time, although there were to be a few romances in the late '40s and '50s, Enid's sexual encounters with men were largely over. Pat believed Enid never really fell in love with any of her myriad lovers or husbands. Despite spending a good deal of her enormous energy pleasing them, she was largely indifferent – her children were her real emotional attachments.[25] Yves Vidal, the distinguished Parisian art collector who spent a lot of time at La Fiorentina, remarked that '[b]efore anything else Enid was a mother. Most of the things she did, marrying all those men, were for the children more than herself.'[26] Though perhaps not as close to Caryll, who spent his formative years at Eton, Enid adored Rory and Pat.

In 1948 the three of them went to Australia for an extended visit. Enid displayed quite surprising elements of her personality; she was eager to meet Daisy Bates, who resided with the Indigenous desert peoples along the Nullarbor Plain, and she was interested in wider questions of Indigenous culture and welfare.[27] Enid also spent time with the old Australian gentry families such as the Jamiesons in South Australia and was shocked that they had to chop their own wood. She was delighted to catch up with a Sydney grand seigneur, Ernest Watt, who had introduced her to Roderick Cameron in 1912. Watt was a wealthy grazier and shipowner, a man of deep culture and wit.[28] Enid undoubtedly kept in touch with her friends and family in Australia, despite infrequent visits home.

In her final widowhood Enid lived at first with Rory at La Fiorentina where they entertained lavishly. Increasingly, the guests were invited by Rory, with Enid a reluctant hostess, often late for dinner and silent. Rory was a cultured man of wide learning and talents. His various books show his extensive, sometimes arcane, knowledge. He particularly treasured his friendships with older beauties like Emerald Cunard, Nancy's mother, to whom he saw a direct link back to the eighteenth century before the prudery of the Victorian age.[29] Strangely, Enid was shocked to learn that Rory was gay; he was in his forties when he told her. For all her knowledge of men she had not perceived the most fundamental aspect of her son's character.

Theirs was a privileged world. Enid was invited to the twenty-fifth anniversary of Prince Louis of Monaco's reign. She hoped that his son, Rainier, would marry Pat, a rather fanciful wish since she was not a Roman Catholic. The family was invited to his wedding to Grace Kelly. Enid had contributed much to the economy of Monaco over the years, since she was an avid gambler in the deluxe casinos in Monte Carlo. When she went there with Furness, Enid on one occasion wore a beautiful Molyneux dress with lace flowers into which was sewn a real diamond. She wore the Furness tiara with pear-shaped diamonds, setting off her silver hair, which was always dressed by the famed

Alexandre. Apparently the tables were silent as she made her way through the rooms.[30]

By 1950 Enid began to spend a lot of time in her bedroom painting, surrounded by numerous animals. She had been introduced to Nassau in the Bahamas by her sister-in-law Anne Tiffany and now spent several months there every year. She also purchased a Kenyan property, Ol Orion, for Caryll for £10,000 in the '50s and spent several months there each year as well. Enid still dressed formally for dinner but the extravagances of her life in Kenya with Duke Furness in the 1930s were over. The days of Happy Valley had ended with the murder of the Earl of Erroll in 1941 – as Kenya moved towards independence such decadence was no longer tolerated. Rather she increased her interest in animals, adding chimpanzees and lions to her menagerie.[31]

By her sixties Enid was suffering from a heart condition that slowed down her usually energetic lifestyle. When Pat moved to South Africa, Enid accompanied her with all their wild animals. Her interest in horseracing went from being a spectator to breeding and training with the assistance of the Australian trainer Tommy Smith. Enid employed Beryl Markham, the famed pilot and hunter from Kenya, but this was not a happy match between two independent and strong women. With Enid a wealthy widow and Markham impoverished and with her glory days behind her, the differences in the women's lives at this point were in stark contrast. Yet Enid admired Beryl's achievements by her own efforts.

Enid Lindeman led a life that reads like a fairytale – although perhaps an X-rated one, so replete was it with notoriety, sex, gambling and drugs. Many envied the rise of the middle-class Sydney woman to the very heights of British nobility and American money, yet she suffered much sadness in the deaths of various husbands. She also battled with severe chronic pain from the riding accident in the '30s. Her reputation as a black widow who killed all her husbands for money is entirely undeserved. At the centre of this fabled and almost unbelievable life lay a deep devotion to her children and sympathy for those less fortunate than herself. Unlike many sacred monsters, she truly did have a heart of gold, even if its reach remained personal and close to home.

CHAPTER 14

Tilly Devine
(1900–1970)

From London streetwalker to wealthy Sydney madam and standover merchant.

Alongside her long-standing rival Kate Leigh, Tilly Devine occupies a unique position in Australian history. Both women led notorious gangs of pimps, prostitutes and drug sellers. Both were audacious and ran enduring criminal enterprises. American bank robber Bonnie Parker operated with her partner, Clyde Barrow, while Kate 'Ma' Barker was a support to, not a leader of, the Barker gang; other figures such as actor and chorus girl 'Texas' Guinan in New York ran a famous speakeasy; but none organised their own criminal networks, oversaw its operations with standover men and police protection, or took part in public violence. American gangsters were ruthless men – Al Capone, 'Bugs' Moran, Hymie Weiss and 'Big Jim' Colosimo – whose empires ran on ethnic and religious lines. Women in their world were 'molls', 'dames', prostitutes, wives, mothers and daughters, not cunning leaders and entrepreneurs. In this regard, Australia struck an early blow for gender equality, albeit in the underworld of terror and violence.

Tilly Devine and Kate Leigh were not well-educated madams like Caroline Hodgson ('Madame Brussels') in late

Victorian Melbourne, or crusading prostitutes like Shirley
Brifman in the 1960s or Kim Hollingsworth in the 1990s;
rather, they were tough, savage and merciless criminals.[1]
Tilly and Kate formed the basis of the composite character
Delie Stock in Ruth Park's novels set in the slums of Surry
Hills *The Harp in the South* (1948) and *Poor Man's Orange*
(1949).[2] Tilly's reputation has been sanitised in some
quarters in the forty years since her death. She featured
in an Australian War Memorial exhibition as an example
of a World War I bride, and a café in Canberra is named
in her honour. The authoritative Australian Women's
Register calls Tilly 'colourful', a euphemistic term for this
ferocious and formidable woman.[3] Peter Kenna's play *The
Slaughter of St Teresa's Day* (1973) was more in keeping
with her notoriety, and a 2009 exhibition at the Justice
and Police Museum in Sydney attempted to rectify the
surprising sentimentality about this vicious criminal.[4]
The inner eastern suburbs of Sydney, including notorious
'Razorhurst' (Darlinghurst) – as described by the salacious
newspaper *Truth* on 23 September 1928 – of the inter-
war years, with its armed gangs, executions of rivals, drug-
running and prostitution, has now been gentrified, except
for the former bohemian enclave of Kings Cross.

Matilda Mary Twiss was born at 57 Hollington Street,
Camberwell, near Southwark in South London. This area,
mentioned in the Domesday Book, had been a rural idyll,
but by 1900 it was an area infested with noxious factories,
the so-called 'stink industries' banned from across the
Thames, crime and slums, the misery relieved by many
music halls.[5] George Gissing's novel *The Nether World*
(1889) conveyed the 'evil smells' of the district. Charles

Booth, the reforming author of *Life and Labour of the People of London* (1903), depicted this area in his maps of London in 1898–99 as inhabited by 'savages' and criminals existing in the haze of permanent alcoholic overindulgence.[6] The Twisses lived in 'one of the vilest slums in the whole of London'.[7] Tilly's father, Edward Twiss, was a bricklayer, often out of work, and the family lived in poverty so relentless and destructive that it is now hard to imagine.

Like other children of the slums, Tilly left school barely literate at the age of twelve or so, and was sent to work in one of the local factories, where conditions had not changed since Charles Dickens wrote *David Copperfield* in 1850. She soon left this employment for a far more prosperous one as a streetwalker along the fashionable Strand, where the Savoy Hotel was built in 1889. Tilly was a pretty, solidly built young woman, with a foul temper and the street cunning and manners of Camberwell. Her earnings as a prostitute were substantial. At the age of sixteen, she met James Devine from the 4th Tunnelling Company of the Australian Imperial Forces. Like many servicemen on the lookout for bright company in boisterous Soho, he told Tilly he owned a kangaroo farm back home.[8]

Their relationship from the outset was filled with violence, combative anger and boozing. Tilly and Jim married in the Church of the Sacred Heart of Jesus in Camberwell in August 1917. Strangely for a young married couple, Jim insisted Tilly earn a good income as a prostitute and acted as her 'protector'. Even at the young age of fifteen, Tilly had accumulated a substantial police record for offences ranging from assault to theft and prostitution. In October 1918, she was arrested for soliciting on the

Strand and paid a fine of forty shillings rather than go to jail. By that time she had also had two children, a girl who died at birth and a son, Frederick, whom she left with her mother when she sailed to Australia in 1919. Jim had already embarked for home with his fellow Diggers.[9] The Devines lived in his rented flat in Glenmore Road, Paddington, now an exclusive enclave but then a seedy area of the inner eastern suburbs. Tilly soon returned to her old job as a streetwalker.

She was highly successful. With her beautiful, pale complexion, buxom figure, and 'deep, husky, fascinating voice', she charged ten shillings for a half-hour encounter, then a top price.[10] Tilly chose to work on her own with Jim, rather than enter a brothel where police protection money was paid and harassment of sex workers was far less. Jim expanded his activities as a drug dealer – at this time only cocaine and opium were listed as illegal, dangerous drugs in Australia – and as a chauffeur and a standover man. Tilly earned so much that soon she and Jim were able to drive around in a Cadillac; often she entertained clients in the back seat of this luxury vehicle, cutting the cost of a hotel room and allowing a quick get-away.[11] She also purchased a fruit shop in Bondi Junction for Jim so he could appear to have a legitimate source of income.

Between 1921 and 1925 Tilly was arrested on seventy-nine occasions for prostitution-related offences and she spent several terms in Long Bay Prison, where she was dubbed 'Pretty Tilly'.[12] Along with another woman, Elsie, Tilly was arrested in 1923 for attempted robbery of a client. (This may have been the commencement of her activities as a manager rather than a worker in the sex industry.) That year

Tilly and Jim were involved in a shooting incident at a party where guests' wallets and purses were stolen. This departure from the *modus operandi* indicates that the Devines were now part of an emerging criminal gang network.

Several big changes in legislation ensured the vibrancy of an underworld culture selling drugs and sly grog. In 1916, after years of agitation from Protestant reformist groups such as the Women's Christian Temperance League, the hours when it was legal to sell alcohol in a hotel were curtailed. The days of the 'six o'clock swill' – when patrons rushed to the bar before six o'clock closing to swill as much alcohol as possible – were ushered in with some rapidity.[13] Rather than curb consumption of alcohol, the legislation produced sly grog dealers like Kate Leigh.[14] Following the American and British lead, soon after World War I prohibitions were also enacted to ban the importation of opiates and cocaine.[15] Opium, since the 1660s in England, had been widely used in teething syrups for infants, as a sleeping draught, and as a remedy against diarrhoea. Many respectable citizens, especially women, who were prohibited from consuming alcohol in public venues, became addicted to laudanum from patent medicines. Cocaine had originally been used in the soft drink Coca-Cola as a pep-me-up. Throughout the 1920s and 1930s cocaine was a popular party drug used by wealthy socialites through to streetwalkers. Prohibition created a lucrative source of income for gangsters in Sydney by the early 1920s.

Tilly was part of this shift. Given that her days on the streets of London and Sydney had left her with numerous scars on her face, chest and arms – police photographs of her taken in 1925 reflect her fading beauty and disfigurements, all part of her occupation's hazards – she seized on a loophole in the New South Wales *Police Offences (Amendment) Act* (1908) that made it an offence for a male to operate a brothel or act as a pimp, and like Madame Brussels in Melbourne in the late nineteenth century, Tilly saw her opportunity to run her own business. She purchased a derelict house in Palmer Street, Surry Hills, and refurbished it, adding the distinctive red light outside. She proved to be a benevolent dictator, generous in her payment to workers but ruthless with those who concealed their earnings. By the end of the decade she owned eighteen brothels, largely in the Surry Hills, Darlinghurst, Woolloomooloo and Paddington areas. With the substantial earnings from these bordellos, she bought a house for herself and Jim in middle-class Maroubra. The Devines were hardly welcome neighbours, with their raucous parties, loud quarrelling and domestic violence.[16]

In May 1925 Tilly was convicted of slashing a man with a razor and sentenced to two years' imprisonment. She had walked into a barber's shop and slashed him as he sat in the chair, uttering the words, 'This is for Mary.' Presumably this was a revenge attack on a customer who had injured one of her girls. Tilly always commanded great respect and admiration, tinged with a modicum of fear, from her stable of prostitutes. Yet if one was abused or injured she took decisive action on their behalf.[17] She did her best to protect them from the incursions of her rival Kate Leigh's drug pushers, often with immense force and violence.[18] Unlike the United States, where gangsters flourished in the wake of Prohibition and used machine guns as their

Tilly Devine in Sydney in the
early 1930s. SMH News picture
by Staff; Fairfax Media 5085583.

weapon of choice, Sydney gangs favoured the razor. The
Pistol Licensing Act (1927) made it harder to possess pistols
and other weaponry. The razor was easy to conceal and
made no noise, a great advantage in killing or wounding
by stealth. It could also be used simply to maim or identify
a rival.

In 1927 the sensationalist tabloid newspaper *Truth* in a
series of exposés chronicled the rise and extent of the razor
gangs. The tabloid coined various terms – 'Razorhurst',
'Gunhurst', 'Bottlehurst', 'Dopehurst' – to characterise
their theatre of activities.[19] On 1 January 1928 it proclaimed
'Razor Terror' in Sydney's inner eastern suburbs. By this
it meant three gangs in particular: Kate Leigh's, Tilly
and Jim Devine's, and, until recently, Norman Bruhn's.
Bruhn was murdered in June 1927, shot in a laneway in
Darlinghurst.[20] The mainstream *Sydney Morning Herald*
of 28 June 1927 also employed the term 'razor gangs'.

American terms such as 'racketeers' and 'gangsters' had also entered common parlance, even before popular Hollywood films such as *The Public Enemy* (1931) appeared.

In 1929 with bipartisan support for the New South Wales *Vagrancy (Amendment) Act*, with its draconian 'consorting clause', the police formed a consorting squad to target madams like Tilly and Kate Leigh, as well as their standover men and pimps. Under this new Act, Leigh was sentenced to a prison term and then another for cocaine dealing.[21] Tilly enjoyed a modicum of police protection, as well as employing manoeuvres to undermine the letter of the law. For instance, in her brothels she rented out rooms to respectable tenants so she could maintain the charade of operating as a landlady.[22] But this did not stop her street fights and brawls. In early 1929 she was arrested for her involvement in a fight with Elsie Kaye and Vera Lucas in the courtyard off the Central Criminal Court, in which she nearly severed one of her opponent's fingers. All three women were fined.[23] Tilly also threatened a butcher who sold her rotten meat, poking his chest with a knife and saying, 'Give me my fucking money back, or I'll put this knife through your fucking chest.' The case did not end up in court.[24] Kate and Tilly, accompanied by members of their gangs, brawls often conducted brawls outside one or the other's brothels. Guns were used when forty mobsters fought in Kellett Street, Kings Cross, in mid 1929. Victims were slashed with razors, though none made a formal complaint to the police for fear of retribution.[25] On 5 September 1929 the police confiscated all the weaponry held at the Devines' home.

In 1930 the *Crimes Amendments Act* was passed, allowing for six-month jail terms and a flogging for unlawfully possessing a razor. Tilly's luck ran out when she was charged with consorting, riotous behaviour and assaulting a police officer in January 1930. She was defended by an ex-Labor mayor of Sydney, R. D. Meagher, who promised that Tilly would leave the country for two years if released.[26] Tilly told an amazed court that she had to return to London to tend her ailing mother and see her son whom she had abandoned in 1919. As she wrote in *Truth* of 29 June 1930, '[m]y dear mother is very sick at this time and I am nursing her back to health …' Most of the letter was a diatribe against Kate Leigh, who was then serving yet another lengthy jail term.

Though ordered to stay out of the country for two years, Tilly returned in January 1931 after only nine months' absence. At their home in Maroubra she found Jim entertaining a strange woman he claimed was the new housekeeper. In a rage, Tilly hit him. He retaliated with a threat to shoot her with a rifle. When they ran out onto the street screaming and cursing, neighbours called the police, who arrested Jim for attempted murder and possession of an unauthorised razor. At the trial, which began on 16 January 1931, Tilly refused to testify against him and the case was dismissed. What the incident signalled was the deep rift between Tilly and Jim. Two months later, Jim was attacked with a knife when he opened the door.[27] He later earned the nickname 'Scarface Big Jim Devine'. Jim's violence, alcoholism and erratic temper became a liability to Tilly's enterprises and her personal safety.

A few weeks later Tilly was in court charged with stealing £2 from George Hudson. In court she let fly with abusive language and insults to the magistrate, who sent her to jail for a month.[28] Stealing and risking further imprisonment when she was already a wealthy woman shows a lack of critical judgment on her part. Yet the Depression hit Tilly's cash flow, for her wealth resided in her property investment. With mass unemployment, evictions and unprecedented poverty in Sydney, the money for sly grog, visits to prostitutes and gambling was curtailed for many men. In early 1932 Tilly was sentenced to six months' imprisonment on charges of consorting. In an outburst in *Truth* of 7 February 1932, Tilly let fly with accusations of dope peddling against Kate Leigh. Yet a NSW Police Report in 1933 believed that the cocaine rings of the previous decades had largely been eliminated.[29]

Always alert to market forces, Tilly ran a three-tiered system of prostitution. At the top, her well-educated, more refined girls catered to politicians, businessmen and senior police officers out of decorous Darlinghurst terrace houses replete with bars, or their clients visited them in their own homes. Earning as much as £5 as well as tips and presents, these women could reap financial rewards unobtainable to professional women. Many were not full-time call girls but young women supplementing their meagre earnings from legitimate employment. On the next tier were housewives trying to feed their families, low-paid workers, single mothers and women from the bush. Tilly often provided food and accommodation, as well as banking a proportion of their earnings for them. At the bottom operated the 'boat squad' who catered to the dockside crowd. They were in the front line of the game, where savage beatings, robbery and even murder lurked.[30] Tilly also engaged some women as shoplifters in department stores Mark Foys and David Jones, and then sold the stolen goods.

By the mid 1930s Tilly and Kate Leigh realised that their public campaigns against each other, played out in the pages of *Truth*, were detrimental to both of them. They decided on a truce, each carving out her own specialty in criminality without interference or the chance of the police being informed. At the same time, their incomes were undermined by the way the entertainment industry was changing. Nightclubs in Sydney after 1936 were permitted to sell alcohol after 6pm, thereby ruining the fortunes of sly grog dealers. At the outbreak of war in September 1939 many customers enlisted in the armed services, causing even more financial strain on Kate and Tilly.

Yet it was war that saved their criminal enterprises. With the arrival of American servicemen from early 1942, suddenly there was a surfeit of customers for sex, gambling, drinking and drugs. Kate took care of the drinking and drugs, leaving Tilly to the sexual services arena. They were by no means alone in these activities, and sharp new operators entered the rich field. Tilly was still not immune from prosecution: in June 1943 she was charged with owning a 'disorderly house'.[31] She was also arrested for maliciously wounding one of her prostitutes, Ellen Grimson, who was an alcoholic cocaine addict. Appearing before Mr Justice Street, Tilly explained that Grimson was often drunk and forgot to turn out lights. Tilly took a knife to her face after repeated warnings about the blackout and saving electricity. She got six months' imprisonment for this offence.

Tilly's personal life had also reached a turning point. In March 1943 she filed for divorce from Big Jim, tired of his beatings and abuse, his promiscuity with young, more attractive, women, and his alcoholism.[32] They had not lived together since 1940, after Jim was sentenced to yet another jail term for stealing. He continued to harass her for money, often using violence to obtain it. Tilly had naively thrown a party for their twenty-fifth wedding anniversary in August 1942 despite their separation. Jim disgraced her by turning up hours late, drunk and ready to pick a fight, then he paraded his latest girlfriend in front of Tilly and all her guests. Jim finished off the party by fracturing Tilly's skull. She was admitted to St Vincent's Hospital and required weeks of recuperation.[33]

Despite her personal and professional challenges, in some ways the war years gave Tilly a new lease of life. She hosted parties for servicemen, not riotous sexual and drinking binges, but simply good old-fashioned fun. A keen supporter of the British and Australian war effort, she donated thousands of pounds to veterans' welfare associations. She also gave generously to children in hospital.[34] In some ways, Tilly saw herself as a benevolent matriarch, dispensing largesse and kindness through her Surry Hills domain. In her own mind, her violence and revenge on those who crossed her was always justified.

After her release from prison, Tilly met Eric Parsons, a seaman and barman a few years younger than herself. They started an affair in 1944 and Parsons moved in with Tilly fairly quickly. The relationship was tempestuous, to say the least. In February 1945 Tilly let fly with her temper and shot Parsons after he had been drinking heavily. The police were called to the house after neighbours heard a row and gunshot. Parsons denied he had been injured. At St Vincent's

Hospital he said he had no idea who had shot him. After some intense interrogation he admitted that indeed Tilly had pulled the trigger over a fight about Mrs Mary Parsons, or, as Tilly put it, 'over a bit of a yike over his missus'. Tilly was arrested and charged with attempted murder. Parsons refused to testify and she was released.[35] They married on 19 May 1945. Tilly wore all her diamond rings, a powder-blue outfit and blue ribbons in her blonded hair, as well as far too much make-up. His nephew George later recalled that on his marriage, Eric ceased to be an independent man but was now a Flash Harry.[36]

In 1948 Tilly sailed first class to England to visit her ailing father. On her arrival in Southampton, she called a press conference to keep up her reputation back in Sydney. Her use of a chauffeured Daimler as transport was in stark contrast to the slum her father still lived in. On her return, Tilly put on an elaborate party for her fiftieth birthday. *Smith's Weekly* of 23 September 1950 covered the 'Lobster Spread', at which Tilly gave renditions of her favourite music hall numbers from her youth. By this time she was nicknamed 'Diamond' Tilly Devine, the 'tough peroxide blond from Camberwell Green ... [who] is probably one of Sydney's wealthiest citizens ...'[37] Tilly was annoyed that the *People* article elicited many requests for money from her old home stamping ground, Camberwell.

Tilly went to the Melbourne Cup in 1951, a rather risky move, as she had jumped bail in Melbourne in 1934. This time she was arrested for consorting at Flemington Racecourse. She wore a fur coat despite the heat and diamonds on every finger, so she was hardly inconspicuous. She told the magistrate she had cancer. Sentenced to twelve months' imprisonment, she served only five weeks.[38] Not one to harbour grudges, Tilly went again in style the following year to enjoy the Melbourne Cup. In 1953 she decided to return to London to witness Queen Elizabeth's coronation. Tilly and Eric watched from a vantage point on their allocated seats on Pall Mall, near where Tilly had walked the streets in 1915 and 1916.[39]

This was perhaps Tilly's last hurrah. Eric had to have an eye removed in London, and on her return the Australian Taxation Office besieged her. In 1955 she owed £20,000 in back taxes, which required a serious sale of her property assets to cover the huge amount.[40] Eric died of cancer in November 1957, leaving Tilly devastated and alone. By 1959 she owned only one brothel, in Palmer Street. Like Al Capone, she may have colluded with corrupt police, but the tax investigators were relentless and eager to recover lost taxes. As the NSW Royal Commission into Crime revealed in 1961, the nature of organised crime was rapidly changing, with longer opening hours in hotels and legal off-course betting.[41]

In January 1964 Kate Leigh died, after years spent as a recluse in her little flat in Devonshire Street, Surry Hills. Tilly attended Kate's funeral at St Peter's Catholic Church, Surry Hills. Many old acquaintances, police and former customers came to pay their respects to someone they had seemingly forgotten in her twilight years.

From this time Tilly was increasingly thin and frail, suffering chronic bronchitis.[42] Her rivals and associates had all died, leaving her as a relic from another age, out of step in the new world. She closed her last brothel in 1968 after a series of threats from new crime entrepreneurs such as Joe Borg. A firebomb was thrown into the brothel and her house was ransacked. Even for Tilly, who would have fought back with more violence in her heyday, this was terrifying. Once one of Sydney's wealthiest women, who had earned her money by her own hand and not through inheritance or marriage, Tilly lived in poverty on the old age pension. In 1969 she went to the Sacred Heart Hospice in Darlinghurst when she was diagnosed with stomach cancer. One nun, Sister Mary St Joseph, who grew attached to Tilly, arranged for visits and outings on her behalf.[43] She died in Concord Repatriation Hospital on 24 November 1970, and was cremated after a Catholic requiem mass to a tiny congregation.

Unlike the tributes to Kate Leigh, those to Tilly were harsh and unforgiving. One journalist went so far as to say she was 'a vicious, grasping, high-priestess of savagery, venery, obscenity and whoredom'.[44] No doubt this was all true. But Tilly Devine, one of Australia's most notorious gangsters and madams, had simply outlived her time of glory.

CHAPTER 15

Sunday Reed
(1905–1981)

Born into the Melbourne Baillieu family, Sunday snared
Sidney Nolan and helped create Australia's best art.

Sunday Reed was a renowned patron of the arts in Australia. Along with her husband, John Reed, she supported artists such as Sidney Nolan – with whom she conducted a passionate affair for many years – Joy Hester, Albert Tucker, John Perceval and Charles Blackman. Born into the wealthy Baillieu family, Sunday was a rebel, feisty and determined to make her mark in a male-dominated world. Her notorious love affairs, her commitment to art with Australian themes and her challenges to conventional morality mark her as a woman of flair, intelligence and determination.

The Baillieu family arrived in Victoria in 1853, when James Baillieu jumped ship by swimming ashore to Queenscliff. His antecedents were a fascinating lot. Etienne Baillieux fled to England from Liège early in the French Revolution. The family were lacemakers and embroiderers, creative endeavours of which Sunday was remarkably proud. Etienne's son, Lambert Baillieu was a dancing master and musician. Welsh-born James was the third of Lambert's fifteen children. Once in the colonies, James found employment as a boatman in the health service in Queenscliff. In 1858 he married Emma Pow from Somerset. Not content with his lowly job, in 1881 James built a hotel, where the Victorian governor holidayed. His second son, William Baillieu, was the financial genius behind the family's spectacular rise to wealth. The family company, Mutual Trust, employed six of the Baillieu brothers, with the daughters marrying close associates of William.[1] Family loyalty was placed at a premium, a value instilled in Sunday as a child.

William built a vast commercial empire based upon real estate. When he narrowly avoided bankruptcy by some dazzling financial manoeuvres in the depression of the early 1890s, his reputation was impugned. Undeterred, he went into mining in Maryborough, Victoria, armed with British capital. Within a decade, he and some of his brothers were astoundingly wealthy. Sunday's father, Arthur Sidney Baillieu (1872–1943) built his own fortune upon real estate. Her mother, Ethel Ham, was also Australian-born. Arriving in Victoria in 1849, Ethel's father, David Ham, made money as a miner at Ballarat, then as a stockbroker with business interests in Queenscliff.[2] His reputation was secured when he was appointed to the Victorian Legislative Council in 1880. Ethel was a gifted painter whose professional aspirations were severely limited by marriage. Like her daughter later, she was a prominent patron of the arts, supporting Frederick McCubbin and Arthur Streeton.

When Sunday – Lelda Sunday Baillieu – was born in October 1905, the family had not yet overcome the odium caused by their business dealings in the previous decade. They were rich, but newly rich, unlike respected old families such as the Hentys, the à Becketts, or the Cunninghams.[3] There was a taint of the sly, ruthless and recently-made-good hanging over them. The Baillieu men were simply not yet gentlemen. This polite appellation awaited William's elevation to the House of Lords in 1936. Sunday always felt the intense masculine camaraderie of her family. She had two elder brothers, Jack (known as King) and Darren, and a younger brother, Everard. Unlike many wealthy parents, Ethel and Arthur were close to their children, with Sunday particularly close to her father, a far more sensitive and imaginative man than his rambunctious brothers.[4]

Sunday's early life was secure and privileged. When she was five, her parents moved to Balholmen in Toorak, then a small exclusive enclave.[5] Grand houses were surrounded by hectares of beautiful lawns and gardens, allowing a high degree of privacy for residents. The Baillieu boys were sent to Geelong Grammar School, leaving Sunday in the care of governesses. She was not destined for a career, so she learned domestic skills at home. Her one outlet was gardening. At the age of fifteen she attended St Catherine's School in Toorak.[6] At this time, the school operated as a finishing school rather than an academically orientated institution such as Presbyterian Ladies College, where Nettie Palmer, Ethel Florence (Henry Handel) Richardson, Nellie Melba and Dame Jean McNamara were educated. At school, Sunday felt out of place and was viewed as a mere parvenue with disreputability still hanging over the family's reputation. Her maid, Clare Pitblado, was her best friend, an indication of her isolation and lack of friends.[7]

Holidays as a teenager were spent at the family home, Merthon, at Sorrento, now immortalised in

Arthur Streeton's paintings *Nocturne* (c. 1920) and *Point King, Sorrento* (1920).[8] As it was for many wealthy Melbournians, the holiday period was extended and leisurely, commencing in November and terminating around Easter. Entertainment was kept within the family. There Sunday felt at ease and relaxed.

Like Maie Casey, Sunday was expected to make her debut at a court presentation. The Baillieus had many business and social connections in London, so her path to the royal event was smooth. By 1924 the dress expectations for ladies had slightly relaxed, though they were still elaborate and expensive, requiring ostrich plumes and a white evening dress often with a four-metre train. Sunday wore a beautiful shift with a string of pearls.[9] Attractive, slim and athletic from her years of swimming, she looked magnificent. After this rite of passage, Sunday was considered a young woman rather than a girl, and allowed far more freedom. What she did with this new freedom was to mark the rest of her life.

Sunday went to Paris where she gained a sophisticated elegance in her dress. Chic modern clothes looked perfect on her. She favoured white, cream and pale blue in tailored clothes, a style she maintained all her life. She did not rush into cropping her hair, though by the time she returned home the following year she had an Eton crop, a short hemline and smoked cigarettes. She also learned to drive early. This was not quite what the Baillieu family anticipated from Sunday's expensive presentation. Then her life changed when she met handsome and debonair Leonard Quinn in Sydney, sometime in 1925. Affecting the persona of a rich young American, Quinn was a petty thief accustomed to living on his wits. He was entirely unsuitable for Sunday as he represented everything her family would hate – a Boston Roman Catholic and a charlatan. Moreover, her mother Ethel, had become a Christian Scientist, an American religion popularised by Nancy Astor in England.[10] When her beloved brother King died suddenly of typhus in 1926, Sunday was besieged by grief, an emotion that Leonard was quick to manipulate.[11]

Sunday's engagement was announced just before her twenty-first birthday. The wedding took place at St Mary's Star of the Sea Catholic Church in Sorrento, unlike the usual society events for young ladies from Toorak. Her parents hosted a modest reception at Merthon, where Leonard disgraced his bride by becoming drunk very quickly.[12] Sunday was assured of a comfortable allowance from her father, which permitted her and Leonard to travel to Europe and live without worrying about work. They headed for Paris after the wedding, where Sunday moved in an outer ring of the Hemingway circles. Her French lessons paid off and she could behave like an accomplished participant rather than a wealthy cultural tourist. As with another fashionable couple, Zelda and F. Scott Fitzgerald, Sunday and Leonard also moved to the Côte d'Azur where Sunday luxuriated in the beach life. Coco Chanel had made a healthy tan fashionable so this choice was even more palatable, and Sunday was particularly taken by the absence of sharks.[13]

The Quinns moved to England for the years of 1928 and 1929 and settled in the picturesque village of Broadway in the Cotswolds. They moved back to Paris as the marriage disintegrated. Sunday was devastated to learn that she had contracted gonorrhoea from Leonard and required an immediate hysterectomy. He simply abandoned her to her grief of dashed dreams and lost children. At the young age of twenty-five, Sunday was thrown into the bewildering symptoms of a sudden menopause, which was not at that time treated with hormone therapy. Her parents were neither hostile nor reproving, and she spent her long recuperation with them in Melbourne before returning to Paris. When Sunday was painted by Agnes Goodsir, an Australian artist long resident in Paris, she had lost her freshness and soft features.[14] Life in Paris alone held no appeal for Sunday, and she returned home in 1931.

On her return, Sunday was fortunate to met John Reed, a sensible, good-looking young solicitor, born into wealth and privilege in northern Tasmania. He and his sister, Cynthia Reed, hated the strict, Non-conformist Church Wesleyan piety that dominated their upbringing.[15] Reed was a quiet, reflective man who found solace in nature. Educated at Cheltenham College in England, Geelong Grammar, and Gonville and Caius College, Cambridge, John was a far more appropriate match for Sunday. He was introduced to modern art by artist and journalist Clarice Zander, the owner of the New Gallery in Melbourne.[16] Clarice's acquisition of the exhibition of British Contemporary Art in 1933 was a masterly coup. John shared an apartment with engineer Fred Ward, an influential Modernist furniture designer whose collection is now housed in the Powerhouse Museum in Sydney.

Sunday and John met at a tennis party in Toorak in 1931 and he was immediately smitten by her vitality and beauty. She was also attracted to the rather stiff and formal solicitor, whose background matched her own. Even at the outset of their affair, Sunday's sexual appetites vastly ran ahead of John's, though it was all well managed when they later married. Her libido simply went elsewhere. During their engagement John came to know her moody self-absorption, her tendency to retreat to the sickbed at any sign of stress and her myriad minor physical ailments, yet he was not deterred. Rather like Leonard Woolf's care for Virginia, John was the devoted attendant to a highly strung, demanding and selfish woman of talent.[17] Like those famous denizens of Bloomsbury, Sunday and John entered into a virtual *mariage blanc.*

Sunday's parents were delighted with this appropriate choice of partner while the Reeds were notably less enthusiastic. A divorcee was perfectly fine in a sophisticated Lubitsch comedy in Hollywood, but it was certainly out of the question in Australia in the 1930s. Sunday was, after all, a woman who was sterile because of an unmentionable disease. And she was not even divorced, but technically still a married woman. Most likely Arthur Baillieu paid Quinn off in order to release his daughter, who was formally divorced in June 1931. Sunday and John were married in St Paul's Anglican Cathedral on 13 January 1932 in a small side chapel, not before the central altar. This was the Church's concession, in view of the status of a divorcee remarrying with a former husband still alive. But the marriage did not appear in the cathedral's records, given the Anglican strictures on divorce. Sunday signed her certificate 'Sunday Baillieu Quinn' then crossed out 'Quinn'.[18] The new couple honeymooned overseas.

On their return to Melbourne later in the year, Sunday began her commitment to modern art in earnest. She purchased a painting by Adrian Lawlor, an emerging artist and writer, with articles in the progressive literary journals *Vision* and *New Triad*.[19] Associating with artists George Bell and William Frater, she mixed in the same art circles as Maie Casey. Sunday and John also met another of Casey's colleagues, Sam Atyeo, who had a far more profound influence upon their tastes and sensibilities. Born into a working-class family in Melbourne, Sam exhibited at Fred Ward's gallery and at Cynthia Reed's shop at 367 Little Collins Street in June 1933. In the 1940s he became a diplomat.[20] He and Sunday conducted a passionate public affair with John's approval in 1933. (Thirty years later, in 1963, John curated an exhibition of Atyeo's work for George's Gallery.) What Atyeo's partner, Moya Dyring, felt or thought of the affair at the time was irrelevant to Sunday, blown away by her own needs and desires. Dyring, nevertheless, later collaborated on projects at Heide, John and Sunday's future home, which they opened to a wide circle of artists.[21] Perhaps in response to their partners' affair, John and Moya engaged in a tepid liaison. Sam also had an affair with Sunday's sister-in-law, Cynthia; all in all, a highly incestuous little group. Moya later painted both Sam and Cynthia, the latter in a most unflattering light. These claustrophobic couplings were to become a core feature of Sunday's life.

Sunday was beset with grief when her mother, Ethel, died after a long illness in late 1932. The overwhelming masculine ruggedness of her family was even more apparent after her mother's death. That year Sunday enrolled in the George Bell–Arnold Shore School in Bourke Street.[22] The only Modernist school in Melbourne, it taught potential artists as well as dabblers and Toorak matrons.[23] Students such as Sunday and Maie Casey wanted to become serious artists, but the demands of their social lives and class, plus their limited ambition, relegated them to the ranks of the gifted amateur. Sunday had the foresight to realise she would never become a professional artist and destroyed most of her work, gauged less than perfect and original by her own exacting standards.

While their personal lives were caught up with Sam, Cynthia and Moya, John and Sunday also became serious art collectors, commencing with Sam's works.[24] They were facilitators, not patrons, they frequently protested; friends of artists, not simply their financial supporters.[25] Yet their patrician upbringing and their financial abundance, along with their deep need to be involved in creativity, rendered them archetypal patrons, albeit in a modern Australian setting. For Sunday, her childlessness and her failure as an artist required a direct imaginative expression. In 1935 the couple moved to their new home, Heide, in Heidelberg. Perhaps no location represents more communal creativity and transformation than Heidelberg, for it was here in the later 1880s that Tom Roberts, Frederick McCubbin and Arthur Streeton captured the beauty of the Australian environment.

The house was in keeping with its artistic and cultural heritage. Balholmen provided a source of substantial furniture, at odds with the Modernist paintings Sunday collected. She also included her mother's old Streeton and McCubbin paintings. The house was surrounded by a decaying garden, but Sunday oversaw its restoration, along with the help of friends, as a creative outlet. Guests recalled they were expected to pitch in with chores in the garden, whether they liked it or not. This was despite the employment of domestic and garden staff to do the basic work of maintaining the property in the initial stages.[26] Strict dietary rules were rigorously enforced upon guests, long before the raw food regime was popularised.

That year a major change occurred in Sunday's life. John, a partner in the prestigious law firm of Blake and Riggall, was asked to resign after an alleged affair with his secretary. He then made the dubious move of entering the Baillieus' commercial networks, which meant a financial dependency upon Sunday and her family. John did not inherit from his own family until 1956. By the mid 1930s the Baillieu empire, under the banner of the Collins Group, invested heavily in the Tasmanian pulp wood industry, real estate and mining ventures associated with BHP and formerly Mount Morgan. Sunday's Uncle William had been dubbed 'Australia's Money King' and was successful in outbidding the Australian government agent's tender for a major loan in London. William's son Clive maintained his father's business acumen, later becoming a chairman of Rio Tinto.[27]

The impact of John's new circumstances and her tempestuous affair with Sam began to take their toll on Sunday's health. Along with her old servant, Clare, she went to the United States in 1937 to recuperate and gain some distance from her problems. By 1938 her spirits and energy had revived and, back in Australia, she suddenly had a new focus for her life. Sunday met young Sidney Nolan through John initially, when Nolan brazenly asked for £50 to finance his hoped-for overseas training.[28] John later recalled, 'Nolan ... was a kind of wild-cat spirit, unformed, uncertain of his destiny, but arrogantly confident that the fates were on his side …'[29] Working for Fayfield Hats as a signwriter, Nolan spent a lot of his day studying Modernism from books. A series of casual jobs left him despondent. He pondered whether he should become an artist or a writer. It was this connection to literature that sealed his initial bond with Sunday. He entered the world of Heide where he was surrounded by money, a high European aesthetic and the Modernism of artists like Atyeo. For Sunday, this was her chance to nurture a great talent to her own designs, at least initially.

On the spur of the moment Nolan married Elizabeth Patterson, a student at the Gallery School. Rather than existing solely in the world of art and creativity, Nolan also ran a little pie shop in Lonsdale Street, before landing a commission with the de Basil Ballet Company to design sets for their productions in Sydney. When compared to the attractions of Heide, the marriage fell apart despite the birth of a daughter, Amelda, in 1940. Yet at this artistic refuge, the management of a ménage à trois had difficult logistics to surmount, not that this bothered Sunday in the slightest; she had located her potential genius and he was her life work for the moment. Conscripted into the army in April 1942, Nolan reluctantly left the security of his new home. For his art, the dry Wimmera landscape, where he was stationed, ignited his imagination and led him to produce his first paintings in his own style. The letters Nolan wrote to Sunday in this period are cool and intellectual, concerned with Kierkegaard, Dylan Thomas, William Blake and André Gide. Reading them gives no indication they were lovers or so much as intimate friends.[30] Nolan always detested the accusation he was a 'kept man'.[31] Back at Heide, Sunday prepared his canvases, mixed paints and purchased books.[32] She would have been well advised to note the dispassionate tone of his correspondence. The consequences of all this assistance were to explode later over the ownership of the finished works after he left for London in 1951.[33]

Sunday was not solely preoccupied with Nolan, however. The artist Joy Hester was increasingly drawn into the Heide set, which also included Arthur Boyd, Albert Tucker and John Perceval.[34] Joy found inspiration within this domain, drawing *Gethi in a Tree*. The image referred to Sunday's doll, Gethsemane, which she treated as a substitute child. There is an added poignancy, as later Sunday adopted Joy's baby son, Sweeney, when Joy was struck down with Hodgkin's disease. As the men went to war, Sunday and Joy consolidated their friendship through their mutual interests in art and literature.

When Arthur Baillieu died in 1943, Sunday inherited a considerable estate, though not the family house, Merthon.[35] That year, John left work as a solicitor at the Baillieu company. In his new liberation he founded the avant-garde magazine *Angry Penguins*, with poet and critic Max Harris, as well as the publishing company Reed and Harris. The capital, however, came from Sunday. The Ern Malley hoax in 1944, in which poets James McAuley and Harold Stewart created the fictitious Ern Malley and his impressionistic poems to prick the Modernist pretensions of the Angry Penguins movement, was a *succès de scandale* and largely finished the magazine.[36] For Sunday this was a disappointing outcome for her literary hopes. She had little time to fret over it, however, for Nolan was commencing his series of Ned Kelly paintings. *Ned Kelly*, *The Encounter* and *The Chase* were all painted in 1946. In the process of representing the Kelly legend, Nolan transformed post-war Australian painting. Nolan and Sunday fed each other's creativity. Later, he wrote to John Reed, 'I do not ever feel that the Kellys belong to anyone other than Sun.'[37] Nolan left for Brisbane when he completed the series in 1947. Outwardly, Sunday was dignified, as letters from Joy Hester indicate; her inner turmoil, grief and anger were kept largely at Heide.[38] Joy innocently reported that she visited Cynthia at her home in Wahroonga, Sydney, in January 1948, just before Cynthia's affair with Nolan, and later socialised with the new couple.[39]

Sunday was apprehensive about the longevity of her affair and artistic collaboration with Nolan, yet her life took on a new challenge when she adopted Sweeney, the son of Joy Hester and Albert Tucker. Joy declared that she saw herself primarily as a painter and was glad to have a wealthy couple take over the care of her young son. When Joy moved to Sydney to live with artist Gray Smith, she welcomed the opportunity to go alone.[40] For Sunday, Sweeney was the child she had been unable to conceive and nurture. Her longing for Nolan had not ceased however, and she fretted and became more depressed over a relationship she correctly feared was over. What she did not realise was that Nolan had begun living with her sister-in-law Cynthia in Sydney. Cynthia had largely alienated her entire family with the recent publication of a toxic portrayal of them in *Daddy Sowed a Wind!* (1947). When she and Nolan married in March 1948, they decided to see the Reeds straight after. This was hardly a conciliatory gesture and Sunday's sense of double betrayal was overwhelming and enduring. Later in 1971, Nolan's savage collection of poems *Paradise Garden* tore through his relationship with Sunday and John in the 1940s.[41]

The Reeds sought solace in travel, venturing to Paris, Belgium, England and Italy. They took some of the Ned Kelly series with them, their faith in Nolan's genius remaining steadfast. But Sunday no longer felt the same ease with sophisticated Parisian life as she had in the 1930s, and even as they stayed on, they felt alien and provincial. Sweeney was sent to a family in Tours, making his life even more chaotic and insecure. During this childless time, Sunday and John negotiated for a short exhibition of Nolan's work to be shown at the Maison de l'UNESCO.

When the Reeds returned to Melbourne in 1949, the focuses of their cultural aspirations – Nolan, Arthur Boyd and John Perceval – had moved away. Brisbane-born bookseller and librarian Barrett Reid guided the Reeds in their new period of patronage. Through him they met and nurtured Charles and Barbara Blackman, Robert Dickerson, Nadine Amadio, George and Mirka Mora, as well as Judith Wright.[42] John kept in touch with Albert Tucker, informing him about this new pool of talented artists.[43]

Like Nolan and Hester before them, this group was as passionate about literature as art. Life at Heide took on a new dimension as Sunday decided to home-school Sweeney, perhaps not a good idea for a child already so indulged and neglected at various times. At the age of nine, after years of frustration on both sides, he was sent to Geelong Grammar as a boarder, a tremendous change for a child who had not been encouraged to learn self-discipline.[44] The arrival of Peregrine and Fern, the children of his mother and Gray Smith, as half-siblings hardly assisted his sense of security.

In 1953 John re-established the Contemporary Arts Society (CAS).[45] By 1956 it was the premier gallery showing contemporary Australian art in Melbourne. This was a momentous year for John as he finally inherited his estate, the family sheep farm at Deloraine and was now free of his financial dependency upon Sunday. He could afford to indulge his passions with his own money. Often profligate with funds, the newly renamed Gallery of Contemporary Art (GCA) was a financial hole into which he poured his money.[46] Through the influence of artists Ian and Dawn Sime, Sunday and John were introduced to American Abstract art. This movement was hardly to their taste and it remained a fleeting interest. Far more important to Sunday was the restoration of the house and the construction of her Heart Garden.

Within a year the GCA was losing money at a speedy rate. Because of a certain inflexibility the Reeds would find themselves surpassed in the fickle, bitchy world of art. In the very week the GCA was launched, John Perceval chose to open an exhibition at the Australian Galleries in Collingwood. Cocooned by decades at Heide, neither Sunday nor John were accustomed to the more aggressive world of the open art market and its critics.[47] When the gallery was reopened as the Museum of Modern Art of Australia (MoMAA) in June 1958, Sunday relocated much of her collection at Heide to this new enterprise. Waging war against the Melbourne *Herald*'s art critic Allan McCulloch was hardly a smart move. But McCulloch's assessment that the Reeds were far too isolated and introverted in their patronage and tastes had a strong ring of truth.[48] They should have called it the Museum of Contemporary Melbourne Art, such was their parochialism.

The vexed question of the Nolan paintings remained. In 1957 the Whitechapel Gallery in London organised a Nolan retrospective. The paintings at Heide were not included, despite Nolan's entreaties. Sunday '… became hysterical with grief' at the mere thought of relinquishing them.[49] To do so meant abandoning her hopes for reconciliation with him. Seven years later, Fred Williams was asked to conserve the paintings, many of which had been damaged by Sunday's cats' urine. Subsequently, the paintings went into a bank vault. Pamela Warrender, the chairman of the MoMAA, undertook the emotionally fraught role of accompanying the paintings to a 1964 exhibition in London, where she had to deal with Nolan and his anger over the paintings kept at Heide. John accused Nolan of behaving like 'an executioner' towards both him and Sunday, whom he believed had provided enduring love and support.[50]

While Sunday continued to feel a searing, relentless attack on her very being regarding Nolan, she was able to support other emerging artists such as Charles Blackman, purchasing his *Golden Alice* from the Alice in Wonderland series. When Nadine Amadio went to live at Heide, her first impression of the house was the beauty of this painting.[51] The Reeds' coterie, however, was rapidly diminishing. They did not purchase new works by Arthur Boyd or John Perceval, as they had moved out of the Heide

circle. In 1959 Russian painter Danila Vassilieff died at
Heide, while the following year in Prahran, Joy Hester
finally succumbed to Hodgkin's lymphoma. Another
major change occurred when a second Heide was built.
Everything in the original house, including the piano,
books and furnishings, was abandoned, left to fester along
with Sunday's increasing bitterness over her lost cultural
domains. Yet it also produced renewal. Instead of Victorian
comfort, Sunday now moved to cool clean 1960s design
– a beautiful building designed for displaying art brought
much pleasure back into her life.

In May 1965 John's life changed radically once more
when he resigned from MoMAA.[52] The museum closed
that year after tottering financially for a decade. The
construction of the new Heide was more than enough to
fill John's time, since the process went on for several years.
Yet, in the end, Sunday's vision for her new enterprise,
Heide II, was rewarded. In this fresh environment she
adopted new tastes, including brightly coloured plastic
bowls from Finland. Even in her sixties she felt all the
enthusiasm of a teenager for Beatlemania.[53] It is hard to
imagine the Toorak patrician attending a Little Richard
concert, yet she absorbed all the latest popular music
and art with gusto. Her next project was a bookstore in
Exhibition Street, Melbourne. Barrett Reid warned her
of the financial pitfalls of this enterprise but, never one to
listen, Sunday learned the hard way.

An even harder lesson came with the release of Nolan's
collection of poems, paintings and drawings *Paradise
Garden* in 1971. In it Nolan portrayed himself as a
Candide seduced by a 'subtle tart'. Sunday was mocked

and humiliated for her infertility and her age, while John was a knowing, weak cuckold. The poems made painful reading. Sunday told her friend Jean Langley that she was 'quite blind with sadness. I would die and be lost forever if I tried to repress these thoughts ...'[54] She certainly did not deserve this vicious public treatment, which detracted from Nolan's own reputation. Sunday also had to endure more sadness, as Sweeney grew up an irresponsible and wild young man, trying this and that before failing and trying something else, squandering his parents' money.

In 1972 Sunday decided she would donate her Nolan paintings to the nation.[55] In 1977 she finally relinquished the Nolan oeuvre she possessed to the National Gallery of Australia. Cynthia Nolan had committed suicide in November 1976, perhaps making the decision easier. Yet with this long-standing rival gone, Sunday was distressed to learn that in January 1978 Nolan married her friend Mary Boyd Perceval, whom she had supported when she left the alcoholic John Perceval.[56] When Mary and Sidney Nolan visited Melbourne later that year, Mary went to Heide II and her husband sat in the car. A phone call to Nolan soon after was so distressing that Sunday burned his entire correspondence going back into the late 1930s. Yet the demon of her obsession for forty years did not die.[57] Further horror was to come when John was diagnosed with cancer and in March 1979 Sweeney committed suicide. He left no farewell note to his parents. John wrote months later '... our world has fallen apart ... It is hard at our age to learn to live without him.'[58]

When the Victorian government purchased Heide II to use as an art gallery, Sunday and John moved back to the original Heide, a painful relocation full of traumatic memories. Sunday did not attend the opening of the gallery. John's health deteriorated rapidly.[59] He died on 5 December 1981. For Sunday, the loss of her life companion and champion was too overwhelming to endure. She committed suicide ten days later. Her ashes were scattered among the trees of Heide.

CHAPTER 16

Rosaleen Norton
(1917–1979)

The Kings Cross resident witch and satanic artist.

Rosaleen Norton holds a unique place in Australian history. An artist who depicted hermaphrodites, women coupling with panthers at a witches' sabbath, penises evolving into terrestrial serpents and seductive Lucifers, she was dubbed the nation's most notorious and well-known witch. The pagan themes of her art went far beyond the sexually alluring depictions produced by Norman Lindsay; they entered into the darkest places of the psyche, where disorder, alien lust and supernatural forces rule. In the repressed years of the 1950s, her appearance alone marked her as a woman dancing to the beat of a different drum from conventional suburban or even bohemian ones. With jet-black hair and naturally pointed ears, Rosaleen wore heavy red lipstick and wildly coloured clothes, an intricately carved cigarette holder her perpetual prop. She also possessed a 'third breast', a thin strand of flesh that hung from armpit to waist, the sign of the demon and witch in medieval cosmology.[1] With her arched eyebrows and steely, unflinching gaze she was the definition of a woman totally at odds with the society around her. She lived for her art, rejecting any form of economic security, in abject poverty in Kings Cross.

Little in her childhood predicted Rosaleen's destiny. Born in the stern and rigid Scottish-settled city of Dunedin, New Zealand, her early environment was highly repressive. Her later art explored the murky moral imperatives very distant from the certainties of the Calvinism practised in New Zealand's southern city. Her father, English-born Albert Norton, was a master mariner employed by the New Zealand Steam Company. His family contained gifted creative people – the distinguished composer Ralph Vaughan Williams was a cousin. Albert was said to possess his cousin's charm and dark good looks with sad magnetic eyes. Rosaleen adored her often absent father. Her mother, Beena Salek Aschman, was born in New Zealand. Her life work was her home and role as mother to daughters Cecily, Phyllis and the much younger Rosaleen. Spoilt and pampered by her mother and sisters from an early age, Rosaleen became accustomed to getting her own way. The family followed the practices of the Church of England, though without any apparent devotion or conviction. Rosaleen later recalled her mother as 'a very difficult woman, hysterical, emotional and possessive'.[2] This revealed a lack of insight into the fact that, with her husband at sea, Beena was left for extended periods on her own to raise the family.

In 1925 the family moved to Lindfield in Sydney, where Rosaleen went to the Church of England Girls School in nearby Chatswood, which she found restrictive and conventional. Even as a child, Rosaleen baulked at discipline and convention. At home she insisted on living in a tent in the backyard and she soon came to admire the world of spiders, toads and lizards. Her parents were obviously far more tolerant and relaxed than she ever gave them credit for. At the early age of three, Rosaleen had begun drawing ghosts, otherworldly creatures and dragons.[3] This, in itself, is remarkable, for most children of this age draw their house, pets and family members. In 1957 she explained that her childhood dreams fuelled her art. At seven she knew she possessed the sign of the witch by several blue marks on her knees. In adolescence her depictions of the macabre and Gothic alarmed her teachers. At fourteen she was expelled from school, the teachers fearing her 'depraved nature' would corrupt other pupils.[4] When she was twelve, she had experimented sexually with a boy, although she did not repeat the painful experience for another five years. Her sexuality, enjoyed with both men and women, ventured into the realms of sado-masochism: she enjoyed being tied up and beaten by men.[5]

Rosaleen enrolled at the East Sydney Technical College in Paddington, studying under the distinguished English sculptor Rayner Hoff. He had arrived in Sydney in 1923 and soon became friends with the artist Norman Lindsay. Known for his controversial war memorial sculptures, as a former soldier in World War I Hoff believed he understood the nature of war better than his critics.[6] Hoff was a fortunate choice of mentor for the rebellious Rosaleen, who had not yet decided on her ultimate career path. She wavered between art and writing, having published stories in the popular conservative journal *Smith's Weekly* at the age of fifteen. Rosaleen's signature theme in her first published work was already fully developed. Editor Frank Marien later recalled that: '[n]ever have we discovered a juvenile author so obviously gifted as Rosaleen Norton'.[7] He had an uncanny ability to spot the talents of cartoonists and pen-and-ink artists such as Stan Cross, Mollie Horseman, and Emile Mercier.[8]

Rosaleen wrote of the macabre, the supernatural and the world-beyond-knowing. Marien offered young Rosaleen a cadetship at the newspaper, although she soon wanted to transfer to the art department. Her unusual imagination did not fit within the strictures of a newspaper so she left at the age of eighteen. With her mother's death around the same time, she also left home somewhat impulsively, heading for the Ship and Mermaid Inn in the Rocks area.[9] Known as 'Beggary Barn' or 'Buggery Barn', it was both 'arty' and decrepit. Jack London and Joseph Conrad had stayed there on trips to Sydney.[10] To support herself, Rosaleen took casual jobs in kitchens and hotels, as a telegram messenger and as a model for Norman Lindsay. These jobs allowed her time to start studying the Jewish Kabbalah and Greek mythology.[11]

In 1935 Rosaleen met seventeen-year-old Duco sprayer Beresford Conroy, whom she married in 1940. When he enlisted for active service, he effectively ended the marriage. Meanwhile, Rosaleen revived her artistic career submitting sketches to the innovative journal *Pertinent*, edited by Leon Batt.[12] It published leading writers of the time such as Dulcie Deamer, Kylie Tennant, George Farwell and Ian Mayleston Mudie.[13] Rosaleen's first drawing was published in October 1941, a study entitled *The Borgias*. In a later issue that year, she published drawings of Merlin, ghouls and goblins, as well as a centaur. Surrealism was a popular mode for young avant-garde artists in the inter-war years but Rosaleen took no influence from this movement; rather, her work stepped back into medieval and earlier pagan themes and representations.

During the war Rosaleen continued with her art, though she waited until 1947 before her notorious work was exhibited at Pakies Club at 219 Elizabeth Street in Sydney. A critic for the *Sydney Morning Herald* described her erotic drawings as 'artistic maladjustment'. Rosaleen also experimented with self-hypnosis as a means of gaining access into the darker terrains of her psyche. These methods were not unique; worldwide there had been an upsurge in spiritualism after World War I, when the grief-stricken tried to contact their lost loved ones. Later the Surrealists in France employed similar techniques. Sir Arthur Conan Doyle was a practitioner of the paranormal, particularly after his son died in the war. With the publication of the work of Swiss psychoanalyst Carl Jung, exploring fundamental archetypes in human consciousness and dreams as a vehicle into the subconscious mind, psychic investigations were widely undertaken by intellectuals and artists. This was not common in Australia, however, which was far less exposed to the new thoughts of Freud, Jung and writers like James Joyce than the United States and Europe in the inter-war period. Rosaleen cited the significant influence of Jung in her book *The Art of Rosaleen Norton* (1952).[14] Jung had few followers in Australia, and it is unlikely that Rosaleen read the more accessible books of his Australian disciple Dr William McCrae.[15] She seems to have read the original texts.

Surrealists Salvador Dali, André Breton and Joan Miró all practised automatic writing and art as a means to enter the subconscious, with varying degrees of success.[16]

Rosaleen also practised this form of creativity. She spoke at length about this process with psychologist Professor L. J. Murphy at the University of Melbourne in 1949, recalling that: 'I had a feeling (intuitional rather than intellectual) that somewhere in the depths of the unconscious, the individual would contain, in essence, the accumulated knowledge of mankind ...'[17]

Her research into mystic texts in the 1940s and '50s led her to study the works of Madame Blavatsky, the Ukrainian founder of theosophy. Incorporating beliefs from Eastern mysticism, with an emphasis on intuition, mystical revelations and reincarnation, theosophy was popular with many distinguished individuals in the later nineteenth century.[18] The movement was moderately popular in Australia – Prime Minister Alfred Deakin was its most noted exponent.[19] Australia was a comparatively secular culture without an established Church. The loose doctrines of theosophy found a ready audience in people wanting some spirituality without the conventions of formal religion.[20]

Rosaleen's other sources of mystical knowledge came from modern European movements devoted to spiritualism and inner revelation. Eliphas Levi – born Alphonse Constant – had originally studied for the Catholic priesthood in Paris in the 1830s. Abandoning this call as he felt he lacked sufficient vocation, Levi went to England where he was influenced by the popular novelist and politician Sir Edward Bulwer-Lytton[21] and Rosicrucianism. Levi later wrote books on magic and other ancient occult practices destroyed by Christianity. Many of his ideas were incorporated into his disciple and translator

Arthur Edward Waite's English version of the tarot cards, still in use today. Rosaleen probably did not read Levi but those who succeeded him.

She certainly read the works of the Welsh mystic Dion Fortune – née Violet Mary Firth (1890–1946) – who had visions of Atlantis at the age of four.[22] Trained as a psychotherapist in London, Fortune was also attracted to mysticism. A follower of the Temple Alpha et Omega in London in 1919, she then went over to the Stella Matutina, a magical order.[23] Such organisations are often fragile in structure, with members cohering around charismatic leaders. They often fail and evolve into new sects. The Temple Alpha et Omega was a breakaway from the original Hermetic Order of the Golden Dawn, founded in England in 1888. Fortune later formed the Fraternity of the Inner Light. She was a prolific novelist and early exponent of the Wicca religion. Her work on the Kabbalah was well received in mystic circles in the 1930s. Such movements were attractive to women as they allowed leadership roles denied them in conventional Christian and Jewish religions.[24]

Another major influence was Aleister Crowley – born Edward Alexander Crowley in Leamington Spa in England in 1875 to devout Exclusive Brethren parents. This alone made him an outsider in Victorian England. His father, however, was acquainted with Aubrey Beardsley, an early influence on young Aleister. Crowley studied at Trinity College, Cambridge. Independently wealthy as a young man after the death of his father, Crowley was able to indulge his passions for occultism, the study of magic, chess and bisexuality. He studied mysticism with Arthur

Waite and W. B. Yeats before he left the Hermetic Order of the Golden Dawn to pursue his interests in yoga and Buddhism. In 1920 he co-founded the Temple of Thelema in Sicily. He was a heavy drug-taker, believing this to be a means of entering into the mystic portals of consciousness.

Crowley's influence was profound and enduring in many areas; an image of him appeared on the cover of the Beatles' *Sgt. Pepper's Lonely Hearts Club Band* (1967). For Rosaleen, his interest in the god Pan was particularly significant. His poem *The Hymn to Pan* (1929) was widely admired.[25] His work was well known in Australia through the publications of P. R. Stephensen, later to end up interned during World War II, with suffragette and co-founder of the Communist Party of Australia Adela Pankhurst, for his strange beliefs.[26] Crowley's works were collected in Australia as *The Spirit of Solitude; An Autohagiography Subsequently Christened the Confessions of Aleister Crowley* (1929). They were not mainstream interests for Australians, who did not have the English tradition of mysticism and modern magic. Where Rosaleen struck others as deviant and odd in her homeland, she might have been regarded merely as eccentric in England. In some ways she was simply ahead of her time; by the 1960s many of these ideas and practices had entered mainstream Western youth culture.

Rosaleen was not simply interested in pagan beliefs; she wanted a soulmate to share them with. In 1949 she became reacquainted with the young Adelaide poet Gavin Greenlees, who also published with *Pertinent*. She may have met him some years earlier in Sydney, but given the difference in age – he was born in 1930 – the friendship was initially casual. In August they hitchhiked from Sydney to

Melbourne to locate a venue for her first major exhibition, which demonstrates just how poverty-stricken they were. Her exhibition was launched in the Rowden White Library of the University of Melbourne, perhaps not the most congenial location for such provocative and unusual works. Forty-six were shown, introduced by the prominent academic Professor A. R. Chisholm, a major scholar both of Rimbaud and Australian poetry. Uproar occurred when the police raided the exhibition, removing four works: *Witches' Sabbath, Lucifer, Triumph* and *Individuation* were declared to be obscene. Complaints had been made that the works were 'lewd and disgusting'. The case went to court; Rosaleen's solicitor pointed out the charge had been lodged under legislation passed in 1836. With support from the University of Melbourne, the case was dismissed with all costs awarded to the police.[27]

Rosaleen did not sell her paintings and drawings at the exhibition, since most of the visitors were poor students. She and Gavin returned to Sydney to live in a flat at 179 Brougham Street in Kings Cross, the underworld hub of drugs and prostitution. The tiny flat was a squalid, cluttered mess, with a welcoming sign proclaiming 'Welcome to the house of ghosts, goblins, werewolves, vampires, witches and poltergeists'. Artist Dulcie Deamer, the so-called 'Queen of Bohemia', had lived in the area since the 1920s. She and Rosaleen were kindred spirits and friends, although Deamer had a more conventional past as the mother of six children.[28] Other prominent artists, such as sculptor Loma Latour and painter Sir William Dobell, had also lived there at some time.[29] Rosaleen showed her work at various coffee shops, including the Californian

Coffee Shop, Kashmir Café and the Arabian Café.[30]
Paintings rarely sold, but they added atmosphere to these
modest establishments.

Although Rosaleen and Gavin had a roof over their
heads, they were arrested for vagrancy in 1951. They were
offered work in a most unlikely place – *The Pastrycook's
Review* – by its editor, Wally Glover, a returned soldier. He
had heard of their arrest for vagrancy and offered them a
respectable source of employment. They were to assist with
the production of images. Rosaleen made the mistake of
allowing Glover the right of ownership of all her work in
return for financial support. With this sudden windfall
they were able to concentrate on their creative projects for
a major book, *The Art of Rosaleen Norton with Poems by
Gavin Greenlees* (1952). Copies were beautifully bound
in red leather and printed on Glastonbury Antique paper.
Both Glover's and Rosaleen's fathers died suddenly on the
same day of the advance copies' release. When the book was
finally released, Rosaleen was ambitious for her work and
sent copies to Professor C. S. Lewis, the author of the *Narnia*
series, to Dame Edith Sitwell and, even more bizarrely, to
Albert Einstein, then at Princeton University. The release
was dogged by controversy and legal intervention. Glover
was charged in August 1952 with producing an obscene
publication and fined £5. The United States Customs
officials burned copies on entry to America. In 1957 Glover
was declared bankrupt largely because of the financial strain
of this unusual publication and copyright was transferred to
the Official Receiver of Bankruptcy.[31]

By the time of the book's release Rosaleen was already
dubbed 'The Witch of Kings Cross', an epithet she carried

One of Rosaleen's fascinating sketches, *Self-portrait with Devil*. Mitchell Library, State Library of NSW P3/211.

for the rest of her life. Rather than attempt to understand her art, it was far easier to assign a conventional label to this eccentric woman. Nevertheless, her paintings and drawings went on permanent display at the Apollyon Café, a rendezvous for tourists wanting a taste of the occult and the bizarre at a safe distance. She was regarded as an exotic animal exhibit to be scrutinised. Newspaper reports that she conducted black sabbaths, however, severely damaged her reputation as a serious artist. The curious went to her flat in the hope of witnessing the occult at first hand or taking away some souvenir from her premises.

In September 1955 a mentally ill woman named Anna Hoffman claimed she had attended a black mass at the flat, accompanied by 'sex orgies and parties', which led to charges against Rosaleen. The judge dismissed Anna Hoffman's allegations, considering her to be 'a menace', nevertheless, the extensive coverage in newspapers damaged Rosaleen's reputation even further.[32] Another dramatic case hit the headlines in October after the vice squad raided Rosaleen and Gavin's flat. The police alleged that two men had photographs of a black mass, with Rosaleen and Gavin engaged in 'an unnatural sexual act'. The photographs had been taken at a ceremony devoted to the god Pan, and then stolen from their flat. The culprits were sentenced to four months' imprisonment for theft.[33] The case did not go altogether well for the couple. Rather than dressing conventionally, Rosaleen attended court in leopardskin shoes, a sign of her deviancy in conservative Sydney. More alarming was her obvious stupor from the drugs methedrine and dexedrine, which left her incoherent and unable to concentrate. These drugs became more popular later in the '60s. Rosaleen and Gavin were released on £100 bail.

At the same time David Goodman, the proprietor of the Kashmir Café where Rosaleen showed her paintings, was charged under the *Obscene Publications Act*. He was fined £5.[34] The court was particularly offended by the *Witches' Sabbath* – retitled *Black Magic* – depicting a muscular young woman copulating with a black panther, with a figure satirising the Virgin Mary watching. Where Rosaleen's hatred of Christianity came from is a mystery, since the Church of England does not generally provoke such strong emotions. Aleister Crowley's rejection of his repressive and doctrinaire Exclusive Brethren upbringing is far more understandable.

For all her notoriety, Rosaleen had famous friends within the establishment. Sir Eugene Goossens, the internationally famous conductor of the Sydney Symphony Orchestra

(SSO), struck up a 'rather indiscreet friendship' with her dating from around 1952.[35] At that time his rehearsal studios in Darlinghurst were close to her flat. Described in his obituary as 'urbane and civilised', Goossens was a protégé of Sir Thomas Beecham and an early supporter of Diaghilev's Ballets Russes in England.[36] Moreover, he championed the young office worker Joan Sutherland in her first major performance. But this sophisticated man was far too cosmopolitan for local tastes in the 1950s. Goossens appreciated that both Rosaleen and Gavin were serious researchers and artists. He proposed that they collaborate on a project using Edgar Allan Poe's *The Fall of the House of Usher* as inspiration. Earlier, Claude Debussy had attempted a musical score based on this macabre and Gothic tale.[37] Nothing came of the Goossens–Norton collaboration. Goossens was a participant in many of the rituals dedicated to Pan and conducted in the Brougham Street flat.[38]

Goossens' reputation was ruined when Australian Customs arrested him in March 1956 for possession of over a thousand 'obscene' photographs, books and pamphlets. Today, much of this material would not raise an eyebrow, but in 1956 it was viewed as deeply depraved, wicked and threatening. Masks destined for use in rites to Pan were regarded as particularly offensive to good public morality.[39] The distinguished conductor did not appear at his hearing in the lower court, pleading guilty through his solicitor. His contract with the SSO was not renewed, and thereafter no major engagements came his way. As the *Sydney Morning Herald* of 23 March 1956 predicted, '[t]he end of his career has been pitiful beyond measure'.

Gavin was also affected by this series of revelations in the newspapers. In October 1955 he was admitted to Callan Park Hospital for the Insane in Sydney's Rozelle. Two psychiatrists, Dr S. G. Sands and Dr R. J. Kierly, believed he suffered from schizophrenia with attendant symptoms of hearing voices and delusions. He was emaciated as well. His conversation was almost exclusively about sex.[40] Rosaleen continued to support Gavin, visiting him often and talking about her projects. She showed herself to be kind, loyal and supportive, an image far different from her public one. In the *Australasian Post* of 20 December 1956, an article entitled 'I Am a Witch' depicted her in the thrall of dark satanic forces. The accompanying photograph, which no doubt she found amusing and satirical, was nevertheless damaging. Rosaleen wore a child's witch's hat and was surrounded by a ritual dagger, a phallic snake's head and her pet cats, which she called her 'familiars'. This was followed by a series of exposés on her life and career. Her attempts at explaining her world view and beliefs were lost on a prurient public eager for salacious details of depravity. Rather foolishly she stated that 'If Pan is the devil, then I am indeed a devil worshipper.'[41]

Since her art did not often sell, Rosaleen decided that she would trade on her reputation as a witch by making and marketing charms and performing hexes for selected clients. Her art became increasingly repetitive as she recycled old images of the black sabbath, devils, and Pan. When Gavin was released from psychiatric treatment, his condition had not improved. His behaviour deteriorated to the extent that he threatened Rosaleen with a knife in January 1964. When the police were called, rather than summon medical assistance, they arrested both Gavin and Rosaleen as vagrants, even though they were living in a house in East Sydney. Gavin was jailed for what was perceived as a domestic violence dispute. Clearly he should not have been released from Callan Park Hospital.[42] He died in 1983.

As the East Sydney house was owned by Gavin's parents, Rosaleen next moved in with her sister Cecily Boothman, who lived comfortably in Kirribilli overlooking Sydney Harbour. This was a far more restful and tranquil world than Kings Cross. With her sister's care and sympathy, Rosaleen tried to put Gavin's savage attack on her in the past. In 1967 she moved back to Kings Cross to a decrepit room in Bourke Street. She again constructed an altar to Pan and covered the walls with her paintings.[43] By this time, with the rise of the alternative youth movements, hippies and anti-Vietnam protests, Rosaleen's art, persona and notoriety were all rather passé. She seemed as contemporary as a flapper or a bobby-soxer. Undeterred, she attempted to recapture the public spotlight with an interview in February 1969 with journalist Nan Javes, in which she described herself as a 'Coven Master'.[44]

The attendant publicity sparked controversy within the evangelical wing of the Church of England in Sydney, which called for a wider investigation. By the early 1970s, readings from tarot cards, runes and the I Ch'ing had become widespread. Teenagers and university students held ouija board parties simply for fun rather than with any devotional intent. Rosaleen's influence was totally overestimated; she alone was hardly responsible for this renewed global interest in reading tarot cards. The Church instigated a commission of enquiry into the occult – it was the sole Protestant Church ever to attempt such a move. More significant might have been the influence of two popular films, *Rosemary's Baby* (1968) and *The Exorcist* (1973). The report was handed down in August 1975. The conventional religion came under criticism for not providing for the spiritual needs of modern Australians, yet it condemned the use of tarot cards and ouija boards, hardly items to rock the moral foundation of any society.

The press was not moderate in its coverage of the enquiry's findings, dwelling on a few sensational aspects. Journalists rather predictably headed to Rosaleen for comment. She was now living near Rushcutters Bay on the less fashionable edges of the eastern suburbs. She agreed with Anglican Dean Shilton's belief that amateurs should not meddle with dark forces. The photograph that accompanied her interview portrayed a haggard, tired-looking woman with dyed-black hair and startlingly pointed, heavy black eyebrows. She looked far older than her years. She held in her hand a three-pronged table fork that presumably denoted the devil's symbol.[45]

By this time Rosaleen's public notoriety had began to diminish. She spent most of her time alone in her flat, listening to classical music, painting or tending to her cats. She had unwittingly become the stereotype of the lonely older woman lavishing love on her cats. In late 1978 she was diagnosed with colon cancer. A year later she entered the Sacred Heart Hospice in Darlinghurst where she was tended by the nuns. She died on 5 December 1979. Her paintings went on sale at auction in early 1980, alongside works by Sir Arthur Streeton and Arthur Boyd. Few sold.

Interest was revived when Wally Glover re-released *The Art of Rosaleen Norton*. He produced a supplement in 1984. By this time, although her paintings were not fashionable, she had begun to be mythologised and was the subject of a play entitled *Rosaleen: Wicked Witch of the Cross* by Barrie Lowe.[46] It was no more frightening than Frank Baum's character the Wicked Witch of the West, who alarmed young Dorothy from Kansas. Rosaleen's life, so full of rebellion and fuelled by an enduring determination to live out her own vision of herself, was reduced to bathos, yet just thirty years earlier, she had been depicted as Australia's most notorious and dangerous woman.

CHAPTER 17

Charmian Clift

(1923–1969)

*The poor New South Wales countrywoman who fought her
way to fame and, in the process, destroyed herself.*

Charmian Clift was a surprising writer. Her modest
background from the New South Wales seaside town
of Kiama, her initial public attention as a beauty queen,
and her limited education at Wollongong High School
were not the prototype for a successful travel writer
and popular *Sydney Morning Herald* columnist. At the
age of eighteen, she relinquished a baby daughter born
out of wedlock. Her life with husband, novelist George
Johnston was stormy, competitive and often aggressive,
with vitriolic, alcohol-fuelled fights. The grinding
poverty in which they lived with their three children in
their modest home in Greece, and the nurturing of career
aspirations, always made their relationship volatile and
often destructive. Charmian's later role as breadwinner
for the family, as Johnston's health deteriorated with
tuberculosis, was not conducive to a happy marriage,
while in the 1960s tough gender expectations allowed
little initiative for talented married mothers. Her suicide
in 1969 was a profound loss to Australian literature and
journalism.

Charmian was born in the small New South Wales coastal town of Kiama near Wollongong in 1923. The area was developed by British squatters in the 1840s for its abundant supply of cedar trees. These squatters were often not gentleman pastoralists but rough, aggressive men intent upon attaining wealth and upward social mobility.[1] In *Walk to the Paradise Gardens* (1960) Charmian used her birthplace to great effect. Her unfinished autobiography, 'The End of the Morning', developed her almost photographic ability to recall landscapes and characters of the hilly seaside village.[2] The fictional Lebanon Bay, a tribute to the old cedar forests long gone, was portrayed from the viewpoint of both the insider and the wiser, more sophisticated observer from outside. Her attempts to psychologically flee the restrictions and narrow vista of her early years, long after her physical removal, remained a complex process throughout her life.

Charmian's father, Sydney Clift, was born in 1887 in Huntington in windswept East Anglia. Her grandfather had been born in Benares (Varanasi) in India, where his father was stationed as a sergeant in the 7th Division Grenadiers. For Charmian this exotica felt like part of her DNA. Sydney trained as a fitter and turner in Derby before immigrating to Australia in 1909. Charmian's mother, Amy Currie, was born in Inverell in 1886, the daughter of a coachbuilder. In her autobiography, Charmian claimed her grandmother was a delightful 'beautiful Irish Jewess' and her grandfather of mixed French and Scottish origins. Her paternal grandmother was also Jewish.[3] In her essay 'Portrait of My Mother', she maintained that even 'skivvying for a boarding house in King's Cross' did not dim Amy's glow.[4] For Charmian this heritage took her soaring above the mundaneness of a more typical Australian heritage, providing her with a fanciful romantic mythology to cultivate in her imagination. She freely admitted her family of origin were 'tremendous embroiderers', without fully understanding that she was the most accomplished weaver and embroiderer of them all.[5]

Her parents married in Christ Church Saint Laurence in George Street, Sydney. As a bastion of Anglo-Catholicism in Sydney, this seemed an unlikely site for two professed agnostics. The marriage was at one level content, although her mother's dissatisfaction with the confines of her life later swept through Charmian's psyche, propelling her to success in the wider world. Both her parents, despite their rudimentary education, were lovers of serious books and interested in ideas. She later wrote that her father made her read Laurence Sterne, Rabelais, Balzac and Cervantes, as well as children's books such as *The Wind in the Willows*.[6]

Life in Kiama was not all concerned with the heavy canon of Western literature; the beautiful environment was an important influence of young Charmian, who recalled in her first travel book, *Mermaid Singing* (1956), that '[m]y own Australian childhood had been wild and free'.[7] Her love of swimming came from days at the dangerous beaches surrounding the hamlet. Life with her school mates, often from the rough communities around the nearby quarries, displayed her independent mind, nurtured by literature and fantasy in her home, and made her an uneasy, odd companion. Clever and talented, she was a delight for teachers unaccustomed to children with aspirations beyond the mundane world.

When she was twelve Charmian won a scholarship to Wollongong High School, which provided educational

Charmian Clift, winner of the
Pix beach glamour competition,
1941. Private collection.

opportunities lacking in Kiama. Despite her talents, she left after two years, returning to Kiama and engaging in odd part-time jobs.[8] Her life then spun into anguish when she was raped by an unnamed family friend. The impact of this ordeal was to haunt her the rest of her days.[9] She now wanted to escape Kiama at all costs. In 1941 she entered a beach glamour competition for the populist magazine *Pix*, which had been established three years before. Noted for its covers featuring voluptuous young women, the magazine was racy yet oddly prurient in its approach to life. But for Charmian, winning that competition was her ticket out of obscurity into the cosmopolitan world of Sydney.

The distinguished novelist Ruth Park later described the youthful Charmian: 'Her walk, carriage, quick glancing expressions, radiant health and vitality were what drew the eye.'[10] This vitality and zest for living life to the full as a young woman were noted by others. Alan Ashbolt's obituary in the *Sydney Morning Herald* in 1969 appreciated the 'sort of pagan vitality or inner glow of mischief which illuminated her whole personality ...'[11] Her stunning beauty and fine physique, honed by many years at the beaches around Kiama, were legendary. Both men and women were dazzled by her physical perfection, her wit and her good humour, at least in the early days.

Her dreams of an altogether different life were initially limited by her employment as an usherette at the Minerva theatre in Potts Point. The manager David Martin insisted his female staff don evening frocks which were to be worn with grace and refinement. He was a canny entrepreneur with a rare flair for glamour.[12] For Charmian relocation to the big city brought temptations, affairs with married men, and, even more disastrously, an unwanted pregnancy. At the age of eighteen she was not in a position to keep the little girl she bore at the Women's Hospital on Crown Street, Surry Hills. Her parents and older sister, Margaret, would not tolerate the shame for one thing, and there was little provision in the 1940s for single mothers.[13] Her daughter, Suzanne Chick, has written movingly of discovering that Charmian was her birth mother.[14] Like other relinquishing mothers, Charmian never got over the loss of her first child to adoption.

Charmian and Margaret joined the Australian Women's Army Service in April 1943. For many young women the war offered the opportunity to expand their horizons and to contribute in a way that was unthinkable during the previous world war. Charmian was quickly identified as officer material. She later claimed she was the youngest woman officer appointed.[15] Relocated to Broadmeadows in

Melbourne in 1944, she undertook the training with verve. She was fortunate that her new duties included editing a magazine for the Ordnance section. Charmian met an influential mentor, Bruce Kneale, a former journalist for the Melbourne *Argus*, who encouraged her fiction writing. With his support she placed a short story, 'Other Woman', in the *Australia National Journal* in 1945.[16]

Through Kneale, Charmian met George Johnston, Australia's first accredited war correspondent. A rendition of their introduction at the Hotel Australia restaurant in May 1945 concluded his semi-autobiographical novel *My Brother Jack* (1964), with his alter ego David Meredith meeting the beautiful young Lieutenant 'Cressida Morley'. At the outset, Charmian and Johnston found each other amusing company. Nothing came of it, however, for he was a married man with a baby, and off to China for another dangerous assignment. Charmian was also emotionally unavailable. She had announced her engagement to Leo Kenny, the scion of a wealthy, well-connected Victorian Catholic family. She was later dismissive of this liaison, remarking that 'I did like flashing that half-hoop of family diamonds around the barracks for a while, and was reluctant, really, to have to give it back.'[17] Their backgrounds were too different to ever endure a long-term involvement.

Charmian was not demobilised until May 1946, from when she went to work as a journalist for the *Argus*. Running into Johnston in the lift of the newspaper offices, their mutual attraction was re-ignited. Yet Johnston did not seem a good prospect, initially, for such a lively and ambitious young woman. He was born in 1912 in eastern

Melbourne where his father, John Johnston, had risen from the lowly occupation of labourer to an engineer on the tramway. His mother, Minnie Wright, came from a far more cultured and affluent background in Bendigo. Johnston had been apprenticed as a lithographer before accepting a cadetship at the *Argus* in 1933. Five years later he married Elsie Taylor; their daughter, Gae, was born in 1941. His career as a war correspondent in both the Pacific and European fronts was distinguished. Johnston witnessed the signing of Japan's surrender on the warship *Missouri*. The numerous books he published during the war captured the immediacy of combat on several fronts.[18] On his return to life as a civilian journalist in October 1946 he was a celebrity.

For Charmian, it was not simply professional admiration; she fell deeply and suddenly in love with Johnston. He represented much she desired – an older, more experienced man, successful by his own efforts in rising from the limitations of his background, well known, and offering her an escape from a dreaded suburban non-existence. For him, Charmian offered a comrade with literary ability, aspirations that mirrored his, as well as a physical beauty and sexuality that was at once enticing and youthful. In an early draft of his novel *Clean Straw for Nothing*, Cressida/Charmian '… represents the unobtainable prize, something more than he can ever hope to have achieved'.[19]

Their hot affair was soon noticed by office colleagues – and Elsie Johnston. Charmian and Johnston went to live as a couple in the Post Office Hotel in inner Melbourne in 1946, much to the surprise and indignation of many who had seen his former affairs fizzle out quickly. They were portrayed as the 'koala version of the Mailers or the Fitzgeralds', as travel writer Colin Simpson later acerbically remarked.[20] Yet this was not to be the case – Charmian was a talented journalist and writer, not a driven figure like Zelda Fitzgerald, who could only rely on her beauty and charm. Even during the heady, lust-fuelled first stage of their romance, Charmian was extending her professional range with articles and short stories.

Adultery in 1946 was a serious matter, especially between two workmates. Even though Johnston was the married party in question, Charmian was summarily sacked. Johnston handed in his resignation, which was accepted. For both of them, these events were disastrous professional setbacks, filled with disbelief and shame. They were thus thrown together in a way that might not have evolved in more temperate circumstances. They moved to Sorrento on the Mornington Peninsula in the off-season, where their relationship was tested. Johnston was jealous and possessive, a point that perhaps Charmian should have taken more notice of right at the start. In *Clean Straw for Nothing*, his alter ego proclaimed, '<u>And she is his.</u> The most precious thing he ever owned. To lose her would be to lose everything ... For Cressida is Golden Boy's real laurel.'[21] This is dangerous talk – it is the language of the domestic violence perpetrator who views his partner as personal property. For Johnston had also sacrificed his promising career, perhaps in haste.[22] But his 'prize' – Charmian – carried a heavy burden and obligation through the marriage.

A new start was needed. The couple moved to Manly in Sydney where they married on 7 August 1947. Their collaboration on a joint enterprise, a novel entitled *High Valley* (1948), went well for two writers with such different methods of putting words to paper. It won the *Sydney Morning Herald*'s literary prize for 1948. The prize money of £2000 was an enormous amount at a time when post-war austerity still ruled.[23] In November 1948 Charmian gave birth to their son, Martin. Before her confinement, she painted her toenails different colours. Not that it helped – the birth was painful, like being 'in a torture chamber'.[24] Whatever joy she attained in her new role as a wife and mother, she was nevertheless relegated to this status while Johnston's career began to flourish. In 1948 there were no public debates about work–family balance. A mother's place was firmly in the home. Charmian's one outlet was the parties they hosted. Yet even these attracted intense suspicion later on. Ruth Park wondered whether Charmian and Johnston were really professional writers, or merely poseurs who talked about writing at parties, yet got down to little.[25] Park is unfair and perhaps jealous that she and her partner D'Arcy Niland did not attract the same amount of public attention and popularity. Niland later wrote the bestseller *The Shiralee*, so this enmity is surprising.[26]

Charmian began writing radio scripts for the Australian Broadcasting Commission (ABC). These paid poorly but allowed her to hone her craft. With two children now, after the birth of daughter Shane, the couple needed to work at jobs perhaps not as congenial to creativity as they might have liked. In 1951 Charmian's life suddenly changed when Johnston was appointed as the bureau chief of the Associated Newspaper Services' London office. Ruth Park recalled their jubilation at a lunch attended by actor Peter

Finch. Charmian proclaimed, 'We've got the world by the scruff' – quite a different sentiment from having the world at your feet.

For Charmian, London offered a window on to a more sophisticated world, though the possibilities were curtailed by domesticity and two children. She and Johnston worked collaboratively on a novel, *The Piping Cry*, a situation fraught with tension as he maintained his day job as a reporter and her slower, more private methods of creation clashed with his. More often Johnston's was a day and evening job, since he had to telephone copy at 2am to reach the Melbourne office. Unfortunately, the manuscript was rejected by publishers. Along with this rejection Charmian had to bear hints that Johnston was repeating the pattern of his first marriage with shallow sexual liaisons.

All was not grim, however. The family went on a pleasant holiday to Italy and France in 1952. This infatuation with old Europe was to sustain Charmian for the rest of her life, as it did indeed for Johnston, who relied on Charmian's travel diary for material in *Clean Straw for Nothing*.[27] In mid 1952 they embarked on another collaboration set in seventeenth-century China entitled *The Big Chariot*. For Charmian it was a disaster. She was a slow, deliberate writer, not a journalist like her husband, accustomed to high-speed production in noisy environments. She was relegated to the role of a research assistant for this endeavour and for his novel *Pagoda*. Her own book *Mermaid Singing* outlines her feelings of resentment and her fears that she was disappearing into domesticity.

With Johnston plagued by pneumonia, the family went to Greece in April 1954. This holiday was pivotal to a new phase in their lives. Johnston published the novel *The Cyprian Woman* (1955) about the holiday, in which the Charmian character is not shown in a positive light but as a woman on the lookout for sexual intrigues. Despite her indignation at the fictionalised portrayal, Charmian held her resentments in check. They decided to relocate permanently. For Charmian the sunny islands offered freedom for the two children to play and dream as she had done in Kiama. For Johnston and herself she imagined a life devoted to writing full-time. This was a highly risky business. Even with a low cost of living in Greece compared with London, the expectation of earning a living from creative writing was at best optimistic.[28]

There were other motives that propelled the move. Charmian knew of Johnston's affair with a colleague and wanted to take him away from the daily temptation of attractive young women eager to score with a famous war correspondent. On the other hand, the core motif that runs through his autobiographical novels is the persistent and flagrant infidelity of Cressida. Johnston's behaviour and hypocrisy, though not uncommon in that era, showed the inherent difficulties for a woman with children to maintain her independent existence. Motherhood placed an iron-bound cage around any woman's body and psyche in the 1950s.

The family left London in cold and blustery November 1954, settling in warm, and initially inviting, Kalymnos. *Mermaid Singing* revealed Charmian's almost childlike delight in the heat, the beautiful bright colours and the sea. The ochres, bright pinks and azure blues contrasted dramatically with the shadowy greyness of London, with its constant drizzle and impenetrable skies. The rocky island was famous for its sponge divers whose seasonal stint finished just as the family arrived. This made the small communities on Kalymnos appear far more lively, carefree and happy than usual. It was a deceptive and temporary charm that encircled Charmian. The children were less than enthusiastic, though; suddenly they were in an alien environment, away from their friends and surrounded by children who did not speak English.

Charmian and Johnston published *The Sponge Divers* in 1956. Its production had again caused the build-up of considerable tensions and resentments. The release of *Mermaid Singing* produced jubilation, for it showed she was not just the beautiful, talented wife of a famous writer and journalist, but an artist in her own right. Unfortunately, despite positive reviews, it did not capture the popular imagination and sales were poor. Because of where they were living, she was not able to arrange publicity and conduct interviews with influential reviewers. This was a severe handicap. Charmian's decision to change publishers from Faber to Collins certainly did not help.

In August 1955 the family relocated to the more populated island Hydra, which had the misfortune to be right on the tourist track. They went ahead and purchased a house, making their life in Greece more tangible and permanent. Yet a more immediate issue for Charmian was her realisation that she was again pregnant. Her hopes for professional advancement and esteem seemed to be slipping out of her reach, as another baby would enmesh her even more firmly in domesticity. Jason was born in April 1956, an event she recalled in her travel book *Peel Me a Lotus* (1959). The employment of a nurse, Zoe, certainly assisted her to find some time to think and write. Impelled by financial urgency, however, Johnston started publishing detective stories under a pseudonym – Shane Martin. He, too, had legitimate gripes that supporting a family and hack work took him away from his serious endeavours.

Charmian nevertheless found time for another diversion. By 1958 her affair with a young French artist, Jean-Claude Maurice, had given an explosive edge to an already tense marriage. That Johnston had conducted affairs in London hardly mattered; double standards applied. In Greece in the 1950s, they were even more rigid. The local and expatriate communities marvelled at the lovers' doings, much to the humiliation of Johnston.

Charmian's work was not going well despite her romantic interest. The path to publication of *Peel Me a Lotus* was tortuous and slow, with rejection, rewriting and all its attendant anxieties. With never-ending financial worries and continued illness, Johnston became far more withdrawn. His chest problems were diagnosed as tuberculosis. Around this time, he and Charmian ceased their sexual relationship.[29] This was not good timing. Johnston brooded upon these resentments, magnifying them until they spilled out into his fiction with disastrous effects. In *Clean Straw for Nothing*, not only is Cressida/Charmian portrayed as a faithless wife deserting her husband at his greatest time of need, but he also strips her of her professional identity.

It wasn't all gloom, however. The Canadian poet and later international singer Leonard Cohen stayed with them in Hydra and he later wrote affectionately about

Charmian.[30] Her and Johnston's time in Greece was marked substantially by boozy confrontations, wounding arguments more ferocious than those in *Who's Afraid of Virginia Woolf?* With a constant stream of visitors and hangers-on, all of whom witnessed this publicly performed domestic carnage, Charmian's creativity shrank. Ruth Park, who '… deplored the public soap opera of her life with George Johnston …' went so far as to call her a 'failed writer … this flashing, faulty woman'. More kindly, journalist Valerie Lawson felt that 'the balance in the marriage was not right'.[31] Scarce funds were channelled into entertaining strangers and purchasing prodigious amounts of alcohol. Charmian began to lose her vitality, health and emotional balance; her beauty was damaged by emotional stress, haphazard nutrition and excessive alcohol.

In mid 1960 Johnston and Charmian met a wealthy young English couple, Peter and Didy Cameron, who proposed a house swap, with the advantage for the Johnstons of a splendid country house for weekends. Within months the family had relocated to a small village in the Cotswolds. The younger children, who had not really been brought up in an English-speaking environment, were shell-shocked, while Charmian was now resentful, cold and rightly wondered whether this hasty move to a drizzling climate assisted Johnston's recovery. Funds were precarious despite a few royalties from various publishers.[32] For Charmian the publication of *Peel Me a Lotus* (1959) and *Walk to the Paradise Gardens* (1960) did not provide the satisfaction she expected. The family returned to Hydra in April 1961.

In 1962 Charmian began her novel *Honour's Mimic*, published in London in 1964. This was a new departure, for it was a novel of which she was the sole author and also not a travel memoir. The subject, an unlikely romance between an Australian woman and an illiterate Greek sponge diver, was a bleak assessment of love and loyalty. She began an autobiographical novel, 'The End of the Morning', set in Kiama, which was never completed.[33] In September 1962 her mother died, causing Charmian intense grief and periods of guilt. Amy had not seen her wayward daughter in over a decade, and had had no personal contact at all with her three grandchildren brought up in distant Greece. Charmian fell into a period of what is so dismissively called 'writer's block', a devastating condition for any professional writer who depends on creativity and its uncertain ensuing funds. Around this time her passionate affair with the English biographer Anthony Kingsmill flourished, especially when Johnston went home to Australia in February 1964 to publicise his novel *My Brother Jack*.[34] Her young lover moved into the marital home and lived with her and the children until they returned home to Australia six months later.

For the children this move was a total change from their upbringing; for Charmian, it was professional obliteration. Johnston's novel was hailed as a masterpiece, while her publications lay obscured and forgotten. She was relegated to the role of the 'literary wife'. Old friends were shocked at the physical and emotional transformation from the beach beauty to a haggard, prematurely aged woman, captured later in Ray Crooke's portrait. She was no longer the trophy Johnston had won in Melbourne – he was now the star, around which all wanted to revolve. Johnston leased their new home in Mosman, Sydney. Charmian later told her friend Grace Edwards that she was 'a low-life prole', one of the 'great unwashed', unsuited to the life in snobbish north shore Mosman.[35]

Yet all this was to change. Charmian was offered a column writing for the women's pages of the *Sydney Morning Herald*. Her subjects ranged over all sorts of topics of daily life to the meaning of life, and everything in between. In the foreword to a selection edited by Johnston after her death he wrote that, 'Above all she was an implacable humanist. Her great gift was her ability to reach all types of people, and on all levels, young as well as old, rich and poor, men as well as women … with her undeviating insistence on the simple and ancient verities and values of being …'[36] Her ongoing generosity to his creativity was not in doubt. Charmian adapted *My Brother Jack* for a television play on the ABC, where she showed 'a true, vivid talent for that medium'.[37]

There were other traumas to absorb in her relocation. Her brother Barre died and Johnston's health deteriorated, exacerbated by chronic depression and moodiness. She remarked that he was also 'often pretty heavily drugged',[38] making life at home frequently intolerable. Charmian now had to earn a living for her family, yet this caused immense resentment. Johnston had old-fashioned ideas about being the breadwinner in his family. Certainly, too, the public attention given to Charmian's column did not allow him to express gratitude or admiration. Rather, he was resentful as she sped out in taxis, went to openings and other events important to her work, and of the obligations to her employer, which she took seriously.[39] Charmian blossomed in her new role and her appearance mirrored this new confidence. New clothes, hairdo, make-up and even stiletto heels after years of sandals and bare feet in Greece, all contributed to her new professional persona. Not that producing a column was easy: it required strict discipline that she had not practised since her army days a quarter of a century earlier.

Johnston spent much time in hospital and underwent major surgery in 1966 and 1968.[40] He worked on *Clean Straw for Nothing*, his sequel to *My Brother Jack*, which had won the Miles Franklin Award in 1964. For Charmian, this prospect filled her with dread, as she wondered how her alter ego, Cressida, would be portrayed and what would be revealed. She also quarrelled constantly with their daughter, Shane, now in her late teens, perhaps jealous of her beauty and youth, with all its attendant possibilities.[41] Charmian fretted over the lost potential of her earlier unpublished work; she drank heavily, and was often depressed and melancholy. The award of a Commonwealth Literary Grant in late 1968 gave her the money and thus the time to devote herself to her fiction.[42] Yet it did not allay her deep anxieties. The turbulence of her marriage took a huge toll on her spirit and energy; the impending publication of Johnston's new novel, which she believed dramatised her numerous love affairs, was the final blow for this defiant woman. Her shadow identity as Cressida Morley in Johnston's books vanquished the real woman both literally and symbolically. What is even more worrying is that the persona of Cressida Morley was invented by Charmian as her fictional alter ego, and this was appropriated by Johnston for his semi-autobiographical novels. Not only did he cannibalise her life for his books but he took her fictional identity as well.

Ever present was the thought of exposure in Johnston's new novel. She later said she had not read *Clean Straw for Nothing* (1969), though clearly she had read some passages about herself which she regarded as less than flattering. She penned an extraordinary article early in 1968 in which she put her fears into the public domain, declaring that '[nothing] could force me back into the old side-stepping role. Nor all my professionalism could lure me into listening dispassionately.'[43] Overall, his portrayal is not as bitter and vicious as it could have been, given the soap opera of their lives in Hydra.[44]

On 8 July 1969 Charmian took a fatal dose of barbiturates, having asked a friend the evening before to accompany her on an extended holiday to get away from her life in Sydney. She had been drinking heavily all that fatal day and arguing with Johnston about her excessive drinking. Charmian wrote a sad but recriminatory letter of farewell to Johnston:

> Darling, Sorry about this. I can't stand being hated
> – and you hated me so much today – I am opting
> out and you can play it anyway you choose from
> now on. I am sure you will have a distinguished and
> successful career … I will cease upon the midnight
> and no pain – isn't that something?[45]

This was a terrible legacy to leave anyone, with its charges of fault and neglect. The horror in the family continued, as Johnston died the following year, and both Shane and Martin ended their own lives.

CHAPTER 18

Lillian Roxon
(1932–1973)

*A refugee from the Nazis who came to Brisbane and
eventually defined the world of rock'n'roll journalism in
New York.*

When Germaine Greer published her provocative treatise *The Female Eunuch* in 1970, she dedicated it to Lillian Roxon, a fellow member of the libertarian Sydney Push, 'whose energy has never failed despite her anxieties, and her asthma, and her overweight'. The words were both flattering and deeply cruel.[1] The most prominent early rock journalist besides Lester Bangs in the United States, Lillian was a charming, combative and influential writer in a new genre that was edgy, defiant, and rebellious.[2] Her publication, *Lillian Roxon's Rock Encyclopedia* (1969), proudly proclaimed her own construction of the discipline, attributing to raw popular music a respectability that it previously lacked. In turn, Lillian was called the 'mother of rock and roll journalism'.[3] Her life as an independent, assertive and confident woman was often lonely in a world dominated by hard, swaggering and rambunctious men, both on stage and at the typewriter. She died alone after a massive asthma attack in her home in New York City in 1973.

Lillian Roxon's early life was full of turbulence and travel. Born Liliana Ropschitz in Savona, Italy, she changed her name and her identity as she moved through her life. Her parents were well-educated, cultured Poles from Lvov (Lviv) in Galacia. Established in 1256, Lvov was an important academic and cultural centre now incorporated into Ukraine. Passing through the control of various powers over the centuries, this area was attacked by the Red Army in 1920. For Jewish residents like Liliana's family this event was significant, for the Russians were virulently anti-Semitic. Her father, Izydor, was prevented from studying medicine in his homeland. Instead, he studied at the esteemed University of Padua, established in 1222 with such distinguished alumni as Galileo, Casanova and William Harvey. On graduation, Izydor established a fashionable practice at Alassio on the Italian Riviera. Her mother, Rosa Breitman, was an intelligent woman whose life was centred on the family and home. Liliana's brother Milo was ten years older. In 1936 her younger brother, Jacob (Jack), was born.

The family was initially privileged and able to spend their holidays in Vienna and the Polish resort town of Zakopane, near Slovakia. This came to an abrupt end with the German–Italian pact in 1938. Liliana's parents decided to emigrate and arrived in Australia under Polish passports in July 1939 aboard the *Dunera*, which brought refugees from Nazism to Australia.[4] Izydor and the family relocated to Queensland, where he was able to practise medicine. They settled in the inner-city suburb of New Farm, a beautiful and once wealthy multicultural area, and anglicised their name to Roxon. Liliana became Lillian. Though Brisbane was a provincial city in the '40s, it was soon alive to the beat of American jazz and the jitterbug.

General Douglas MacArthur planned strategies for the war in the Pacific from July 1942 in the AMP Building in Queen Street. The city and surrounding areas were inundated with nearly 100,000 American service personnel among a population of just 345,000.[5] Dance halls like the Trocadero and the grand ballroom of the City Hall buzzed with American dances and songs, seen before only in films. New Farm Park by the river was a favourite trysting place where sex was often fast and furious.

In 1944 Lillian was sent to board at St Hilda's School at Southport. Founded in 1912, St Hilda's was the most exclusive girls school in Queensland, catering largely for the wealthy pastoralist families. Although her background was far removed from those of her fellow pupils, she excelled academically. She later claimed she was expelled, and in 1947 she enrolled at the elite, selective Brisbane State High School.[6] Students during the war produced the innovative magazine *Bajai*, which nurtured writers Thea Astley and Barbara Patterson (later) Blackman and arts administrator Charles Osborne.[7] Judith Wright published with this talented group of students. With her cultured European upbringing, again Lillian stood out, forming friendships with teachers like Rhyl Sorensen. At this time Lillian fell in love with a young actor, Peter Munro, who later died of cancer aged twenty-two. This was a harbinger for her subsequent unlucky romantic life.[8]

Lillian's social life centred around the Pink Elephant Café, a bohemian meeting place frequented by a gay and creative crowd, where waiters dressed in full drag. Located in upper Queen Street near the beautiful Customs House, the café had been financed through Donald Friend's coterie. The owners of the Ballad Bookshop, Barrie (later Barrett) Reid and Laurie Collinson, who became part of the Reeds' Heide circle in Melbourne, were core members of this refuge from conservative Queensland society.[9] Lillian attended Charles Osborne's twenty-first birthday party at the café, along with the troupe from the visiting Ballet Rambert.[10]

In 1949 Lillian decided to attend the University of Sydney, boarding in a guesthouse in Bondi. Anne Coombs, the chronicler of the Push, described Lillian as 'a bright, naïve, middle class girl' in 1949.[11] At university Lillian soon met the faster crowd inhabited by people such as Margaret Elliott (later film producer Margaret Fink) and Aviva Canton (later Layton). She was drawn into the Sydney Push, a group of anti-materialist, anti-careerist rebels and libertarians who met in the Royal George Hotel in Sussex Street and the Tudor Hotel in Phillip Street, as well as the Lincoln coffee house.[12] Some of the members were exceptions – such as CSIRO physicist Dr Gilbert Bogle, now famous for his mysterious death with lover Margaret Chandler in 1963.[13] Dominated by educated men who had dropped out of the privileged world of university studies, when that was available to very few in the '50s, the Push nurtured elements of nihilism and unproductive disillusionment. The hard drinking and casual sex, in an era before oral contraception, demanded far more from its women members than its men. Nor were its men, in particular, in the league of the French existentialists, who produced major philosophical and cultural works.[14] Insider Neil C. Hope characteristically remarked, '[t]he Push was not a repository of dedicated thinkers drawn into its vortex by an inexorable logic. It was an atmosphere, congenial to like temperaments, a refuge, a fireplace and a home ... a union of outsiders ...'[15] David Malouf recalled that: '... that world ... used people up very quickly ... people were brilliant at the age of twenty-three or twenty-four. But hardly a single one of them ever came to anything.'[16]

Lillian's entanglement in the Push represented a rejection of bourgeois femininity with its aspirations of a 'good' marriage and children. She said in a letter to Aviva Layton around 1959: 'If I do not marry Glenn I'm going to travel around the world and have fun and settle down when I am thirty with a nice American with dough ...'[17] Her unpublished novel set in this period captures the mood of a young, voluptuous and beautiful woman who opts for independence. The description of an illegal abortion illustrated the pain that might accompany the freedom.[18] In contrast with other Push members, Lillian had had strong career aspirations since her days at St Hilda's; she sent in her first article to *Woman* (later *Woman's Day*) when she was fourteen.[19] She merely took from the Push what she needed. There is an apocryphal story that young men in a Christian college at the University of Sydney were sung a song, the refrain of which proclaimed, 'Beware Karl Marx, Professor John [Anderson, the prophet of libertarianism] and Lillian Roxon.'[20]

Despite the hedonism around her, Lillian was still a virgin in 1950, a plight she discussed in a letter to her friend Barbara Blackman. Not that offers were not frequently forthcoming to this witty, exuberant, plump and delectable young woman. She chose an architecture student, George Clarke, for her initiation in sexual experience, her 'happy

Lillian Roxon, 10 January 1972, when she was on the Sydney *Sun Herald* staff. Picture by Staff; Fairfax Media 10980070.

release from that wretched condition'. They began living together, still called 'living in sin' until the late '60s, in Windsor House in Jamison Street, Sydney, along with her brother Milo. Fortunately, the landlady lived off the premises, allowing bohemian residents more freedom than usual. Clarke later went on to become one of Australia's leading town planners.[21]

Other friends from that time included David Malouf, then a retiring young student from the University of Queensland, and Zell Rabin, later a famous journalist working for Rupert Murdoch in New York.[22] Lillian disarmed Malouf by offering him, on first acquaintance, a copy of Magnus Hirschfeld's *Sexual Anomalies and Perversions* (1944). Her party game was his test of sophistication.[23] He passed splendidly; to such a degree that Lillian later introduced him to her parents.

Lillian graduated from the University of Sydney in 1955 and in January the following year her father died. Lillian made a visit to New York City to try her luck and this saw the beginning of her career as a rock journalist. Zell Rabin was already established there, so she had a friend who could lead her through the maze that was cosmopolitan New York. She tracked down such luminaries as Woody Guthrie, the initial inspiration of young Bob Dylan. However, she returned to Sydney before long and her mother purchased a flat in Double Bay for her. This signalled a massive cultural and social step away from the Push, with its bare and decrepit lifestyle. She began working on Frank Packer's racy magazine *Weekend*, edited by Donald Horne, in January 1957.[24] This offered an unsurpassed apprenticeship with a master craftsman as mentor and adviser. *Weekend* was a precursor to tabloid celebrity magazines so common now. Articles included one with the intriguing title, 'Why Queensland Will Become a Second Hollywood'.[25]

In 1959, Lillian got the opportunity to return to New York to stretch her cultural and professional horizons. She first worked for Murdoch's *Daily Mirror* under the direction of its bureau chief, Zell Rabin. She found a small apartment in Hudson Street in West Greenwich Village, a good location to pursue the emerging music scene as it changed from folk music and beatniks to protest and rock genres. But dissatisfied with the type of subject given to her as a 'woman' journalist, Lillian headed for London for the summer as part of the *Sydney Morning Herald* team. On her return to New York in October 1960, the pace of change in the United States was accelerating, with the election of the young and charismatic John F. Kennedy as president. Donald Horne, now the new editor of *The Bulletin*, attempted to lure her back to Sydney, but Lillian instinctively felt that destiny had brought her to New York. As she reported to her mother: 'New York is hot and exhausting, a sort of huge Brisbane, but I don't mind. I love it with a tireless and quite uncritical devotion.' What she had seen in Brisbane to compare it to the pace of New York remains a mystery.[26]

Lillian moved to the Lower East Side on East 11th Street, to live in a cheap, rundown old Irish neighbourhood. After several years of insecure freelancing, she began working for the *Sydney Morning Herald* in 1963. She celebrated her new security by moving to East 21st Street near Gramercy Park and the Flatiron district. Lillian scored a professional coup when she got a few words from Sybil Burton, the humiliated wife of Richard Burton, during his affair with Elizabeth Taylor, for *Woman's Day*. This popular Australian women's magazine sent her on assignment to the Mexican film location of *Night of the Iguana* starring Ava Gardner, Richard Burton and Deborah Kerr. The following year she wrote an insightful piece on Jacqueline Kennedy. Her work also covered the race riots and civil rights movement.

In early 1965 Lillian returned to Sydney, primarily to visit her mother who was emotionally lost without her daughter. Rosa died soon after Lillian's return to New York. She pondered her mother's closed life full of bitterness and regret, making her even more enthusiastically determined to embrace life with all its disappointments and joys. Her old Push buddy Neil Hope had died in a car accident the year before and in the following year Zell died of melanoma at the age of thirty-four.[27] Lillian was devastated. Her confidante in New York had been such a solid presence in her life.

Lillian's professional career prospered. She was right at the centre of the new 'happenings'. She wrote to Aviva Layton in May 1965 that she went to '... an Oldenburg happening in Al Roon's Steam Baths [located in the Riverside Plaza Hotel on West 75th Street]', a black tie party in honour of hairdresser Vidal Sassoon and 'cocktails with Miss bloody Australia at QANTAS ... Thursday, *Seventeen* magazine is having a happening. Erk. I have been to half the bloody avant-garde theater groups in town ...' She also reported that she witnessed an impromptu performance by the artists Robert Rauschenberg and Roy Lichtenstein another time at Al Roon's pool. Andy Warhol was also present.[28]

In May 1966 Lillian went to London to catch up on the fashions, and she was delighted with the Biba boutique and the styles along Carnaby Street and King's Road. She met up with old Push friends John Taylor, Ruth Biegler and journalist Paddy McGuinness, now the unofficial leader in London. Always at the right spot at the very right time, Lillian went to the Beatles' last performance in the UK.[29] Previously she had interviewed Brian Epstein, the manager of the Beatles, asking him '... are you a millionaire?' signalling the realisation that rock music had become a huge industry, where vast fortunes could be made and lost.[30] This was her breakthrough interview in a career that was to define her enduring reputation. Danny Fields, the editor of *Datebook*, a teenage magazine, recognised her potential with this interview. She also encountered Linda Eastman, a young photographer for the snobbish magazine *Town and Country*.[31] The synergy of these new friendships came together as Fields later wrote Linda McCartney's biography.[32] The three of them covered the Rolling Stones' first visit to New York in 1966. Lillian was fascinated with Linda Eastman, the beautiful blonde journalist, Jewish and ambitious like herself. Nor did Lillian forget her Australian background, supporting the Easybeats on their first trip to the States in 1966.[33] She also had a brief fling with lead singer Stevie Wright.

Lillian had an instinct for pinpointing the next trend, writing about the emergence of the hippies in San Francisco in early 1967, months before the 'Summer of Love' was documented.[34] She embarked on her personal summer of love with teenaged Canadian drummer David Wynne, who started working for her. He later returned to his more conventional origins, becoming a senior diplomat.[35] For Lillian, this relationship, though brief, was important. She felt dispirited and defeated by her constant battles with her weight, ever mindful of her father's cruel remarks in her girlhood.

Her professional ambitions widened when she conceived a project to systematically document the rock scene. Rock was slowly being taken seriously. Lillian wrote that Norman Mailer, Timothy Leary and Allen Ginsberg 'all settl[ed] raptly ringside the night The Byrds first played [in New York]'.[36] Beginning in 1968, she researched all the personalities and genres for her magnum opus, *Lillian Roxon's Rock Encyclopedia*. Her celebrity status at Max's Kansas City, a club at 213 Park Avenue, ensured she had access to anyone who was anybody in the rock world. This venue, described by Andy Warhol as '… the exact spot where Pop Art and Pop Life came together in the sixties …', drew celebrities and the talented from the arts and music in a fertile cross-mix. Raunchy, decadent and influential, Max's Kansas City lured all the luminaries and wannabes.[37] Lillian reported that '[I]t looked pretty sleazy, at least it would have to an outsider, but in that crowded cellar any night there was more money and more power than the rest of Tin Pan Alley put together.' Limos waited outside the venue until 4am to take the rich and famous away to who knows what.[38] At the centre Lillian held court. She knew the entire Warhol Factory crowd, Leonard Cohen, Jim Morrison, Janis Joplin, Lou Reed, Philip Glass and the Velvet Underground.[39] Lillian wrote that '[G]oing to a Warhol party (I really mean this) currently rates higher than being asked to Jackie Kennedy's for brunch.' At one party at Warhol's The Factory, Tennessee Williams, Rudolf Nureyev, Montgomery Clift, and Judy Garland all laughed with habitués and other guests.[40]

Lillian's fame and reputation as a journalist were acknowledged when she was asked by the Beatles to cover the Lennon–McCartney tour in New York in May 1968. Her article entitled '101 Hours' was a *tour de force*. It appeared in the September 1968 issue of the popular culture magazine *Eye*, where Lillian was a contributing editor. At the same time, Linda Eastman renewed her friendship with Paul McCartney. By the end of the stay they were lovers and Linda left for England.[41] Lillian never saw or spoke to her 'closest friend' again, as Linda's life ascended into the pop stratosphere. Lillian was devastated not to be invited to their wedding in March 1969. She did, however, write a positive article in *Woman's Day*; but her anger simmered slowly and relentlessly. Lillian had her revenge, taken sweetly in 1973, when she reviewed a McCartney TV special in the New York *Sunday News* of 22 April.[42] This assessment is still regarded as one of the most dismissive pieces ever written by a major journalist. Lillian wrote pointedly: 'I can tell you right now … [Linda] did not marry a millionaire Beatle to end up in a Liverpool saloon singing "Pack up your troubles in your old kit bag" with middle-aged women named Mildred …'[43] Linda was devastated to learn of Lillian's death, and was racked with guilt at her sudden departure and abandonment of her American friends so effortlessly.[44]

Lillian went on to make other combative friendships with powerful women. The most notable was with '… the big G, Germaine Greer in London … She is seven feet tall and a bully and about the only female I know who is NOT a eunuch …'[45] They had met in 1959 when Melbourne was abuzz with the filming of *On the Beach*. Lillian was amazed to meet Greer, who then had purple hair and wore red stockings. Their reacquaintance in London in 1968 was full of fun. Lillian was particularly impressed by Greer's knitting pattern for a 'cock sock', her column in the provocative underground Dutch magazine *Suck*, and her celebrity status, confirmed by a photograph by Lord Snowdon.[46] Greer first visited New York City in late 1968, when Lillian was exhausted from reporting on the presidential elections. Trouble arose over Lillian's choice of accommodation and things got worse from there. Lillian was trying to write her book, however, she went out of her way to show her visitor around Max's Kansas City and its famous habitués.[47] Greer, who described herself at the time as 'superwhore, supergroupie …', wrote a vitriolic account mentioning Lillian, for London *Oz* in February 1969. Another article in *Suck* advised readers, 'Anyone who wants group sex in New York and likes fat girls, contact Lillian Roxon.'[48] This public ridicule was cruel, especially since Lillian's weight had ballooned from her use of cortisone medication for her severe asthma. Her phone number was listed in the New York directory and endless telephone calls from prospective sex partners followed this piece, distressing Lillian.

Lillian's professional status prospered despite this ignominy. In 1969 her book, *Lillian Roxon's Rock Encyclopedia*, was released to tremendous praise. Using careful research, she estimated the career and significance of various performers and genres, viewed through her lens not just as passing ephemeral wonders but often as legitimate artists. She was more sure-footed in her appraisals of those she had heard and met, rather than the early rock'n'rollers of the 1950s. Motown was clearly not much on her radar either. For all its limitations, *Lillian Roxon's Rock Encyclopedia* was a monumental achievement which carved out an entire discipline. It has been rather forgotten now.

Nik Cohn's *Pop from the Beginning*, also published in 1969, was essentially English in its tone, and lacked the immediacy of Lillian's interaction with many major players. Enduring magazines, like *Rolling Stone*, established in 1967, have kept their momentum by their very conspicuous presence. Lillian and her friend, journalist and later contributing editor to *Vanity Fair* Lisa Robinson nurtured the talents of other rock journalists, including Lester Bangs, Jon Landau, Richard Meltzer and Lenny Kaye. The salon at Max's Kansas City, where they discussed ideas and methods, were high-testosterone duelling matches, tempered by Lillian's good interpersonal skills and ability to listen carefully to others. When she died, the group fell apart.[49]

Lillian's pace of recreational and professional achievements was conducted at a high-powered level. Considering that she worked full-time for the Fairfax press, as a contributing editor to *Eye* and freelanced for various other publications while researching a major reference book involving long hours at Max's Kansas City, it is no wonder her health began to deteriorate. She did not have the support of a committed partner who could provide solace and love. She was an independent woman with many friends but no one special in her life, and a celebrity in her own right after the extraordinary success of her book, feted in newspapers and on television shows. Yet, as she confided to Richard Neville, the editor of *Oz* magazine in London, she had made no money out of its success.[50] She had naively signed a less than satisfactory contract, an altogether familiar story for first-time authors. This lack of financial largesse could never detract from the monumental achievement and the accolades accorded her by her peers, usually so dismissive of women's capabilities. She lamented: 'True, I've been offered ten books but they are all dreadful. The worst was called "Under Thirty".'[51]

Lillian was not simply attuned to fashions and shifts in the music industry, she was a first-class journalist with a strong antenna for social change in its earliest manifestations. She recorded the historic march of 25,000 women down Park Avenue to celebrate the jubilee of women's suffrage in the United States. The march is commonly regarded as the beginnings of second-wave feminism, but this overlooks a blow which occurred five years earlier in her home town of Brisbane when three women chained themselves to the bar of the Regatta Hotel to protest against discrimination against women in hotels.[52] A march like this was an important historic moment that was widely publicised. Lillian wrote a long and incisive article entitled 'There is a Tide in the Affairs of Women' for the *Sydney Morning Herald* of 28 August 1970, in which she spoke of her own excitement and disappointment that many women spectators jeered the marchers. Some even carried placards proclaiming '"M-O-M" for "Men Our Masters"' and 'actually scuffled with their marching sisters ...' She ended this appraisal by writing: 'If the idea of change makes you uncomfortable, don't worry. You're not alone. All of us ladies agree that this time getting there is not going to be half the fun. But being there is going to be an important part of a brave new world.' She also reported on the drug arrests of Robert Kennedy Jr and Robert Shriver, noting how drug issues affected not just the poor and marginalised.[53] Her friend Danny Fields summed up the era when he remarked that '... people look back on those speed [amphetamines] years and they think, "Did I spend those years wallpapering an apartment with stamps when I could have written a play?"'[54]

In the two years before her death, Lillian's asthma became progressively worse, despite treatment. Her letters to an always sympathetic Aviva Layton began to deal far more with Zen diets (and why they did not work), her medication, which made her obese, and her battle with asthma. One happy occasion during this time was when she went to a fancy dress party dressed as Dame Nellie Melba and took first prize.[55] She contemplated leaving New York as it is '... brilliant and glittering and hard and ruthless, a terrible cheat and a liar, but it is also full of tender little surprises, and if it's in a giving mood, it has a lot to give ...'[56] She thought of Italy, London, or even returning to Australia 'before I have no eggs left – with a nice, mythical man called Kevin'.[57] Lillian's frantic lifestyle was the very opposite of what was needed to manage her life-threatening illness. Her drive for professional success did not abate. A daily radio program called 'Lillian Roxon's Discotheque' went out from March 1971 to over 250 stations. The show ran for six months. This alone would have constituted a full-time job for most people. She also ran a column in *Mademoiselle* magazine entitled 'The Intelligent Woman's Guide to Sex' from March 1972 and she took on more assignments for new rock magazines, such as the short-lived *Fusion*. All this extracurricular activity and her fame caused ructions at the Fairfax office.

In 1973 Lillian returned to Brisbane, meeting up with old friends from school with whom she had always corresponded. This shows a generous side to her character, an unexpected loyalty from a woman feted in New York. She admitted to Rhyl Sorensen, 'New York is killing me, but I can't live without it.'[58] Her addiction to this city was as lethal as heroin. She and Richard Neville caught up with Mick Jagger in Sydney. Lillian was amused by Jagger's description of Linda and Paul McCartney as 'the lovely couple'.[59] Lillian saw many of her old Push friends now on the Whitlam government bandwagon of arts boards, with mortgages and private schools for their children. In the Push they had been temporarily absent from the bourgeois origins of their youth but had now slipped back, however awkwardly.

When Lillian returned to New York, her health had not improved. Subject to mood swings from her illness and medication, along with feelings of deep insecurity, she was no longer the amusing, witty companion of old. Her last days were poignant, in retrospect. She argued with her boss, Derryn Hinch, about what he paid her when he suggested that she needed an air-conditioned apartment.[60] She spent her last evening at Max's Kansas City supporting a friend of Danny Fields, dressed in a long black gown with an Iggy Pop badge positioned on her chest. As a person who constantly talked on the phone to her friends, an alarm went out two days later when her phone went unanswered. Lisa Robinson and Danny Goldberg called the police who broke into her apartment, finding her dead.[61] The *New York Times* of 12 August was extravagant with praise in its obituary, though the *Sydney Morning Herald*, for whom she had worked for decades, was restrained and brief. At her funeral many rock journalists were present and respectful of their great pioneer and champion.[62] Her brother, Jack Roxon, and some friends established the Lillian Roxon Memorial Asthma Research Trust.

In New York City she had carved out an enviable career as a journalist and rock chronicler, producing the inaugural encyclopedia of the genre. Intensely loyal and loving to all her family, Lillian did not take the vituperative path of Germaine Greer, who castigated her mother in public. Her generosity with her time, advice and connections helped many young artists, and she was loving, sympathetic and nurturing, despite her notorious reputation. Yet Lillian's poor health and immense drive to work and accomplish great things took a lethal toll. To die alone, with no one to help her, was far from what this courageous woman deserved.

Endnotes

Chapter 1 Mary Broad Bryant

1   Reprinted in *Historical Records of Australia* (*HRA*), 1915, vol. 2, pp. 809–810.
2   C. M. H. Clark, *A History of Australia*, vol. 1 (MUP, 1969, first published 1962), p. 91.
3   Ibid.
4   Ibid., p. 69.
5   B. H. Fletcher, 'Phillip, Arthur (1738–1814)', http://www.adb.online.anu.edu.au/biogs/A020292b.htm.
6   Arthur Phillip's undated memorandum to the Secretary of State is contained in *Historical Records of NSW* (*HRNSW*), vol. 1, part 2, pp. 50–54.
7   Fletcher, op. cit.
8   C. H. Currey, *The Transportation, Escape and Pardoning of Mary Bryant* (Sydney, Halstead Press, 1986, first published 1963), p. 1.
9   *The Voyage of Governor Phillip to Botany Bay; with an Account of the Establishment of the Colonies at Port Jackson and Norfolk Island* (London, 1789).
10   John White, *Journal of a Voyage to New South Wales* (ed. A. H. Chisholm), (Sydney, Angus & Robertson, 1962, first published J. Debrett, London, 1790), p. 88.
11   *Journal of Ralph Clark*, 21 June 1787, cited in Clark, op. cit., p. 84.
12   Refer to Currey, op. cit., pp. 1–3, for more details.
13   Refer to *HRNSW*, vol. 1, part 2, p. 79. There is much discussion among historians and demographers as to the exact number. I have tried to balance the numbers in my estimation.
14   David Collins, *An Account of the English Colony in New South Wales*, vol. 1 (London, T. Cadell Jr & W. Davies), p. 55.
15   Watkin Tench, *Sydney's First Four Years: A Narrative of the Expedition to Botany Bay and a Complete Account of the Settlement at Port Jackson, 1788–1791* (printed by the Library of Australian History, 1979), pp. 149–150.
16   Ibid., pp. 165–166.
17   Phillip to Lord Sydney, 11 April 1790, *HRA*, series 1, part 1, p. 168.
18   Currey, op. cit., p. 9.

19   Secretary Charles Long to Governor Phillip, 27 June 1792, *HRA*, vol. 1, series 1, p. 359.

20   Collins, op. cit., p. 153.

21   Currey, op. cit., p. 11.

22   John Eastey, *Memorandum of the Transaction of the Voyage from England to Botany Bay, 1788–1793* (Sydney, Trustees of the Public Library of NSW with Angus & Robertson, 1965), p. 127.

23   James Scott, *Remarks on a Passage to Botany Bay, 1787–1792* (original ms in Mitchell Library, Sydney, Trustees of the Public Library of NSW with Angus & Robertson, 1963), p. 62.

24   Frederick A. Pottle, *Boswell and the Girl from Botany Bay* (London, William Heinemann, 1938), p. 27. These sarsaparilla leaves were presented by Yale University to the Mitchell Library in 1956.

25   William Bligh, *Remarks on Log Book of HMS* Providence, *1792–93*, p. 236 cited in Currey, op. cit., p. 26.

26   Ibid., p. 22.

27   Ibid., p. 28.

28   Ibid., p. 3.

29   Edward Edwards, George Hamilton and Basil Thomson, *Voyage of HMS* Pandora *Dispatched to Arrest the Mutineers on the* Bounty *in the South Sea, 1790–91* (reprinted London, Francis Edwards, 1915).

30   'A list of Convicts, Deserters from Pt. Jackson, delivered to Captain Edward Edwards, of HMS ship, *Pandora* by Timotheus Wanjon, Esq., Governor of the Dutch Settlement at Timor, 5 October 1791', *HRA*, series 1, part 1, p. 369.

31   This material is cited in Peter Ackroyd, *London: The Biography* (London, Chatto & Windus, 2000), p. 250.

32   *Dublin Chronicle*, 21 July 1793 reprinted in *HRA*, vol. 2, pp. 800–802.

33   www.oldandsold.com; Ackroyd, op. cit., pp. 290–302.

34   C. B. Tinker (ed.), *The Letters of James Boswell*, vol. 2 (Oxford at the Claredon Press, 1924), p. 426.

35   Frederick A. Pottle, *Pride and Negligence: The History of the Boswell Papers* (New York, McGraw-Hill, 1982), pp. 83–86, 182.

36   Cited in Pottle, *Boswell and the Girl from Botany Bay*, op. cit., p. 26.

37   Ibid., p. 23.

38   Ibid.

39   Governor Phillip to Lord Grenville, Dispatch no. 1, 5 November 1791, *HRA*, series 1, vol. 1, p. 269.

40   Cited in Pottle, *Boswell and the Girl from Botany Bay*, op. cit., pp. 27–28.

41   Ibid., p. 25.

42 Entry in A. W. Jose, *Australian Encyclopedia* (Sydney, Angus & Robertson, 1927), p. 211.
43 Jonathan King, *Mary Bryant: Her Life and Escape from Botany Bay* (Sydney, Simon & Schuster, 2004), p. 276.
44 Rex Rientis, 'Watling, Thomas (1762– ?)', http://www.adb.online. anu.edu.au/biogs/A020524b.htm?hilite=thomas%3Bwatlin.
45 Elizabeth Guilford, 'Morgan, Molly (1762–1835)', http://www.adb. online.anu.edu.au/biogs/A020223b.htm.
46 Wendy Birman, 'O'Reilly, John Boyle (1844–1890)', http://www. adb.online.anu.edu.au/biogs/A050426b.htm.

Chapter 2 Mary Cockerill and Walyer

1   Cited in Glenn Howroyd, *Sun Herald*, 28 June 1986.
2   Carol Brill, 'Flights of Fancy – The Legendary Bushrangers Michael Howe and Mary Cockerill', unpublished paper kindly forwarded to me with permission to quote. Ms Brill is a direct descendant of the Cockerell family which employed Mary in the 1810s.
3   Marcus Clarke, *Old Tales of a Young Country* (Melbourne, Mason, Firth, McCutcheon, 1871), chapter 6, read as an electronic book 16 November 2009.
4   Information supplied by Carol Brill in email to Kay Saunders, 24 October 2009.
5   'Heaven and Hell Together', http://www.heavenandhelltogether. com/, Cockerell family site.
6   Kim Pearse and Susan Doyle, 'New Town: A Social History' (Hobart City Council, 2002), cited in Carol Brill, 'Mary Cockerill aka Black Mary and the Cockerell Family', unpublished ms in possession of the author by kind permission of Ms Brill.
7   James Bonwick cited in James Boyce, *Van Diemen's Land: An Environmental History* (Melbourne, Black Inc., 2008), p. 32.
8   K. A. Green, 'Ingle, John (1781? –1872)', http://www.adb.online. anu.edu.au/biogs/A020003b.htm.
9   John West in *The History of Tasmania* (ed. A.G.L. Shaw), (Sydney, Royal Australian Historical Society and Angus & Robertson, 1971, first published 1852), p. 359.
10 Ibid., p. 360.
11 'Heaven and Hell Together', op. cit.
12 Ibid.
13 J. E. Calder, 'Early Troubles of the Colonists', *Hobart Mercury*, 17–27 November 1873.
14 Alan Atkinson, *The Europeans in Australia. A History. Volume Two: Democracy* (Melbourne, Oxford University Press, 2004), p. 69.

15 Ibid.

16 Boyce, op. cit., p. 55.

17 *Historical Records of Australia* (*HRA*), 3, no. 2, pp. 80, 703.

18 L. L. Robson, *A History of Tasmania Volume 1: Van Diemen's Land from the Earliest Times to 1855* (Melbourne, Oxford University Press, 1983), p. 86.

19 J. E. Calder, *Some Accounts of the Wars, Extirpation, Habits etc. of the Native Tribes of Tasmania* (Hobart, Fullers Bookshop, facsimile edition, 1972, first published 1875), p. 46.

20 Robson, op. cit., p. 69.

21 James Bonwick, *The Lost Tasmanian Race* (London, Sampson Low, Manston, Searle & Rivington, 1884), p. 41.

22 Robson, op. cit., p. 81.

23 Governor Macquarie's Proclamation, 14 May 1814, *HRA*, 1, no. 8, pp. 262–265.

24 Robson, op. cit., p. 90.

25 West, op. cit., pp. 359–360.

26 Rev. R. Knopwood to Davey, 30 August 1814, *HRA*, 3, no. 2, pp. 77–79.

27 Edward Curr, *An Account of the Colony of Van Diemen's Land to 1824* (Hobart, Platypus Press, 1967, first published 1824), p. 180.

28 *Hobart Town Gazette*, 27 July 1816.

29 Robson, op. cit., p. 85.

30 Lyndall Ryan, *The Aboriginal Tasmanians* (Sydney, Allen & Unwin, 1996, first published 1981), pp. 23–29.

31 Carol Brill to Kay Saunders, email, 24 October 2009.

32 Thomas Wells, *Michael Howe: The Last and Worst of the Tasmanian Bushrangers* (Hobart, Andrew Bent, 1818), reproduced in Curr, op. cit., p. 190.

33 Davey to Macquarie, September 1816, *HRA*, 3, no. 2, pp. 591–592, 603–604.

34 Sworn statement of John Yorke reproduced in Curr, op. cit., pp. 187–188. In the account in the *Sydney Gazette* of 20 May 1815 there was nothing about the murder of a woman, only the cold-blooded killing of a man.

35 Report in *Sydney Gazette*, 25 January 1817 and Yorke deposition in Curr, op. cit.

36 Lieutenant Governor William Sorell to Governor Macquarie, 30 June 1817 and 11 September 1817, *HRA*, 3, no. 2, pp. 238, 262–263, 276–277.

37 Wells, op. cit., pp. 188–190.

38 *Hobart Town Gazette*, 8 June 1816.

39   Clarke, op. cit.

40   Calder, 'Early Troubles', op. cit.

41   Sorell to Macquarie, 18 November 1818, *HRA*, 3, no. 2, pp. 363–364.

42   *Hobart Town Gazette*, 24 October 1818.

43   Bonwick, *The Lost Tasmanian Race*, op. cit., p. 31.

44   *Hobart Town Gazette*, 3 July 1819.

45   Robson, op. cit., pp. 80–101.

46   Ryan, op. cit., pp. 88–94; see also N. J. B. Plomley (ed.), *Friendly Mission: The Tasmanian Journals and Papers of George Augustus Robinson, 1829–1834* (Hobart, Tasmanian Research Association, 1966); Cassandra Pybus, *Community of Thieves* (Melbourne, William Heinemann, 1991).

47   Ryan, ibid., pp. 110–113.

48   Ibid., p. 141.

49   Julia Clark, 'Walyer' in Heather Radi (ed.), *200 Australian Women* (Broadway, Women's Redress Press Inc., 1988), p. 11; see also Henry Reynolds, 'The Black War: Tasmania's First Land Rights Movement', *Island Magazine*, 2, no. 1, 1988, pp. 104–107.

50   Ryan, op. cit., p. 150.

Chapter 3 Eliza Fraser

1   Elaine Brown, 'Fraser, Eliza (1798–1858?)', http://www.adb.online. anu.edu.au/biogs/AS10171b.htm?hilite=fraser%3Beliza.

2   Yolanda Drummond, 'Progress of Eliza Fraser', *Journal of the Royal Queensland Historical Society*, 15, no. 1, 1993, p. 16.

3   Kay Schaffer, *In the Wake of First Contact: The Eliza Fraser Stories* (Melbourne, Cambridge University Press, 1995), p. 4 for more details. This is the most impressive account of the entire Eliza Fraser story. Readers are directed to this study for a more complex rendition of her stories and their interpretation. See also Raymond Evans and Jan Walker, '"These Strangers, Where Are They Going?" Aboriginal–European Relations on Fraser Island and the Wide Bay Region 1770–1905', *Occasional Papers in Anthropology*, vol. 8, 1977, pp. 39–105.

4   The whole first narrative of Eliza Fraser is reproduced in Barry Dwyer and N. Buchanan, *The Rescue of Eliza Fraser* (Noosa, Noosa Graphics, 1986), appendix 7.

5   Evidence of Robert Hodge cited in John Curtis, *Shipwreck of the Stirling Castle* (London, George Virtue, 1838), pp. 31–32.

6   Olga Miller, 'K'gari, Mrs. Fraser and Butchulla Oral Tradition' in Ian McNiven et al, *Constructions of Colonialism: Perspectives on Eliza Fraser's Shipwreck* (London, Leicester University Press, 1998), p. 34.

7   Henry Youlden, 'Shipwreck in Australia', *The Knickerbocker*, vol. 41, no. 4, 1853 cited in Schaffer, op. cit., p. 36.

8   Curtis, op. cit., p. 33.

9   An excellent summary is found in Elaine Brown, 'Eliza Fraser: An Historical Record' in McNiven et al, op. cit., pp. 19–20; Schaffer, op. cit., chapters 2 and 3.

10   Curtis, op. cit., pp. 220–240.

11   Cited in Brown, 'Eliza Fraser: An Historical Record', op. cit., p. 20.

12   Cited in Schaffer, op. cit., p. 87.

13   Miller, op. cit., pp. 30–31.

14   Curtis, op. cit., p. 143.

15   See Dwyer and Buchanan, op. cit.

16   Ibid.

17   Reported in Curtis, op. cit., p. 79; see also Brown, 'Eliza Fraser: An Historical Record', op. cit., pp. 22–23.

18   Refer to Schaffer, op. cit., pp. 45, 47, 49–60.

19   Curtis, op. cit., p. 181; see Brown, op. cit., pp. 19–22.

20   Cited in Brown, ibid., p. 25.

21   Schaffer, op. cit., p. 42; Michael Alexander, *Mrs. Fraser on the Fatal Shore* (London, Michael Joseph, 1971, reprinted 1976), p. 106.

22   Don Grady, 'Elizabeth Guard (1814–1870)', http://www.teara.govt.nz/en/biographies/1g23/1.

23   Schaffer, op. cit., p. 44.

24   Ibid., pp. 43–49.

25   H. S. Russell, *The Genesis of Queensland* (Sydney, Turner & Henderson, 1888), p. 250. I discussed his depiction of the Mrs Fraser story at the Clem Lack Memorial Lecture at the Royal Queensland Historical Society on 21 August 2009.

Chapter 4 Lola Montez

1   Bruce Seymour, *Lola Montez* (New Haven, Yale UP, 1995), chapter 1. This is the most reliable and well researched of the considerable literature on Lola Montez.

2   Lola Montez, *Autobiography and Lectures* (London, James Blackwood, n.d.), p. 8.

3   Ibid., p. 11.

4   Horace Wyndam, *The Magnificent Montez: From Courtesan to Convert* (London, Hutchinson, 1935), p. 45.

5   Her autobiography makes some references to these events.

6   Michael Cannon, *Lola Montez: The Tragic Story of a 'Liberated Woman'* (Melbourne, Heritage, 1973), p. 10, and 'Montez, Lola

(1818–1861)', http://www.adb.online.anu.edu.au/biogs/A050313b.
htm?hilite=montez.

7   The material on Paris and Bavaria is taken largely from Seymour, op.
    cit., chapters 8–17.

8   Ibid., p. 147.

9   Cannon, *Lola Montez: The Tragic Story of a 'Liberated Woman'*, op. cit.,
    p. 12.

10 Seymour, op. cit., p. 259.

11 Ibid., pp. 273–282.

12 Ibid., pp. 293–294.

13 Ibid., pp. 295–300.

14 Cited in Cannon, *Lola Montez: The Tragic Story of a 'Liberated
    Woman'*, op. cit., p. 47.

15 Montez, op. cit., p. 49.

16 Ibid.

17 Janet R. Fireman, 'Lola Montez' in Glenda Riley and Richard W.
    Etulain (eds.), *By Grit and Grace: Eleven Women Who Shaped the
    American West* (Golden, Col., Fulcrum Press, 1997), p. 58; see also
    J. F. Varley, *Lola Montez: The Californian Adventures of Europe's
    Notorious Courtesan* (Spokane, A. H. Clark, 1996), and Seymour, op.
    cit., chapters 24 and 25.

18 Fireman, op. cit., pp. 58–59.

19 Ibid., pp. 59–60.

20 S. Korzelinski, *Memoirs of Gold-Digging in Australia* (translated
    and edited by S. Robe), (St Lucia, University of Queensland Press,
    1979), p. 148.

21 Geoffrey Serle, *The Golden Age: A History of the Colony of Victoria,
    1851–1861* (Carlton, Melbourne University Press, 1963),
    pp. 363–364.

22 *The Age*, 22 September 1855.

23 Serle, op. cit., pp. 341–343.

24 E. H. Pask, *Enter the Colonies, Dancing: A History of Dance in
    Australia 1835–1940* (Melbourne, Oxford University Press, 1979),
    p. 35.

25 Korzelinski, op. cit., p. 57.

26 Weston Bate, *Lucky City: The First Generation at Ballarat,
    1851–1901* (Carlton, Melbourne University Press, 1989),
    pp. 109–110.

27 Seymour, op. cit., p. 344.

28 Ibid., pp. 348–352.

29 Montez, op. cit.

30 Ibid., p. 366.

31   Richard Waterhouse, '"Lola Montez" and High Culture: The
      Australian Elizabethan Theatre Trust in Post-war Australia', *Journal
      of Australian Studies*, March 2001, http://www.highbeam.com/
      doc/1G1-20152561.html.

**Chapter 5 Ellen Tremaye (Edward De Lacy Evans) and Marion ('Bill')
Edwards**

1   For more details see Lindy Scripps, 'Jemmy the Rover' in Heather
     Radi (ed.), *200 Australian Women* (Broadway, Women's Redress
     Press, 1988), pp. 7–8.
2   *Columbia Encyclopedia*, sixth edition, 2008, accessed 26 November
     2009.
3   William Telfer, *The Wallabadah Manuscript; The Early History
     of the Northern Districts of New South Wales* (ed. Roger Milliss),
     (Kensington, UNSWP), 1980, p. 103. The manuscript was written
     around 1901.
4   Jillian Oppenheimer, 'Kitty Gallagher' in Radi, op. cit., p. 3; The
     Australian Women's Register entry http://www.womenaustralia.info/
     biogs/AWE3691b.htm. The Register is not correct on her birth date.
     She was already married in 1798 so she could not have been born in
     1785.
5   The best single source for this chapter is Lucy Chesser, *Parting With
     My Sex: Cross-dressing, Inversion and Sexuality in Australian Cultural
     Life* (Sydney, Sydney University Press, 2008).
6   Ibid., pp. 6–11.
7   'The Male Impersonator', *Herald* (Melbourne), 8 September 1879.
8   *Bendigo Advertiser*, 5 September 1879 cited in Chesser, op. cit., p. 20.
     The references from the Bendigo newspapers are taken from Chesser.
9   Ibid.; *Bendigo Independent*, 6 September 1879.
10   Ibid., p. 200.
11   *Argus*, 6 September 1879.
12   Chesser, op. cit., p. 11.
13   Ibid.
14   *Argus*, 27 August 1901.
15   Chesser, op. cit., pp. 28–29. The material on the affair is taken from
     Chesser's account.
16   *Bendigo Advertiser*, 6 December 1879.
17   *Bendigo Advertiser*, 8 September 1879.
18   *Adelaide Advertiser*, 29 August 1901.
19   *Bendigo Independent*, 5 September 1879.
20   O. Penfold, 'A Case of Man-personation by a Woman', *Australian
     Medical Journal*, 2, no. 4, 1880, p. 147.

21 Chesser, op. cit., p. 27.

22 Ibid., p. 31; see also Gail Reekie, 'She Was a Loveable Man: Marion/ Bill Edwards and the Feminisation of Australian Culture', *Journal of Australian Feminist Lesbian Studies*, vol. 4, 1994, pp. 43–50.

23 Mimi Colligan, 'Edwards, Marion (Bill) (1874–1956)', adbonline. anu.edu.au/biogs/AS10143b.htm.

24 Ibid.

25 Chesser, op. cit., pp. 238–270.

26 *Argus*, 22 October 1906.

27 Cited in Chesser, op. cit., pp. 247–248.

28 Ibid., pp. 266–267.

29 Colligan, op. cit.

Chapter 6 'Madame Brussels' Caroline Hodgson

1 Philip Bentley, 'Hodgson, Caroline (1851–1908)', http://www. adbonline.anu.edu.au/biogs/AS10228b.htm.

2 John Sadlier, *Recollections of a Victorian Police Officer* (Ringwood, Penguin, 1973, first published 1913), pp. 176–178; see also Paul de Serville, *Pounds and Pedigrees: The Upper Class in Victoria, 1850–80* (Melbourne, Oxford University Press, 1991), pp. 41–51; his death notice referred to his illustrious family.

3 Chris McColville, 'The Location of Melbourne Prostitutes, 1870–1920', *Historical Studies*, vol. 19, no. 74, 1980, pp. 86–97.

4 Cyril Pearl, *Wild Men of Sydney* (London, W. H. Allen, 1958), p. 202.

5 Ibid., p. 203.

6 Bentley, op. cit.

7 Ibid.

8 Raelene Frances, *Selling Sex: A Hidden History of Prostitution* (Sydney, Allen & Unwin, 2007), pp. 134–135.

9 Philip Bentley, 'Edifices of Venereal Renown and Gilded Palaces of Sin' (BA Hons thesis, Monash University, 1993), pp. 36–37.

10 J. Parsons, *Thirty Six Years Among Criminals* (1906) cited in Graeme Davison et al, *The Outcasts of Melbourne: Essays in Social History* (Sydney, Allen & Unwin, 1985), p. 100.

11 John Stanley James, *The Vagabond Papers* (ed. Michael Cannon), (Melbourne University Press, 1969), pp. 231–232.

12 Davison et al, op. cit., p. 80.

13 Frances, op. cit., p. 157.

14 Andrew Brown-May and Shurlee Swain (eds.), *The Encyclopedia of Melbourne* (Melbourne, Cambridge University Press, 2005), p. 575.

15 Geoffrey Serle, 'Gaunson, David (1846–1909)', http://adbonline. anu.edu.au/biogs/A040266b.htm.

16   Pearl, op. cit., p. 204.

17   Ibid., p. 203.

18   Geoffrey Cox, 'Music at St. Patrick's Cathedral: A Profile', http://
      www.stpatrickscathedral/org.au/music/recording-of-the-music-of-
      the-choir-3html.

19   *Truth*, 18 December 1900, 23 September 1900, 5 July 1900.

20   Judith A. Allen, *Sex and Secrets: Crimes Involving Australian Women
      Since 1880* (Melbourne, Oxford University Press, 1990), p. 74.

21   Pearl, op. cit., p. 202.

22   David Dunstan, 'Gillott, Samuel (1838–1913)', http://adbonline.
      anu.edu.au/biogs/A090014b.htm?hilite=gillott.

23   George Meudell, *The Pleasant Career of a Spendthrift* (Melbourne,
      Robertson & Mullen, 1929), pp. 274–275. Another version was
      released in 1935; see Diane Langmore, 'Meudell, George Dick
      (1860–1936)', http://adbonline.anu.edu.au/biogs/A100477b.
      htm?hilite=meudell.

Chapter 7 Helena Rubinstein

1   Helena Rubinstein, *My Life for Beauty* (Sydney and London, Bodley
      Head in Australia, 1965), p. 118; M. Fabe, *Beauty Millionaire: The
      Life of Helena Rubinstein* (New York, Thomas Cromwell, 1972),
      p. 17; Maxene Fabe's biography is full of mistakes and perpetuates
      many myths about the life of Helena Rubinstein, for instance that
      Helena's father wanted her to study medicine.

2   Lindy Woodhead, *War Paint: Elizabeth Arden and Helena
      Rubinstein: Their Lives, Their Times, Their Rivalry* (London, Virago,
      2004, first published 2003), p. 441. Woodhead undertook research
      in Poland and located the original birth certificate, thereby refuting
      Rubinstein's *Australian Dictionary of Biography* entry which has her
      born in 1870.

3   Ibid., p. 30.

4   Ibid., pp. 32–33.

5   J. R. Poynter, 'Rubinstein, Helena (1870–1965)', http://adbonline.
      anu.edu.au/biogs/A110484b.htm?hilite=rubinstein. This entry
      contains many errors that have been rectified in Woodhead's book.

6   Rubinstein, op. cit., p. 28.

7   Woodhead, op. cit., p. 25.

8   Patrick O'Higgins, *Madame: An Intimate Biography of Helena
      Rubinstein* (New York, The Viking Press, 1971), p. 146. This is a
      delightfully candid book.

9   Ibid.; Poynter, 'Rubinstein, Helena'. Poynter's family came from
      Coleraine and he possessed considerable family knowledge of

Helena's early time in Victoria. See also Helena Rubinstein, *The Art of Feminine Beauty* (New York, Victor Gollancz, 1930), p. 12. In her later autobiography she said she worked for Lord Hopetoun, Australia's first governor-general; Peter and Sheila Forrest, *All for Queensland: The Governors and the People* (Darwin, Shady Tree Press, 2009), pp. 125–141.

10   Woodhead, op. cit., p. 43.

11   Ibid., pp. 44–45.

12   Ibid., pp. 46–47; Rubinstein, *My Life for Beauty*, pp. 26–27; O'Higgins, op. cit., p. 149 contains the most frank account of Rubinstein's time in Australia in her own words.

13   Woodhead, op. cit., p. 49.

14   Advertisement in *Table Talk*, March 1903.

15   Woodhead, op. cit., p. 52.

16   Rubinstein, *My Life for Beauty*, pp. 30–31.

17   Ibid., pp. 27–29.

18   Ibid., p. 32.

19   Woodhead, op. cit., p. 70.

20   *The Australasian*, 30 January 1909, interview with Helena Rubinstein.

21   Maggie Angeloglou, *A History of Make-Up* (London, Studio Vista, 1970), pp. 99–107.

22   M. C. Cohen and K. Kozlowski, *Read My Lips: A Cultural History of Lipstick* (San Francisco, Chronicle Books, 1998), pp. 17–19.

23   *Table Talk*, December 1905.

24   M. Cannon, 'Brodzky, Maurice (1883–1973)', http://www.adb.online.anu.edu.au/biogs/A070425b.htm?hilite=brodsky.

25   *The Australasian*, 30 January 1909, interview with Helena Rubinstein.

26   Rubinstein, *My Life for Beauty*, p. 43.

27   *Argus*, 3 November 1911; *Sydney Morning Herald*, 25 September 1909; *Adelaide Advertiser*, 6 March 1912.

28   Cohen and Kozlowski, op. cit., p. 23.

29   Woodhead, op. cit., p. 78.

30   Rubinstein, *My Life for Beauty*, pp. 39–40.

31   Ibid., p. 81.

32   Rubinstein, *My Life for Beauty*, pp. 44–45.

33   Ibid., p. 48.

34   Ibid., p. 53.

35   Ibid., p. 54; Woodhead, op. cit., pp. 89–91.

36   Ibid., p. 58.

37   Woodhead, op. cit., pp. 103–109.

38　Ibid., p. 110.
39　Ibid., p. 118.
40　Ibid., pp. 119–121.
41　Rubinstein, *My Life for Beauty*, p. 74.
42　Ibid., p. 62.
43　Ibid., pp. 71–74.
44　Woodhead, op. cit., pp. 170–177.
45　Ibid., p. 230.

Chapter 8 Adela Pankhurst

1　Verna Coleman, *Adela Pankhurst: The Wayward Suffragette, 1885–1961* (Carlton, Melbourne University Press, 1996), p. 1. Readers are advised to consult this text. It is the most comprehensive study of Adela's life.

2　F. F. Rosenblatt, *The Chartist Movement* (London, Taylor & Francis, 2006).

3　David Mitchell, *Queen Christabel: A Biography of Christabel Pankhurst* (London, Macdonald & James, 1977), pp. 14–19; Coleman, op. cit., pp. 3–4; see also Emmeline Pethick-Lawrence, *My Part in a Changing World* (London, Gollancz, 1938); E. Sylvia Pankhurst (introduced by Richard Pankhurst), *The Suffragette Movement: An Intimate Account of Persons and Ideals* (London, Virago Press, 1977, first published 1931) provides excellent accounts by participants. A solid overview is contained in David Mitchell's *The Fighting Pankhursts: A Study in Tenacity* (London, Cape, 1967).

4　Coleman, op. cit., p. 5.

5　Emmeline Pankhurst, *My Own Story* (London, E. Nash, 1941); June Purvis, *Emmeline Pankhurst: A Biography* (London and New York, Routledge, 2002). Sylvia also complained in her autobiography of her mother's lack of affection and neglect of her children. Emmeline was callous when Harry was ill with poliomyelitis. He died at the age of 20.

6　Susan Hogan, 'Pankhurst, Adela Constantia Mary (1885–1961)', http://www.adb.online.anu.edu.au/biogs/A120729b.htm?hilite=pankhurst.

7　Coleman, op. cit.

8　Christabel Pankhurst, *Unshackled: The Story of How We Won the Vote* (ed. L. Lord), (London, Hutchinson, 1959).

9　Coleman, op. cit., pp. 46–48.

10　E. Sylvia Pankhurst, op. cit., p. 588.

11　Letter to Helen Fraser Moyes, undated cited in Mitchell, *Queen Christabel*, p. 175.

12 Mitchell, *The Fighting Pankhursts*, op. cit., p. 55; Hogan, op. cit.

13 Patricia Gowland, 'John, Cecilia Annie (1877–1955)', http://www. adb.online.anu.edu.au/biogs/A090484b.htm?hilite=john%3Bcecilia; and J. N. Brownfoot, 'Goldstein, Vida Jane Mary (1869–1949)', http://www.adb.online.anu.edu.au/biogs/A090042b. htm?hilite=goldstein.

14 Adela Pankhurst, *Betrayed: A Play in Five Acts* (Melbourne, Fraser & Jenkinson, 1917). A copy of this turgid drama is held in the John Oxley Library in Brisbane.

15 *Sydney Morning Herald*, 22 July 1914.

16 *The Woman Voter*, 15 September 1914.

17 A good account of these years can be found in Raymond Evans, *Loyalty and Disloyalty: Social Conflict on the Queensland Homefront, 1914-1918* (Sydney, Allen & Unwin, 1987); Joy Damousi and M. Lake (eds), *Gender and War: Australians at War in the Twentieth Century* (Melbourne, Cambridge University Press, 1995). See also Geoff Hewitt, 'Ahern, Elizabeth (1877–1969)', http://www.adb.online.anu.edu.au/biogs/A070019b. htm?hilite=elizabeth%3Bahern.

18 Coleman, op. cit., pp. 64–65.

19 Mitchell, *The Fighting Pankhursts*, op. cit., p. 55.

20 Ibid., p. 66.

21 Hogan, op. cit.

22 C. M. H. Clark, *A History of Australia: Volume 4: The Old Dead Tree and the Young Tree Green* (Carlton, Melbourne University Press, 1987), p. 40.

23 Coleman, op. cit., pp. 72–74.

24 Mitchell, *The Fighting Pankhursts*, op. cit., pp. 58–59.

25 L. F. Fitzhardinge, *The Little Digger, 1914-1952: A Political Biography of William Morris Hughes*, vol. 2 (Sydney, Angus & Robertson, 1979), p. 277.

26 Coleman, op. cit., pp. 79–80.

27 Hogan, op. cit.

28 Stuart Macintyre, *The Oxford History of Australia*, vol. 4, *1901–1942: The Succeeding Age* (Melbourne, Oxford University Press, 1986), and his book, *The Reds: The Communist Party of Australia from Origins to Illegality* (Sydney, Allen & Unwin, 1998).

29 Clark, op. cit., pp. 239–255.

30 Coleman, op. cit., pp. 107–109; Mitchell, *The Fighting Pankhursts*, op. cit., pp. 213–226.

31 James Barnes and Patience Barnes, *Nazis in Pre-War London, 1930–1939* (Brighton, Sussex Academic Press, 2005).

32   Chris Cunneen, 'Miles, William John (1871–1942)', http://www.
      adb.online.anu.edu.au/biogs/A100489b.htm.
33   Coleman, op. cit., pp. 146–150.
34   Craig Munro, 'Stephensen, Percy Reginald (1901–1965)', http://
      www.adb.online.anu.edu.au/biogs/ A120084b.htm; Cunneen, op. cit.
35   Kay Saunders and Roger Daniels (eds.), *Alien Justice: Wartime
      Internment in Australia and North America* (St Lucia, University of
      Queensland Press, 2000).

Chapter 9 Annette Kellermann
1   Nikki Henningham, 'Letham, Isabel (1899–1995)', http://www.
      womenaustralia.info/biogs/AWE2231b.htm.
2   'Sarah Frances "Fanny" Durack (1889–1956)' and 'Annette
      Kellermann (1886–1975)' in Susanna de Vries, *The Complete Book of
      Great Australian Women* (Sydney, HarperCollins, 2003), p. 2.
3   'She's Game: Women Making Australian Sporting History: Fanny
      Durack' in http://www.womenaustralia.info/exhib/sg/durack.html.
4   Emily Gibson with Barbara Firth, *The Original Million Dollar
      Mermaid: The Annette Kellerman Story* (Sydney, Allen & Unwin, 2005),
      p. 5. This book relies a lot on Kellermann's papers which are lodged in
      the Mitchell Library.
5   Ibid., p. 6.
6   Ibid., pp. 6–7.
7   Jacqui Donegan, 'Banned in Boston: A Biography of Annette
      Kellerman (1886–1975)' (BA Hons thesis, University of
      Queensland), p. 12.
8   G. P. Walsh, 'Kellermann, Annette Marie Sarah (1886–
      1975)', http://www.adb.online.anu.edu.au/biogs/A090547b.
      htm?hilite=kellermann; refer also to John Lucas, 'Making a
      Statement: Annette Kellerman Advances the World of Swimming,
      Diving and Entertainment' in *Sporting Traditions*, vol. 14, no. 2,
      1998, pp. 25–35.
9   Annette Kellermann, *How to Swim* (London, William Heinemann,
      1918), pp. 12–15.
10   Ibid.; Marcelle Wooster, 'A Résumé of Annette Kellermann',
      unpublished manuscript, Fryer Research Library, University of
      Queensland, 1975.
11   Annette Kellermann, *Fairy Tales of the South Seas* (London,
      Sampson, Low, Marston, 1926), p. 11.
12   Kay Saunders, 'James Freeman Cavill (1867–1952)' and 'Sir
      Henry Sydney Williams (1920-2003)' in *Queensland: 150 Years of
      Achievement* (Sydney, Focus Books, 2009), p. 161.

13   Annette Kellermann, 'How I Swam into Fame and Fortune' in
     American Magazine, 1917, quoted in Donegan, op. cit., p. 16.
14   Donegan, op. cit., pp. 15–17.
15   *Sydney Morning Herald*, 26 March 1902.
16   Veronica Raszeja, 'Bathing Costumes Controversy' in *Oxford
     Companion to Australian Sport* (Melbourne, Oxford University Press,
     1994, 2nd edn), p. 58.
17   Ibid.
18   Donegan, op. cit., p. 21.
19   Walsh, op. cit.
20   Wooster, op. cit.
21   Gibson, op. cit., pp. 16–19.
22   Annette Kellermann, 'How I Swam into Fame and Fortune', op. cit.,
     p. 28.
23   Hugh Cudlipp, *Publish and Be Damned: The Astonishing Story of the
     Daily Mirror* (London, Dakers, 1953).
24   Gibson, op. cit., pp. 39–41.
25   Ibid., p. 46.
26   Walsh, op. cit.
27   Donegan, op. cit., p. 36.
28   Gibson, op. cit., p. 45.
29   Ibid., p. 38; Kellermann, 'How I Swam into Fame and Fortune',
     op. cit., pp. 82–83. Her ADB entry calculates she earned $1250 per
     week.
30   http://www.classicfilmguide.com/indexef48.html, *Million Dollar
     Mermaid*.
31   Gibson, op. cit., pp. 58–60.
32   Jacqui Donegan undertook extensive research in the USA and failed
     to locate records verifying this event; refer to Donegan, op. cit.,
     pp. 41–46.
33   *Boston Post*, 7 November 1908, cited in Donegan, op. cit., p. 46.
34   Donegan, op. cit., pp. 51–52; B. L. Bennett, 'Dudley A. Sargent – A
     Man for all Seasons', *Quest*, vol. 29, 1978, pp. 33–45.
35   Cited in Gibson, op. cit., p. 89.
36   Donegan, op. cit., p. 53.
37   Gibson, op. cit., pp. 66–72.
38   Ibid., p. 85.
39   Donegan, op. cit., p. 55.
40   Ibid., pp. 57–58; Gibson, op. cit., pp. 107–122.
41   Gibson, op. cit., pp. 128–149.
42   Ibid., p. 46.
43   Donegan, op. cit., p. 50.

44   *Courier-Mail* (Brisbane), 14 July 1945.
45   Gibson, op. cit., pp. 155–161.
46   *New York Times*, 2 September 1918.
47   Donegan, op. cit., pp. 63–64.
48   Gibson, op. cit., pp. 169–172.
49   Donegan, op. cit., p. 68.
50   Gibson, op. cit., p. 95.
51   Gibson, op. cit., pp. 175–176.
52   Ibid., p. 90.
53   Donegan, op. cit., pp. 70–71.
54   *Woman's World* (Australian edition), 1 April 1933.
55   Gibson, op. cit., pp. 182–185.
56   Ibid., pp. 192–203.
57   Esther Williams and Digby Diehl, *The Million Dollar Mermaid* (New York, Simon & Schuster, 1999), pp. 213–215.
58   *Sunday Telegraph* (Sydney), 16 March 1975.
59   Ibid.
60   Gibson, op. cit., p. 218.
61   Walsh, op. cit.

Chapter 10 Lady Maie Casey

1   Maie Casey, *Tides and Eddies* (Penguin, 1966). This is a record of her public not private life.
2   Zara Holt, *My Life and Harry: An Autobiography of Dame Zara Holt* (Melbourne, Herald Books, 1968); P. A. Pemberton, 'Holt, Dame Zara Kate (1909–1989)', http://adbonline.anu.edu.au/biogs/A170548b.htm?hilite=holt%3Bzara. Dame Zara's personal papers in the National Library of Australia reveal many sexual peccadilloes in the higher echelons of society in the 1960s. Never judgmental or cruel, she was a witty observer of life.
3   Maie Casey, *An Australian Story, 1837–1907* (London, Michael Joseph, 1962), pp. 23–24.
4   J. S. Legge, 'Grice, Richard (1813–1882)', http://adbonline.anu.edu.au/biogs/A040339b.htm?hilite=grice%3Brichard.
5   http://www.thewomenshistory.org.au/history/guides/general/provlist.htm. The Royal Women's Hospital, Melbourne, Provenance – Creators and Custodians. It was then termed the Melbourne Lying-in Hospital and Infirmary for Diseases of Women and Children; refer also to his entry in Paul de Serville, *Pounds and Pedigrees: The Upper Class in Victoria 1850–80* (Melbourne, Oxford University Press, 1991), p. 401.
6   Casey, *An Australian Story*, op. cit., pp. 27–31.

7   Ibid., p. 33.

8   Ibid., p. 34.

9   Ibid., pp. 78–94.

10   F. M. C. Forster, 'Ryan, Charles Snodgrass (1853–1926)', http://www.adb.online.anu.edu.au/biogs/A11053b.htm.

11   Maie Casey, *Melba Revisited, 1861–1931*, privately printed by the author, 1975. A copy resides in the Fryer Library, University of Queensland. It is beautifully illustrated.

12   'Marian Ellis Rowan (1848–1922)' in Kay Saunders, *Queensland: 150 Years of Achievement* (Sydney, Focus Books, 2009), p. 34.

13   Casey, *An Australian Story*, op. cit., p. 76.

14   Ibid., p. 115.

15   Ibid., pp. 151–157. The chapter entitled 'The Stranger' concerned her early life with Berthe Tissot, of whom she writes far more warmly than her mother, who was designated 'The Wife'.

16   Ibid., p. 152.

17   Diane Langmore, *Glittering Surfaces: A Life of Maie Casey* (Sydney, Allen & Unwin, 1997), p. 19. This is a well-researched biography and readers are advised to consult this for more details on Casey's life.

18   Diane Langmore, 'Ryan, Rupert Sumner (1884 –1952)', http://www.adb.online.anu.edu.au/biogs/A160186b.htm.

19   John Rickard, 'White, Vera Deakin (1891–1978)', http://www.adb.online.anu.edu.au/biogs/A160637b.htm.

20   Casey, *Tides and Eddies*, op. cit., pp. 27–30.

21   Langmore, *Glittering Surfaces*, op. cit., p. 31.

22   Langmore, 'Ryan, Rupert', op. cit.

23   Casey, *Tides and Eddies*, op. cit., pp. 43–45.

24   Ibid., p. 45.

25   Joan Lindsay, *Time Without Clocks* (Melbourne, Cheshire, 1963), p. 205.

26   Saunders, op. cit., p. 12; W. J. Hudson, *Casey* (Melbourne, Oxford University Press, 1986), pp. 1–75 for his early life and career; W. J. Hudson, 'Casey, Richard Gavin Gardiner (Baron Casey) (1890–1976)', http://www.adb.online.anu.edu.au/biogs/A130426b.htm.

27   Langmore, *Glittering Surfaces*, op. cit., p. 38.

28   Ibid., p. 40.

29   Hudson, *Casey*, op. cit., p. 76.

30   Langmore, *Glittering Surfaces*, op. cit., pp. 47–49.

31   Fred Williams, 'Bell, George Frederick Henry (1878–1966)', http://www.adb.online.anu.edu.au/biogs/A070251b.htm.

32   Maie Casey, 'George Bell in Bourke Street' in *Art and Australia*, vol. 4, no. 2, 1966, p. 166.

33 Christie's sale of estate of Peter Purves Smith, http://www.christies. com/LotFinder/lot_details.aspx?intObjectID=4205918. The Caseys hung this painting in their home in Washington, along with Russell Drysdale, Rupert Bunny, George Bell, Peter Purves Smith and Mary Cecil Allen. For more details refer to Audrey Tate, *Fair Comment: The Life of Pat Jarrett 1911–1990* (Carlton, Melbourne University Press, 1996), p. 58.

34 Casey, *Tides and Eddies*, op. cit., p. 66.

35 Cited in Langmore, *Glittering Surfaces*, op. cit., p. 58.

36 Hudson, *Casey*, op. cit., pp. 105–108.

37 Audrey Tate, 'Jarrett, Patricia Irene Herschell (Pat) (1911–1990)', http://www.adb.online.anu.edu.au/biogs/A170591b.htm; Tate, *Fair Comment*, op. cit., pp. 58–9.

38 Ibid., pp. 57–60.

39 Ibid., p. 62.

40 Langmore, *Glittering Surfaces*, op. cit., pp. 73–74.

41 Kay Saunders, *Between the Covers: Revealing the State Library of Queensland's Collections* (Sydney, Focus Books, 2006), p. 82.

42 Hudson, *Casey*, op. cit., pp. 119–136.

43 Hudson, 'Casey, Richard', op. cit.

44 Cited in Langmore, *Glittering Surfaces*, op. cit., p. 90.

45 Hudson, *Casey*, op. cit., p. 145.

46 Tate, 'Jarrett, Patricia', op. cit.

47 Tate, *Fair Comment*, pp. 96–97.

48 Hudson, *Casey*, op. cit., pp. 167–170.

49 Langmore, *Glittering Surfaces*, op. cit., p. 126.

50 Grace Cochrane, *The Crafts Movement in Australia: A History* (Kensington, UNSW Press, 1992), pp. 83–86, 174–180; *Argus*, 17 January 1945; *The Age*, 17 August 1949.

51 Cochrane, ibid., p. 148.

52 Tate, 'Jarrett, Patricia', op. cit.

53 Maie Casey (editor and compiler), *Early Melbourne Architecture, 1840–1888* (Melbourne, Oxford University Press, 1953). The book was reissued twice more.

54 *Argus*, 24 October 1953.

55 Langmore, *Glittering Surfaces*, op. cit., pp. 130–131.

56 Maie Casey, *From the Night*, illustrated by Frances Burke (self published, n.d.). A copy is held in the Fryer Library, University of Queensland.

57 Tate, *Fair Comment*, op. cit., p. 160.

58 Langmore, *Glittering Surfaces*, op. cit., pp. 225–226; Pat's biographer, Audrey Tate, provides a different version of this decision,

saying it was amicable and does not comment on Richard's funeral;
refer to Tate, *Fair Comment*, op. cit., p. 160.

Chapter 11 Florence Broadhurst

1   *Sydney Morning Herald*, 1 April 1954.
2   Resolutions, in Notebook, n.d. (but an earlier version in her
    handwriting indicates she was about fifteen years old), in Florence
    Broadhurst papers, ML box 2, 4145/2.
3   Helen O'Neill, *Florence Broadhurst: Her Secrets and Extraordinary
    Lives* (Prahran, Hardie Grant Books, 2006), pp. 1–5; Siobhan
    O'Brien, *Life by Design: The Art and Lives of Florence Broadhurst*
    (Sydney, Allen & Unwin, 2004). Readers are advised to consult
    these two excellent books for more details on Florence's life. Her
    papers in the Mitchell Library (ML) are fascinating, as she kept a
    detailed record of her professional life. Even when issues show her
    to be deceitful and negligent in paying her bills she kept them for
    posterity. There is, however, little on her personal life.
4   Ibid., p. 5; Anne-Marie Van den Ven, 'Broadhurst, Florence Maud
    (1899–1977)', http://www.adb.online.anu.edu.au/biogs/AS10059b.
    htm?hilite=broadhurst; the Florence Broadhurst papers in the ML
    box 2, 4145/2 contain many clippings from this period.
5   Ibid., p. 5; *The Queenslander*, 19 November 1921.
6   See Winifred Ponder, *Clara Butt: Her Life Story* (London, George
    Harrap, 1928, reprinted 1978) for a comprehensive study of her
    remarkable career and life.
7   There are extensive newspaper clippings from the tour in her papers
    in the ML box 2; refer specifically to *The Eastern Mail*, Delhi (n.d.),
    Penang Gazette and Straits Chronicle (n.d.), *Malay Mail*, 17 February
    1923, *Bangkok Daily Mail*, 26 March 1923. All articles were
    enthusiastic about her talents.
8   O'Neill, op. cit., pp. 9–10.
9   Ibid., p. 15.
10 Ibid., pp. 15–18; Van den Ven, op. cit.
11 Van den Ven, op. cit.
12 Brochures of the Broadhurst Academy are contained in her papers,
    ML box 2, 4145/2, as well as newspaper coverage which highlighted
    the talents of the staff in each discipline.
13 O'Neill, op. cit., pp. 22–23; refer to extensive coverage of the events
    in China in the *Bundaberg Daily Mail*, 23 July 1927, contained in
    her papers, ML box 1, 4145/1.
14 An anonymous newspaper clipping proclaimed 'Queensland Actress
    Seriously Injured. Car Overturns', ibid.

15   Lindy Woodhead, *War Paint: Elizabeth Arden and Helena Rubinstein: Their Lives, Their Times, Their Rivalry* (London, Virago, 2004, first published 2003), pp. 83–84; Cecil Beaton, *The Glass of Fashion* (London, Weidenfeld & Nicholson, 1954), p. 32. Beaton is catty and snide about Lucile's clothes which he saw as far too feminine and flouncy. Her sister was Elinor Glyn the bestselling author.

16   Letter W. W. Reville-Terry to Florence Broadhurst, 24 January 1929. She worked on commission as indicated in this letter in her papers, ML box 1, 4145/1.

17   The letterhead of Mme Pellier states 'Design and Dress Consultant to Film and Stage', contained in Florence Broadhurst papers, ML box 1, 4145/1.

18   *Sydney Morning Herald*, 1 September 1936, an article by Mme Pellier on the subject of silk fabric; refer also to 'Tambour Beading Frame and Hook', http://www.powerhousemuseum.com/collection/database/?irn=9725.

19   O'Neill, op. cit., pp. 35–37; Van den Ven, op. cit. Cecil Beaton surveyed this world in depth in his memoir *The Glass of Fashion*. In his account it would be hard to ever imagine that two world wars and the Depression cut swathes through wider society outside this wealthy, often titled, enclave of privilege.

20   O'Neill, op. cit., p. 40.

21   Ibid., p. 58.

22   Letter Christina Duncan, Australia House, to Florence Broadhurst, 5 December 1945, in her papers in ML box 1, 4145/1.

23   Licence to operate Slow Passenger Boat is contained in her papers, ML box 1, 4145/1; Van den Ven, op. cit.

24   Finney's Catalogue of Exhibition, 13–24 July 1954, Broadhurst papers, ML box 3, 4145/3; *Canberra Times*, 6 September 1954.

25   O'Neill, op. cit., pp. 52–58.

26   There are numerous newspaper clippings in her papers in the ML stating she was English. The *Daily Telegraph*, 1 April 1954, described her as an English woman who discovered Australia.

27   *Sydney Morning Herald*, 18 May 1954; article by Andrea in *Truth*, n.d., contained in Florence Broadhurst papers, ML box 3.

28   Material is contained in the Florence Broadhurst papers ML, box 1, 4145/1. She organised the preview of Mme Lamotte's Winter Collection in Mrs George Falkiner's home in Bellevue Hill on 31 January 1968.

29   *Daily Telegraph*, 21 January 1958.

30   O'Neill, op. cit., p. 62.

31   *Sunday Mirror*, 28 June 1964, noted Florence was the set decorator; refer to her papers, ML box 3, 4145/3.

32   Van den Ven, op. cit.

33   O'Neill, op. cit., pp. 65–66. Some authors like Van den Ven and O'Brien write that she was married and divorced; O'Neill's research shows however that Broadhurst and Lewis were a de facto couple.

34   Palmer White, *Poiret* (London, Studio Vista, 1973), pp. 119–122. Poiret's business was far more comprehensive with rugs, carpets, furniture and fabrics.

35   O'Neill, op. cit., pp. 72–73.

36   Ibid., pp. 72–90; Van den Ven, op. cit.

37   Loan agreement between Florence Lewis [sic] and Hooker Finance, 17 August 1960, Florence Broadhurst papers, ML box 1, 4145/1.

38   Ibid.

39   Van den Ven, op. cit.; see also the numerous articles in Florence Broadhurst papers in ML box 1, 4145/1, for a fuller coverage.

40   Catriona Quinn, 'Best, Marion Esdale Hall (1905–1988)', http://www.adb.online.anu.edu.au/biogs/A170093b.htm; Penny Sparke, *Elsie de Wolfe: The Birth of Modern Interior Decoration* (London, Acanthus Press, 2005).

41   Letter Peter Hepham Clinic, London, to Florence Broadhurst, 2 May 1973, Florence Broadhurst papers, ML MSS box 3, 4145/3.

42   O'Brien, op. cit., pp. 204–208.

43   'Go with the Flo', *Sydney Morning Herald*, 10 November 2004.

44   O'Brien, op. cit., p. 15.

Chapter 12 Pamela Travers

1   Patricia Demers, 'P. L. Travers', *Dictionary of Literary Biography*, http://www.bookrags.com/biography/pamela-lyndon-travers-dlb; refer also to her biography, *P. L. Travers* (Boston, Twayne, 1991). Demers cites Travers' nationality as born in Australia; 'Pamela Lyndon Travers (1899–1996)' in Kay Saunders, *Queensland: 150 Years of Achievement* (Sydney, Focus Books, 2009), p. 176.

2   *Sydney Morning Herald*, 10 October 1940.

3   http://conservapedia.com/Mary_Poppins.

4   Valerie Lawson, *Out of the Sky She Came: The Life of P. L. Travers, Creator of Mary Poppins* (Sydney, Hodder, 1999), p. 191.

5   Cited in ibid., p. 18; refer also to P. L. Travers papers, Mitchell Library (ML), Sydney, ML MSS 5341/2: Personal Papers. Her papers constitute an extensive archive accessible now to researchers on microfilm.

6   Janet Graham, 'The Cup of Sorrow in Every Woman's Life', *Ladies' Home Journal*, vol. 84, no. 2, 1967, p. 68, cited in Demers, *P. L. Travers*, op. cit., p. 2.

7   Cited in Lawson, op. cit., p. 6.

8   Raymond Evans, *A History of Queensland* (Melbourne, Cambridge University Press, 2007), pp. 118–130; Kay Saunders, *Workers in Bondage: The Origins and Bases of Unfree Labour in Queensland, 1842–1916* (St Lucia, University of Queensland Press, 1982).

9   D. S. Macmillan, 'Morehead, Boyd Dunlop (1843–1905)', http://www.adb.online.anu.edu.au/biogs/A050327b.htm.

10   P. L. Travers, *New York Times* interview, 20 October 1962.

11   Jonathon Cott, *Pipers at the Gates of Dawn: The Wisdom of Children's Literature* (Sydney, Random House, 1983), pp. 215–216. Cott interviewed Travers for this publication.

12   Demers, *P. L. Travers*, op. cit., p. 7.

13   *Southern Highland News*, 17 July 2009.

14   Lawson, op. cit., p. 50.

15   P. L. Travers, interview with Michele Field, *Publishers Weekly*, 21 March 1986, p. 41.

16   Roy Norquist, *Conversations* (Chicago, Rand McNally, 1967), pp. 426–427. Pamela remarked to him that 'This was quite impossible in my kind of family at that time.'

17   Ibid., pp. 52–60.

18   *Sydney Morning Herald*, 26 November 1923.

19   P. L. Travers papers, ML MSS 5341/14: Poems 1920s.

20   Roger Osborne, 'Vance Palmer: Short Fiction and Magazine Culture in the 1920s', *Journal for the Study of Australian Literature*, vol. 6, 2007, pp. 49–56. This article provides a solid overview of publishing in Sydney in the 1920s.

21   For more details on this remarkable man refer to B. G. Andrews and Martha Rutledge, 'Morton, Frank (1869–1923)', http://www.adb.online.anu.edu.au/biogs/A100583b.htm.

22   L. R. McLennan, 'Our Writing Grows Virile', *Sydney Morning Herald*, 22 April 1939.The most comprehensive study of her poetry is contained in Demers' 1991 biography, especially chapter 2, 'Apprenticeship as a Poet'.

23   P. L. Travers papers, ML MSS 5341/18.

24   Lawson, op. cit., pp. 72–88.

25   P. L. Travers papers, box 2. She has several boxes devoted to his writings; refer to P. L. Travers papers, ML MSS 5341, add on 2130 1(2).

26 P. L. Travers papers, ML MSS 5341/22, item 21, interview with Janet Graham; 'Mary Poppins Chooses an Author', *Women's Mirror*, 19 June 1965, and *Saturday Evening Post*, November 1964.

27 P. L. Travers, 'On Not Writing for Children', *Bookbird: International Periodical on Literature for Children and Young People*, vol. 6, no. 4, 1968, contained in P. L. Travers papers, ibid., item no. 8.

28 Lawson, op. cit., pp. 90–93 has a good coverage of Mary's evolution.

29 P. L. Travers, writing from the Beverly Hills Hotel in 1961, reproduced in http://nationaltreasures.nla.gov.au/index/Treasures/item/nla.int-ex6-s28; material relating to Walt Disney MSS 5341/9. This includes letters from Julie Andrews.

30 P. L. Travers papers, ML MSS 5341/3 material relating to AE (George Russell) 1926–1982.

31 R. M. Kain and J. H. O'Brien, *George Russell (AE)* (Lewisburg, Pa., Bucknell University Press – Irish Writers Series, 1976).

32 *New York Times*, 15 February 1906, covered his resignation from *Punch* in some detail. He was an entry in the 1911 edition of the *Encyclopaedia Britannica*.

33 Review by Jason Blake, *Sydney Morning Herald*, 26 May 2009; see also Chelsea Cain, 'The Nanny Diarist', *New York Times*, 22 October 2006.

34 *Sydney Morning Herald*, 23 June 1934, noted her book *Moscow Excursion* (New York, Reynal & Hitchcock, 1934).

35 P. L. Travers papers, ML MSS 5341/3 material relating to AE (George Russell) 1926–1982 contains letters on her health.

36 C. Zilboorg, 'Orage, Alfred Richard (1873–1934)', http://www.oxforddnb.com/index/w101035322.

37 (Melbourne) *Argus*, 29 May 1937, review of Philip Mairet's biography of A. R. Orage (New York, University Books, c1966).

38 C. S. Nott, *Teachings of Gurdjieff: The Journal of a Pupil: An Account of Some Years with G. I. Gurdjieff and A. R. Orage* (London, Routledge & Kegan Paul, 1961).

39 P. L. Travers papers, ML MSS 5341/19, especially item 31.

40 Correspondence of Pamela Travers and Mary Shepard, Pamela Travers papers, ML MSS 5341/8.

41 Lawson, op. cit., pp. 161–163.

42 Ibid., pp. 173–175; P. L. Travers papers, ML MSS 5341/19 papers relating to Gurdjieff.

43 Lawson, op. cit., pp. 178–183.

44 Ibid., p. 200.

45 Radcliffe College presented Pamela with a beautifully bound album of photographs as a memento of her stay. These are kept in her extensive papers in the ML 5341: Add On 2130 2(3).

46   Lawson, op. cit., p. 307.
47   Ibid., p. 348.
48   Letter to Dr Staffan Bergsten, 24 January 1988, P. L. Travers papers,
     ML MSS 5341 Add On 2132 1 (2) item 1. This series contains all
     her correspondence with Bergsten.

Chapter 13 Enid, Countess of Kenmare
1   Caroline Simpson, 'Chisholm, Margaret Sheila Mackellar (1895–
     1969)', http://www.adb.online.anu.edu.au/biogs/A130464b.
     htm?hilite=chisholm.
2   Frank L.Woodhouse, 'Lindeman, Henry John (1811–1881)', http://
     www.adb.online.anu.edu.au/biogs/A050104b.htm?hilite=lindeman.
3   Pat Cavendish O'Neill, *A Lion in the Bedroom* (Sydney, Park Street
     Press, 2004).
4   *New York Times*, 20 October 1900.
5   Dominick Dunne, 'Memento Mori', *Vanity Fair*, March 1991, p. 169.
6   O'Neill, op. cit., pp. 18–20.
7   Dunne, op. cit.
8   O'Neill, op. cit., pp. 34–35.
9   Roderick Cameron, *My Travel's History* (London, Hamish Hamilton,
     1950), p. 207.
10   O'Neill, op. cit., p. 22.
11   James Fox, *White Mischief* (London, Vintage, 1998, first published
     1982), p. 60.
12   O'Neill, op. cit., p. 15.
13   Ibid., p. 21.
14   Gloria Vanderbilt and Lady Thelma Furness, *Double Exposure: A
     Twin Autobiography* (London, Frederick Muller, 1959), pp. 126,
     186–187.
15   Ibid., p. 174.
16   O'Neill, op. cit., pp. 38, 71–74.
17   Ibid., pp. 46, 69, 81.
18   Ibid., pp. 112–113.
19   Vanderbilt and Furness, op. cit., pp. 305–307.
20   *Argus, Sydney Morning Herald*, 18 July 1941.
21   *Sydney Morning Herald*, 16 July 1936. Her marriage to Viscount
     Furness was extensively covered in 1933.
22   Robert Calder, *Willie: The Life of W. Somerset Maugham* (New York,
     St Martin's Press, 1989), pp. 209, 284.
23   G. M. Thomson, *Lord Castlerosse: His Life and Times* (London,
     Weidenfeld & Nicholson, 1973) gives a full account of this
     remarkable man's life.

24   O'Neill, op. cit., pp. 141–161.

25   Ibid., p. 20.

26   Cited in Dunne, op. cit.

27   Cameron, op. cit., p. 220.

28   Martha Rutledge, 'Watt, Ernest Alexander Stuart (1874–1954)',
      htpp://www.adbonline.anu.edu.au/biogs/A120456b.htm.

29   Cameron, op. cit., pp. 3–10.

30   O'Neill, op. cit., p. 16.

31   Ibid., pp. 305–350.

Chapter 14 Tilly Devine

1   Phil Dickie, 'Brifman, Shirley Margaret (1935–1972)', http://www.
      adb.online.anu.edu.au/biogs/A130290b.htm; 'The Queen of the
      Cross', *Sixty Minutes*, 18 April 2010, produced by Sandra Cleary.

2   Joy Hooton, 'Ruth Park: A Celebration', http://www.nla.gov.au/
      friends/ruth/award.html; Bruce Moore, 'Niland, D'Arcy Francis
      (1917–1967)', http://www.adb.online.anu.edu.au/biogs/A150557b.
      htm.

3   See 'Fifty Australians – Tilly Devine', http://www.awm.gov.au/
      exhibitions/fiftyaustralians/15.asp; Australian Women's Register,
      http://www.womenaustralia.info/biogs/AWE2105b.htm.

4   Pauline Askin, 'Ruthless, Real: Sydney Showcases its
      Criminal Women', http://www.reuters.com/article/
      idUSTRES2G0W020090317.

5   Peter Ackroyd, *London: The Biography* (London, Chatto & Windus,
      2000), pp. 691–692.

6   Refer to the London School of Economics, Charles Booth Online
      Archives, 'Poverty Map of London' section for more information,
      http://www.lse.ac.uk.

7   Cited in Larry Writer, *Tilly Devine, Kate Leigh and the Razor Gangs*
      (Sydney, Macmillan, 2001), p. 19. This publication is an excellent
      reference for the larger story of these two women's careers in
      gangland.

8   Ibid., p. 22.

9   Ibid., pp. 22–25; Judith Allen, *Sex and Secrets: Crimes Involving
      Women* (Melbourne, Oxford University Press, 1990), p. 168.

10   Ibid., p. 26.

11   Allen, op. cit., p. 169.

12   Writer, op. cit., p. 29.

13   Lucy Hughes Turnbull, *Sydney: Biography of a City* (Sydney,
      Random House Australia, 1999), p. 352; there had been earlier
      reforms like the *Amended Vagrancy Act* of 1905, the *Gaming*

and Betting Act of 1906, the *Police Offenders Act* of 1908 and all
contributed to a rise in criminal networks that police could not
control or monitor. See also Alfred W. McCoy, 'Two Cities and
Their Syndicates: A Comparative Urban History of Organised
Crime' in Jim Davidson (ed.), *The Sydney – Melbourne Book* (Sydney,
Allen & Unwin, 1986), pp. 104–105; and his book *Drug Traffic:
Narcotics and Organised Crime in Australia* (Sydney, Harper & Row,
1980), chapters 1 and 2.

14 Judith Allen, 'Leigh, Kathleen Mary Josephine (Kate) (1881–1964)',
http://www.adb.online.anu.edu.au/biogs/A100063b.htm.

15 David Pennington, AC, 'The Need for a Rational Policy on Illicit
Drugs', http://museumvictoria.com.au/lectures/read/980602/
rational%20policy%20transcript%20140799x.pdf.

16 Writer, op. cit., pp. 30–31.

17 Allen, *Sex and Secrets*, op. cit., p. 170.

18 Ibid., p. 171.

19 *Truth*, 23 December 1927.

20 McCoy, op. cit., p. 107.

21 Ibid.; Allen, *Sex and Secrets*, op. cit., pp. 172–173.

22 Writer, op. cit., p. 95.

23 Ibid., p. 97; Jim Devine was charged with the murder of fellow
gangster Gregory Gaffney in August 1929. He was found not guilty
on the grounds of self defence and protecting the life of his wife and
the sanctity of his home.

24 Ibid., p. 98.

25 Ibid., pp. 113–114.

26 Allen, *Sex and Secrets*, op. cit., p. 173. Meagher came to
prominence when he defended George Dean who was convicted
of poisoning his wife in 1895; refer to Martha Rutledge, 'Dean,
George (1867–1933)', http://www.adb.online.anu.edu.au/biogs/
A080277b.htm. There was a royal commission conducted into the
case.

27 Writer, op. cit., pp. 154–159.

28 *Sydney Morning Herald*, 23 April 1931.

29 Cited in McCoy, op. cit., p. 107.

30 Writer, op. cit., pp. 199–201.

31 *Sydney Morning Herald*, 18 June 1943.

32 Ibid., 31 March 1943.

33 Writer, op. cit., pp. 260–261.

34 Ibid., pp. 255–257.

35 *Sydney Morning Herald*, 21 February 1945; (Melbourne) *Argus*, 31
March 1945.

36   Writer, op. cit., p. 267.
37   'Study in Scarlet: An Uncrowned Queen of Slumland Drips with Diamonds and Charity', *People*, 15 March 1950.
38   *Canberra Times*, 7 November 1951, and *Sydney Morning Herald*, 7 November 1951.
39   Writer, op. cit., pp. 300–303.
40   Ibid., p. 311.
41   McCoy, op. cit., p. 112.
42   Judith Allen and Baiba Irving, 'Devine, Matilda Mary (Tilly) (1900–1970)', http://www.adb.online.anu.edu.au/biogs/ A080318b.htm.
43   Writer, op. cit., pp. 329–330.
44   Ibid., p. 332.

Chapter 15 Sunday Reed

1   J. R. Poynter, 'Baillieu, William Lawrence (1859–1936)', http:// www.adb.online.anu.edu.au/biogs/A070145b.htm.
2   Janine Burke, *The Heart Garden: Sunday Reed and Heide* (Sydney, Knopf, 2004), p. 13.
3   Paul de Serville, *Pounds and Pedigrees: The Upper Class in Victoria 1850–80* (Melbourne, Oxford University Press, 1991), pp. 269, 289, 304–305.
4   Burke, op. cit., p. 12.
5   E. M. Robbe, *Early History of Toorak and District* (Melbourne, Robertson & Muller, 1934).
6   http://www.stcatherines.net.au/110-years.
7   Burke, op. cit., p. 29.
8   Ann E. Galbally, 'Streeton, Arthur Ernest (1867–1943)', http:// www.adb.online.anu.edu.au/biogs/A120137b.htm; see Ann E. Galbally, *Arthur Streeton* (Melbourne, Landsdowne, 1973, revised edn) for more details.
9   Burke, op. cit., pp. 32–34.
10   J. P. Wearing (ed.), *Bernard Shaw and Nancy Astor* (Toronto, University of Toronto Press, 2005).
11   Burke, op. cit., pp. 41–42.
12   Ibid., p. 48.
13   Ibid., p. 51.
14   Frank Cusack, 'Agnes Goodsir', http://www.daao.org.au/main/ read/2836. Goodsir painted portraits of Tolstoy, Mussolini and Bertrand Russell.
15   Sally O'Neill, 'Nolan, Violet Cynthia (1908–1976)', http://www. adb.online.anu.edu.au/biogs/A150566b.htm.

16 Christine France, 'Alleyne Clarice Zander', http://www.daao.org.au/
main/read/6798. She was later Will Dyson's long-term lover after her
husband's death from injuries sustained in World War I.
17 Burke, op. cit., p. 91.
18 Ibid., pp. 94–95.
19 Gavin Fry, 'Lawlor, Adrian (1889–1969)', http://www.adb.online.
anu.edu.au/biogs/A100010b.htm. Lawlor was later appointed the
art critic for the Melbourne *Sun* and *Art in Australia* after a bushfire
destroyed his home and his collection in 1939.
20 Daniel Mandel, 'Atyeo, Samuel Laurence (Sam) (1910–1990)',
http://www.adb.online.anu.edu.au/biogs/A170039b.htm. Cynthia,
who did not enjoy an allowance from the stern Henry Reed, first
worked for Ward before establishing her own business. Refer to
O'Neill, op. cit.
21 Juliet Peers, 'Dyring, Moya Claire (1909–1967)', http://www.adb.
online.anu.edu.au/biogs/A140076b.htm. She married Sam Atyeo
in 1941.
22 R. Dedman, 'Shore, Arnold Joseph Victor (1897–1963)', http://
www.adb.online.anu.edu.au/biogs/A110617b.htm. John Reed in his
interesting assessment, 'Artobiography', published in *Overland*, no.
101, 1985, wrote enthusiastically about the influence of George Bell
and the original Contemporary Arts Society.
23 Mary Eagle and Jan Minchin, *The George Bell School: Students,
Friends, Influences* (Melbourne, Deutscher Art, Sydney, Resolution
Press, c. 1981), p. 174; M. E. Eagle, 'Purves Smith, Charles Roderick
(1912–1949)', http://www.adb.online.anu.edu.au/biogs/A110322b.
htm.
24 Refer to Richard Haese, *Rebels and Precursors: The Revolutionary Years
of Australian Art* (Ringwood, Penguin, 1991).
25 Burke, op. cit., p. 133.
26 Ibid., chapter 6 for more details; refer also to Brian Adams, *Such is
Life: A Biography of Sidney Nolan* (Sydney, Vintage, 1989), pp. 38–39.
27 Poynter, op. cit.
28 Adams, op. cit., p. 37.
29 Reed, 'Artobiography', op. cit., p. 58. This is an invaluable article
with a firsthand perspective on the creativity in art in the 1930s and
1940s.
30 Letters Sidney Nolan to Sunday Reed, September 1942, 8 November
1942, 29 March 1943, 2 August 1943, contained in Nancy
Underhill (ed.), *Nolan on Nolan. Sidney Nolan in His Own Words*
(Ringwood, Viking, 2007), pp. 113, 122–126.
31 Adams, op. cit., p. 88.

32   Reed, op. cit., p. 60.

33   Ibid., pp. 40–46; Susan Wyndham, 'Was Sunday Reed the Hidden Hand behind Sidney Nolan?', *The Age*, 2 October 2004.

34   Janine Burke, 'Hester, Joy St Clair (1920–1960)', http://www.adb. online.anu.edu.au/biogs/A140509b.htm.

35   Burke, *The Heart Garden*, op. cit., p. 239. Her brother, Everard, inherited the property.

36   Michael Heyward, *The Ern Malley Affair* (London, Faber & Faber, 1993); Adams, op. cit., pp. 75–80; letter John Reed to Max Harris, 25 February 1941, proposing the establishment of *Angry Penguins* in Barrett Reid and Nancy Underhill (eds), *Letters of John Reed: Defining Australian Cultural Life, 1920–1981* (Ringwood, Viking, 2001), pp. 200–201; letter John Reed to Max Harris, 30 March 1943, pp. 207–208; letter 21 June 1944 referred to the concoction of the poems, p. 325.

37   Cited in Burke, *The Heart Garden*, op. cit., p. 256.

38   In a letter to Joy Hester in December 1947, Sunday wrote casually, '[D]id you hear from Nolan?' In January 1948 Joy reported that 'Nolan seems to love Sydney and says she must have been blind when he was here before …' Janine Burke (ed.), *Dear Sun: The Letters of Joy Hester to Sunday Reed* (Melbourne, William Heinemann Australia, 1995), pp. 134, 143.

39   Ibid., p. 143.

40   'Joy Hester and Friends' exhibition in the National Gallery of Australia, 2001, http://www.nga.gov.au/Hester.

41   Adams, op. cit., p. 233; Andrew Sayers, *The Oxford History of Australian Art* (Melbourne, Oxford University Press, 2001), p. 164.

42   Burke, *The Heart Garden*, op. cit., p. 299; Reid and Underhill, op. cit., pp. 461–464.

43   Letters John Reed to Albert Tucker, 23 July 1953, 9 December 1954, 15 March 1956, in Reid and Underhill, op. cit., pp. 487–492, 501–504, 507–510.

44   Letter John Reed to Hugh Montgomery (Master at Timbertop, Geelong Grammar School), 28 June 1960, ibid., p. 534; Burke, *The Heart Garden*, op. cit., pp. 317–320.

45   Reid and Underhill, op. cit., pp. 3, 17–19, 462.

46   Letter John Reed to Michael Sharland, December 1956, ibid., p. 514.

47   Burke, *The Heart Garden*, op. cit., pp. 340–344; Reid and Underhill, op. cit., pp. 12–18, 512–513, 528–533.

48   Letter John Reed to Editor, *Herald*, 1 July 1959, Reid and Underhill, op. cit., pp. 528–529.

49   Burke, *The Heart Garden*, op. cit., p. 351, quoting an interview with Barrett Reid.
50   Letters John Reed to Pamela Warrender, June 1964 and John Reed to Sidney Nolan, 12 October 1964, in Reid and Underhill, op. cit., pp. 600–602, 616–619.
51   Burke, *The Heart Garden*, op. cit., p. 357.
52   Letter John Reed to Elwyn Lynn, 21 August 1965, in Reid and Underhill, op. cit., pp. 650–651. This letter outlines John's grievances on the matter.
53   Burke, *The Heart Garden*, op. cit., pp. 378–380.
54   Cited in ibid., p. 404.
55   Letter John Reed to James Mollinson, Director of the NGA, 27 January 1972, in Reid and Underhill, op. cit., p. 765.
56   Reid and Underhill, op. cit., p. 681. Mary Boyd married Perceval at the age of fifteen.
57   Burke, *The Heart Garden*, op. cit., pp. 419–420.
58   Letter John Reed to Mary Christina Sewell, 27 August 1979, in Reid and Underhill, op. cit., pp. 850–855.
59   Letter John Reed to Mary Christina Sewell, 4 December 1981, in Reid and Underhill, op. cit., pp. 869–870.

Chapter 16 Rosaleen Norton

1   Nevill Drury, *Pan's Daughter: The Magical World of Rosaleen Norton* (Mandrake of Oxford, 1993, first published 1988), p. x. This volume is the most comprehensive assessment of Norton's life and career.
2   This 1949 psychological profile of Rosaleen is quoted in ibid., p. 5.
3   Rosaleen Norton, 'I Was Born a Witch', in *Australasian Post*, 3 January 1957.
4   Drury, op. cit., p. 11.
5   Ibid., p. 47.
6   Noel S. Hutchinson, 'Hoff, George Rayner (1894–1937)', http://www.adb.online.anu.edu.au/biogs/A090329b.htm; see also Earl of Beauchamp et al, *Sculpture of Rayner Hoff* (Sydney, Sunnyside Press, 1934).
7   George Blaikie, *Remember Smith's Weekly* (London, Angus & Robertson, 1967), p. 88.
8   Kay Saunders, *Queensland: 150 Years of Achievement* (Sydney, Focus Books, 2009), p. 41, entry on Jim Case and Mollie Horseman.
9   *Sydney Gazette and NSW Advertiser*, 5 July 1842. The inn was already remarkable by this early date.
10   Lindl Lawton, 'Conrad in Australia', *Signals*, no. 81, December 2007–January 2008, pp. 11–12.

11 Drury, op. cit., p. 17.
12 Leon Batt, *Not for Fools* (Sydney, W. Farrell, 1945).
13 Martha Rutledge, 'Deamer, Mary Elizabeth Kathleen Dulcie
    (1890–1972)', http://www.adb.online.anu.edu.au/biogs/A080276b.
    htm; Stuart Inder, 'Farwell, George Michell (1911–1976)', http://
    www.adb.online.anu.edu.au/biogs/A140153b.htm; Philip Butterss,
    'Mudie, Ian Mayleston (1911–1976)', http://www.adb.online.anu.
    edu.au/biogs/A150504b.htm.
14 Rosaleen Norton and Gavin Greenlees, *The Art of Rosaleen Norton*
    (Sydney, Walter Glover, 1952). A supplement was issued in 1984.
15 Marion Dixon, 'McCrae, William Alexander (1904–1973)', http://
    www.adb.online.anu.edu.au/biogs/A150326b.htm.
16 Jemma Montagu, *The Surrealists: Revolutionaries in Art and Writing*
    (London, Tate Publications, 2002), p. 15.
17 Interview between Professor L. J. Murphy and Rosaleen Norton, 27
    August 1949, cited in Drury, op. cit., p. 30.
18 S. L. Cranston, *Helena Petrovna Blavatsky: The Extraordinary Life and
    Influence of Helena Blavatsky, the Founder of the Modern Theosophy
    Movement* (New York, Putnam, 1994).
19 A. J. Gabay, *Messages from Beyond: Spiritualism and Spiritualists in
    Melbourne's Golden Age, 1870–1890* (Carlton, Melbourne University
    Press, 2001).
20 Jill Roe, *Beyond Belief: Theosophy in Australia* (Kensington, UNSW
    Press, 1986).
21 Refer to Margaret Drabble (ed.), *The Oxford Companion to English
    Literature* (New York, Oxford University Press, 2000), p. 147.
22 Nevill Drury, *Dictionary of Mysticism and the Esoteric Traditions*
    (Bridgeport, Prism Unity, 1992).
23 Alan Richardson, *The Magical Life of Dion Fortune* (Aquarian Press,
    1991).
24 See Mary K. Greer, *Women of the Golden Dawn: Rebels and Priestesses*
    (Rochester, VT, Park Street Press, 1995, first published 1985) for
    more details.
25 John Symonds, *The Great Beast: The Life of Aleister Crowley* (London,
    Rider, 1951).
26 P. R. Stephensen (with new introduction by Stephen J. King),
    The Legend of Aleister Crowley (Enmore, Helios Books, 2007, first
    published 1935). Biographer Nevill Drury believes that Rosaleen was
    particularly influenced by Fortune and Crowley, as these were the
    works available before the *Witchcraft Act* was repealed in the UK in
    1951. Drury, *Pan's Daughter*, op. cit., p. 137.
27 Drury, *Pan's Daughter*, op. cit., pp. 38–47.

28   Rutledge, op. cit.
29   Mary Eagle, 'Dobell, Sir William (1899–1970)', http://www.adb.
      online.anu.edu.au/biogs/A140013b.htm; Jan Roberts, 'Latour,
      Loma Kyle (1902–1964)', http://www.adb.online.anu.edu.au/biogs/
      A150077b.htm.
30   Drury, *Pan's Daughter*, op. cit., p. 54; refer also to *The Art of Rosaleen
      Norton* (introduced by Nevill Drury), (Sydney, Walter Glover, 1952,
      1982 edn), pp. 9–11.
31   Drury, *Pan's Daughter*, op. cit., pp. 55–70.
32   Ibid., pp. 81–83.
33   *Daily Telegraph*, 7 October 1955.
34   Drury, *Pan's Daughter*, op. cit., p. 87.
35   David Salter, 'Goossens, Sir Eugene Aynsley (1893–1962)', http://
      www.adb.online.anu.edu.au/biogs/A140334b.htm.
36   *The Times*, 14 June 1962.
37   Gary R. Thomson, *Great Short Works of Edgar Allan Poe* (Sydney,
      HarperCollins Australia, 2004) for more details.
38   Drury, *Pan's Daughter*, op. cit., p. 86.
39   Gavin Greenlees reported this to Nevill Drury, in ibid.
40   Drury, *Pan's Daughter*, op. cit., p. 88.
41   Rosaleen Norton, 'Witches Want No Recruits', *Australasian Post*, 10
      January 1957.
42   Drury, *Pan's Daughter*, op. cit., p. 94.
43   Ibid.
44   Ibid., p. 96.
45   *Sunday Mirror*, 17 August 1975.
46   Drury, *Pan's Daughter*, op. cit., pp. 102–108.

Chapter 17 Charmian Clift

1   Alan Atkinson, *The Europeans in Australia: A History: Volume Two:
      Democracy* (Melbourne, Oxford University Press, 2004), pp. 210–212,
      304–5.
2   Nadia Wheatley, *The Life and Myth of Charmian Clift* (Sydney,
      Flamingo, 2001), p. 14. This is by far the most comprehensive
      account of Charmian Clift's life.
3   Ibid., pp. 23–34.
4   Charmian Clift, 'Portrait of My Mother' in George Johnston, *The
      World of Charmian Clift* (Sydney, Ure Smith, 1970), pp. 80–81.
5   Ibid., p. 32.
6   Ibid., p. 85.
7   Charmian Clift, *Mermaid Singing* (London, Michael Joseph, 1958,
      first published 1956), p. 75.

8   Nadia Wheatley, 'Clift, Charmian (1923-1969)', http://www.adb.
        online.anu.edu.au/biogs/A130488b.htm.

9   Wheatley, *The Life and Myth of Charmian Clift*, op. cit., pp. 106–
        107.

10   Ruth Park, 'Nothing but Writers', *Independent Monthly*, September
        1989, included in Donna Rath papers, ML MSS 6498/2.

11   Alan Ashbolt cited in Johnston, *The World of Charmian Clift*, op.
        cit., p. 9. The original is in *Sydney Morning Herald*, 12 July 1969.

12   Martha Rutledge, 'Martin, David Nathaniel (1898–1958),' http://
        www.adb.online.anu.edu.au/biogs/A150372b.htm.

13   Wheatley, *The Life and Myth of Charmian Clift*, op. cit., pp. 130–
        133.

14   Suzanne Chick, *Searching for Charmian: The Daughter that Charmian
        Clift Gave Away* (Sydney, Macmillan, 1994).

15   Wheatley, *The Life and Myth of Charmian Clift*, op. cit., p. 153.

16   Ibid., p. 155; it was republished in Connie Burns and Marygai
        McNamara (eds.), *Feeling Restless: Australian Women's Short Stories,
        1940–1969* (Sydney, Collins, 1989).

17   Charmian Clift, 'Betrothing a Daughter' in Johnston, *The World of
        Charmian Clift*, op. cit., p. 78.

18   Garry Kinnane, 'Johnston, George Henry (1912–1970)', http://
        www.adb.online.anu.edu.au/biogs/A140655b.htm. Kinnane is the
        author of an authoritative biography of Johnston published in 1986,
        George Johnston: A Biography (Melbourne, Nelson, 1986).

19   Cited in Wheatley, *The Life and Myth of Charmian Clift*, op. cit.,
        p. 190.

20   Cited in Park, op. cit.

21   This is taken from the manuscript of the novel and cited in
        Wheatley, *The Life and Myth of Charmian Clift*, op. cit., p. 199.
        Underlining in the original document.

22   Kinnane, 'Johnston, George Henry', op. cit.

23   Ibid; Wheatley, 'Clift, Charmian', op. cit.

24   Cited in Wheatley, *The Life and Myth of Charmian Clift*, op. cit.,
        p. 212.

25   Park, op. cit.

26   Bruce Moore, 'Niland, D'Arcy Francis (1917–1967)', http://www.
        adb.online.anu.edu.au/biogs/A150557b.htm.

27   Refer to Kinnane, *George Johnston*, op. cit., for this issue from
        Johnston's point of view.

28   Wheatley, *The Life and Myth of Charmian Clift*, op. cit., pp. 275–
        288.

29   Ibid., p. 379.

30 Max Brown, *Charmian and George: The Marriage of George Johnston and Charmian Clift* (Dural, Rosenberg, 2004), p. 89.

31 Valerie Lawson, 'A Place in Mind', *Sydney Morning Herald*, 4 May 1991.

32 Kinnane, 'Johnston, George Henry', op. cit.

33 Wheatley, *The Life and Myth of Charmian Clift*, op. cit., pp. 420–423.

34 John Hetherington, 'An Australian Author Returns to His Native Land', *The Age*, 8 February 1964.

35 Brown, op. cit., p. 215.

36 George Johnston, *The World of Charmian Clift*, op. cit., p. 10. When I occasionally read her columns as a young woman working in the Department of the Army in Canberra in the mid 1960s, I entered an adult world that Charmian helped explain.

37 Park, op. cit.

38 Charmian Clift, 'My Husband George', *Pol*, no. 9, 1968, p. 85, contained in Rath papers, ML. *Pol* was a racy women's magazine edited by Richard Walsh that addressed important issues just before the resurgence of feminism. It was my secular bible for the new ways of thinking and living in the late 1960s.

39 Brown, op. cit., pp. 196–197.

40 Kinnane, 'Johnston, George Henry', op. cit.

41 Chick, op. cit., pp. 329, 341.

42 Wheatley, 'Clift, Charmian', op. cit.

43 Charmian Clift, 'My Husband George', op. cit.

44 Gary Kinnane believes that Charmian did not read the manuscript. He is at pains to show how Johnston gave a positive account of Cressida's doings. Kinnane, *George Johnston*, op. cit., p. 273.

45 Wheatley, *The Life and Myth of Charmian Clift*, op. cit., p. 616.

Chapter 18 Lillian Roxon

1 Lillian Roxon later stated that 'Germaine Greer and her double-edged dedication changed my life and is she proud of herself? She's braver, crueller and bawdier than I'll ever be, also more generous and patient,' cited in Anne Coombs, *Sex and Anarchy: The Life and Death of the Sydney Push* (Ringwood, Viking, 1996), p. 218.

2 Jim Derogatis, *Let it Blurt: The Life and Times of Lester Bangs, America's Greatest Rock Critic* (New York, Broadway Books, 2000).

3 Yvonne Sewall-Ruskin, *High on Rebellion: The Underground at Max's Kansas City* (New York, Thunder's Mouth Press, 1998).

4 Robert Milliken, *Lillian Roxon: Mother of Rock* (New York, Thunder's Mouth Press, 2005, first published 2002), pp. 13–17.

5   Libby Connors, Lynette Finch, Kay Saunders and Helen Taylor,
        Australia's Frontline (St Lucia, University of Queensland Press, 1993).
6   Milliken, op. cit., p. 29.
7   See Barbara Blackman, *Glass After Glass* (Ringwood, Penguin Books,
        1997); Kay Saunders, *Queensland: 150 Years of Achievement* (Sydney,
        Focus Books, 2009), p. 177; Patrick Buckridge and Belinda McKay
        (eds.), *By the Book: The Literary History of Queensland* (St Lucia,
        University of Queensland Press, 2007), pp. 60, 80; Charles Osborne,
        Giving It Away (London, Secker & Warburg, 1986).
8   Milliken, op. cit., pp. 31–33.
9   Clive Moore, *Sunshine and Rainbows: The Development of Gay and
        Lesbian Culture in Queensland* (St Lucia, University of Queensland
        Press, 2001), pp. 121–133.
10   Milliken, op. cit., pp. 38–39.
11   Coombs, op. cit., p. 26.
12   See James Franklin, *Corrupting the Youth: A History of Philosophy in
        Australia* (Sydney, Macleay Press, 2003), chapters 2 and 8.
13   Cameron Hazlehurst, 'Bogle, Gilbert Stanley (1924–1963)', http://
        www.adb.online.anu.edu.au/biogs/A130243b.htm; refer also to the
        section in Coombs, op. cit., for more details, pp. 162–164.
14   Coombs, op. cit., for more details.
15   Cited in Coombs, op. cit., pp. 202–203; see also Milliken, op. cit.,
        pp. 53–55.
16   Cited in Milliken, op. cit., p. 70; refer also to other assessments.
        Gerard Henderson, 'Left Right out of the Radical Push', *Sydney
        Morning Herald*, 4 June 1996, and Judith White, 'The Push for
        Freedom', *Sun-Herald*, 2 June 1996.
17   Letter Lillian Roxon to Aviva Layton, circa 1959, Aviva Layton
        papers, ML MSS 7869. Apart from the Layton papers, Roxon's
        archive in the ML is on closed access. My attempts to gain access
        during my research trip there in May 2010 were unsuccessful.
18   This novel is contained in Lillian Roxon's extensive papers in the
        Mitchell Library, Sydney.
19   Robert Milliken, 'Roxon, Lillian (1932–1973)', http://www.adb.
        online.anu.edu.au/biogs/A160169b.htm; Barbara Lemon, 'Lillian
        Roxon', http://www.womenaustralia.info/exhib/cal/roxon.html.
20   Coombs, op. cit., p. 73.
21   Papers of George Clarke, 1932–2005, are contained in the Mitchell
        Library, Sydney. He was one of the authors of the City of Sydney Plan.
22   Kay Saunders and Julie Ustinoff interviewed his sister, Milly
        Goldman, in July 2004, researching a book on the Miss Australia
        Quest. Mrs Goldman spoke at length about her brother and his

tragic early death. She and her husband, Dr David Goldman, named one of their sons in his honour. The family was from Lithuania and fled persecution as Jews in 1939. Like many other Jewish refugees they were well-educated professionals. He studied at the University of Queensland where he was editor of the student magazine, *Semper Floreat*. He later worked for the *Courier-Mail*.

23   Milliken, *Lillian Roxon*, op. cit., p. 73.
24   Donald Horne, *Portrait of an Optimist* (Ringwood, Penguin Books, 1988).
25   Milliken, *Lillian Roxon*, op. cit., p. 89.
26   Ibid., p. 108.
27   Milly Goldman interview with Kay Saunders and Julie Ustinoff.
28   Letter Lillian Roxon to Aviva Layton, 27 May 1965, Layton papers, ML MSS 7869.
29   Letter Lillian Roxon to Aviva Layton, May 1966, Layton papers.
30   Danny Fields, *Linda McCartney: A Biography* (Los Angeles, Renaissance Books, 2000), p. 11.
31   http://www.sfmuseum.org/hist6/lindabio.html.
32   Fields, op. cit., pp. 6, 11, 78.
33   Glenn A. Baker, 'Easybeats', http://nla.gov.au/nla.cs-ma-NAMO-3422.
34   *Sydney Morning Herald*, 4 March 1967.
35   Cited in Milliken, *Lillian Roxon*, op. cit., pp. 147–148.
36   Lillian Roxon, 'Will Success Spoil Lillian Roxon?', *Quadrant*, January–February 1971, p. 60.
37   Tony Weinburger, *The Max's Kansas City Stories* (New York, Bobbs-Merrill, 1971).
38   Roxon, op. cit., p. 61.
39   M. J. Taylor (ed.), *The Downtown Book: The New York Art Scene, 1974–84* (Princeton, Princeton University Press, 2006), p. 43.
40   Steve Watson, *Factory Made: Warhol and the Sixties* (New York, Pantheon Books, 2003), p. 206; refer also to Wayne Koestenbaum, *Andy Warhol* (London, Phoenix Books, 2001).
41   Fields, op. cit., pp. 78–96.
42   http://www.economicexpert.com/a/Paul:McCartney:and:Wings. htm; *Sunday News*, 22 April 1973. I happened to see Wings on their Australian tour and concur with Roxon. The band was ill-assorted and Linda McCartney was not a musician but a strange figure that appeared uncomfortable on stage.
43   Fields, op. cit., p. 171.
44   Ibid., p. 172.
45   Milliken, *Lillian Roxon*, op. cit., p. 179.

46   Lillian Roxon, 'The Other Germaine Greer: A Manicured Hand on the Zipper', *Crawdaddy*, 4 July 1971.

47   Lillian Roxon, *Woman's Day*, May 1971, cited in Milliken, *Lillian Roxon*, pp. 184–185.

48   Cited in Milliken, *Lillian Roxon*, op. cit., p. 191.

49   Ibid., p. 166.

50   Ibid., p. 171.

51   Roxon, 'Will Success Spoil Lillian Roxon?', op. cit., p. 63.

52   Saunders, op. cit., p. 7.

53   *Sydney Morning Herald*, 4 October 1970.

54   Cited in Watson, op. cit., p. 152.

55   Undated letter circa 1971 to Aviva Layton, Layton papers, op. cit.

56   Cited in Milliken, *Lillian Roxon*, op. cit., p. 206.

57   Ibid., p. 207.

58   Ibid., p. 216.

59   Ibid., p. 217.

60   Ibid., pp. 220–221.

61   Ibid., pp. 221–222.

62   Fields, op. cit., pp. 172–173.

Acknowledgments

All too often the people who get your manuscript to a beautiful book on the bookstore shelves are a small afterthought in acknowledgments. At HarperCollins all the team offered me warm support as well as invaluable and spirited guidance.

I should like to thank all those librarians who assisted me in my intense labours to bring my twenty 'bad girls' to life – most notably Dr Jeff Rickert at the Fryer Library at the University of Queensland (UQ) and Trudy Johnston and Diane Byrne at the John Oxley Library in Brisbane. The librarians at the Mitchell Library, State Library of New South Wales assisted me with all the collections I read and aided with illustrations. Rebecca Carter, the Document Delivery Librarian at UQ helped me track down rare books, articles and pamphlets. Once on the hunt nothing deterred her mission to get those items to me as quickly as possible. I simply could not have written the book without her help. No challenge was too much for her, indeed she welcomed it.

Mark McGuiness, historian and obituarist, made many welcome suggestions and once again rendered generous support. Shirleene Robinson, with whom I have written more academic work, also read drafts and provided invaluable comments.

Carol Brill, a direct descendant of the Cockerell family in Hobart Town, allowed me access to records and her own work, engaging in an active conversation about the history of Van Diemen's Land and Mary Cockerill in particular. Her generosity is much appreciated.

Barbara Tucker kindly allowed me access to photographs in the Albert Tucker Collection. Her insights into the Heide groups were fascinating.

No doubt all my friends are very pleased to hear of something else apart from Sir Samuel Griffith and his achievements (another recent project). My Zonta group hosted a lunch where a selection of entries had their first public run. In particular thanks to Susan Davies, Rhonda Irwin-Davison, Barbara Kent, Julie Mannion, Iris Scott, Allison Williams and Jennifer West, along with Christina Coles, Bruce Hawker, Tess Livingstone, Andra Muller, Anthe Philippides, Janet Prowse and Lesley Synge, who regularly heard dispatches from the war room of research.

Lastly and most importantly to Donald James, my heart's delight, who supported and encouraged me even though enduring a life-threatening illness and severe pain. He has never wavered as my number one cheer leader and inspiration. When things got tough, he always says, 'You can do it, Kitty.' And so I do.

Index

Ackerman, Richard 22
Adolfi, G. 171
Ahern, Lizzie 146
Allen, William 18, 21, 24, 26
Amadio, Nadine 279, 281
Anderson, Margaret 227
Archdale, Alec 144
Archdale, Betty 144
Arden, Elizabeth (Florence
    Nightingale Graham) 131,136
Arthur, Governor George 44–45
Ashbolt, Alan 305
Asquith, Margot 127
Astley, Thea 322
Astor, Nancy 270
Atyeo, Sam 273, 276
Ayer, Harriet Hubbard 125

Baillieu, Arthur Sydney 267, 272,
    277
Baillieu, Clive 275
Baillieu, Darren 268
Baillieu, Everard 268
Baillieu, Jack 'King' 268, 270
Baillieu, James 266–267
Baillieu, Lambert 266
Baillieu, Lelda Sunday see Reed,
    Sunday
Baillieu, William 267–268, 275

Baillieux, Etienne 266
Baines, Jennie 148
Baker, Frank 160
Baker, Snowy 160
Bangs, Lester 320, 322
Bara, Theda 134
Barker, Kate 'Ma' 251
Baron, Reverend 23, 26
Barrow, Clyde 251
Barton, Charlotte 67
Baruch, Bernard 235
Bates, Daisy 192, 247
Batt, Leon 288
Baxter, John 52, 53, 57, 58, 61,
    63–64, 66
Beardsley, Aubrey 291
Beaton, Cecil 187, 188
Beckmann, Lola 125
Beckmann, Rosalie Silberfeld 119
Beecham, Sir Thomas 297
Bell, Captain 15
Bell, George 184, 190, 273
Bentham, Jeremy 140
Bergsten, Staffan 231
Berkeley, Busby 176
Berry, Graham 114
Best, Marion 210
Biegler, Ruth 328
Black Mary see Cockerill, Mary

Blackman, Barbara (née Patterson) 49, 279, 322, 324

Blackman, Charles 266, 279, 281

Blavatsky, Madame Helena 224, 290

Bligh, Captain William 16, 18, 19, 23–24

Bond, David 209

Boothman, Cecily (née Norton) 286, 299

Borg, Joe 265

Boswell, David 22

Boswell, James 6, 7, 18, 22–26

Boyd, Arthur 277, 279, 281, 300

Breitman, Rosa 321, 327

Brenon, Herbert 169

Breton, André 289

Brifman, Shirley 252

Broad Bryant, Mary see Bryant, Mary

Broad, Dolly 7, 25

Broad, Grace 6

Broad, Mary see Bryant, Mary

Broad, William 6, 7, 25

Broadhurst, Florence Maud 2, 190, 194–212

Broadhurst, Margaret (née Crawford) 195

Broadhurst, William 195

Brodzky, Maurice 126

Brown, Charles 53, 57, 60, 61–62

Bruce, Stanley, Prime Minister 151, 183, 185, 191

Bruhn, Norman 257

Brussels, Madame, see Hodgson, Caroline

Bryant, Charlotte (Charlotte Spence) 11, 14, 20, 21

Bryant, Emanuel 15, 21

Bryant, Mary (née Broad) 1, 5–27

Bryant, William 1, 11–20, 23

Bulwer-Lytton, Sir Edward 290

Burke, Frances 190, 191

Burnand, Madge 222–223, 224, 226, 227–228

Burnand, Sir Francis 222

Burr, Reverend Charles Chauncey 88

Burton, Richard 327

Burton, Sybil 327

Butchulla people 54–63

Butcher, John, Samuel Broom 18, 21, 24, 26

Butt, Dame Clara 196

Cameron, Didy 315

Cameron, Peter 315

Cameron, Roderick 'Rory' 235, 237, 247, 248

Cameron, Roderick Jr 235, 248

Cameron, Sir Roderick 234–235

Campbell, Archibald 35

Carey, Robert 53, 56, 63

Carlisle, Richard 37

Caruso, Enrico 172

Casanova, Giacomo 21–22, 105, 321

Casey, Donn 183, 189

Casey, Jane 183, 189, 193

Casey, Lady Maie 'the Lady Casey' (née Ethel Marion Sumner Ryan) 178–193, 269, 273, 274

Casey, Lord Richard, Baron of
Berwick and Westminster 178,
183–193
Castel, Mr 25
Castlerosse, Enid, Countess of
Kenmare see Lindeman, Enid
Castlerosse, Gerald, Earl of
Kenmare 246
Castlerosse, Valentine, Earl of
Kenmare 245–246
Cavendish, Brigadier General
Frederick 'Caviar' 236–238,
239, 241
Cavendish, Frederick Caryll 238,
241, 247, 249
Cavendish, Georgiana, Duchess of
Devonshire 236
Cavendish, Richard 236
Cavendish O'Neill, Pat 234,
238–239, 241, 246, 247, 248,
249
Cavill, Percy 160
Cescu, Baroness Isa 164
Chamberlain, Neville, Prime
Minister 185
Chaminade, Cecile 159
Chanel, Gabrielle 'Coco' 118,
133, 134, 157, 201, 244, 270
Chaplin, Charlie 168, 174
Charbonnet, Alice 158–159, 161,
162
Charbonnet, Amable 159
Charles, Prince of Wales 164
Chick, Suzanne 306
Chisholm, Professor A. R. 293
Chivers, Sophia 30

Churchill, Sir Winston, Prime
Minister 178, 181, 187, 236
Clarke, Ede 176
Clarke, George 324–325
Clarke, Mervyn 176
Clift, Amy (née Currie) 303, 316
Clift, Barre 317
Clift, Charmian 302–319
Clift, Margaret 306
Clift, Montgomery 330
Clift, Sydney 303
Coats, Peter 239
Cockerell, Ann 30
Cockerell, Arabella 30
Cockerell, Mary (née Crisp) 30,
38
Cockerell, William 30, 37–38
Cockerell, William James 30,
37–38
Cockerill, Mary (Black Mary) 2,
28–44, 48, 92
Cohen, Leonard 314, 330
Cohn, Nik 332
Colette, Sidonie–Gabrielle 130
Collier, John 228
Collins, Lieutenant Governor
David 13, 14, 15, 16, 17, 31
Collinson, Laurie 323
Conrad, Joseph 288
Conroy, Beresford 288
Coombs, Anne 323
Cooper, Gary 244
Cope, Dr David 160
Corralis, Joseph 53, 63
Cotton, Marian 180
Coward, Noël 178, 186, 187, 219

Cox, James 12, 18, 21
Coyne, J. Stirling 78
Craigie, Lieutenant Patrick 73
Crichton, Dick 197
Crooke, Ray 316
Crosby, Mrs 87
Cross, Stan 288
Crowley, Edward Alexander 'Aleister' 291–292, 296
Curtin, John, Prime Minister 148
Cusack, Dymphna 218

Dacre Fox, Norah 153
Dali, Salvador 136, 289
Dangar, Henry 92
Darge, Robert 53, 56, 63
Dark, Eleanor 218
Davey, Lieutenant Governor Thomas 32, 34, 35, 36, 38–39, 42, 44
Davies, Marion 244
Dayman, Robert 53, 56, 63
de Beauvallon, Jean-Baptiste Rosemond de Beupin 75, 76
de la Fuente, Elvira 235
de Landsfeld, Maria de los Delores see Montez, Lola
de Rochefort, Noemie 141
de Valera, Eamon, President 226
de Wolfe, Elsie 210
Deakin, Alfred, Prime Minister 290
Deakin, Vera 182
Deamer, Dulcie 288, 293
Debussy, Claude 297
Dekyvere, Nola 206

Delahunty, Mary 94–97, 102
Delavigne, Doris 246
d'Erlanger, Baroness Catherine 128, 133
d'Espiniary, Countess 206
Devine, Frederick 254
Devine, James 'Jim' 253–257, 259, 262
Devine, Tilly (née Matilda Mary 'Tilly' Twiss) 1, 251–265
Dickerson, Robert 279
Dobell, Sir William 136, 293
Donaldson, Mary 233
Doyle, Michael 53, 57
Doyle, Sir Arthur Conan 289
Drysdale, Russell 184
Dufy, Raoul 136
Dujarier, Alexandre 75
Dumas, Alexandre (père) 75–76, 88
Dundas, George 24
Dunne, Dominick 234
Durack, Fanny 158, 160
Dylan, Bob 326
Dyring, Moya 273, 274

Earhart, Amelia 187
Eastey, John 17
Eastman, Linda see McCartney, Linda
Edward, Prince of Wales 233, 239, 240
Edwards (Howe gang member) 41
Edwards, Captain Edward 20
Edwards, Grace 317
Edwards, John 102

Edwards, Marion 'Bill' (William Ernest Edwards, William McKay, 'Little Willie', 'Bill the Girl-Man') 1, 90–91, 101–107
Edwards, William Ernest see Edwards, Marion 'Bill'
Einstein, Albert 294
Elgar, Sir Edward 196
Eliot, T. S. 219
Elliott, William 53, 56, 57
Elphinstone, Lord 74
Epstein, Brian 328
Evans, Mrs De Lacy see Tremaye, Ellen
Evans, Edward De Lacy see Tremaye, Ellen

Farida, Queen 187
Farwell, George 288
Fellowes, Daisy 236
Fields, Danny 328, 334, 336
Finch, Peter 310–311
Fink, Margaret (née Elliott) 323
Fitzgerald, F. Scott 176, 198, 270, 309
Fitzgerald, Zelda 270, 309
Foch, Marshal 238
Folland, Frank (Noel Follin) 84, 87–88
Follin, Noel see Folland, Frank
Fortune, Dion (née Violet Mary Firth) 291
Fox, William 169–170, 172
Fraser, Eliza (née Slack) 2, 49–70
Fraser, Captain James 50–60, 62
Fraser, John 52

Fraser, Sarah 'Mother' 112
Frater, William 273
Frederik, Crown Prince of Denmark 233
Freud, Sigmund 130, 289
Friend, Donald 322
Furness, Averill 239
Furness, Sir Christopher 239
Furness, Daisy 239
Furness, Richard 'Dick' 239, 241
Furness, Stephen 240
Furness, Viscount Marmaduke 'Duke' 239–245, 249
Furness, Viscountess Thelma Morgan Converse 239–240, 241
Furness, William 'Tony the bastard' 239, 241
Fyans, Foster 53, 54, 59, 60

Gallagher, Frank 92
Gallagher, Kitty 92
Garbo, Greta 235
Gardner, Ava 327
Garland, Judy 330
Gaunson, David 114, 117
Gayrard, Madame Paule 159
Geary (Howe gang member) 42
George V, King 164, 182
George VI, King 184, 243
Gilbert, Ensign Edward 72
Gilbert, Maria Delores Eliza Rosanna see Montez, Lola
Gillott, Sir Samuel 111, 114, 116–117
Ginsberg, Allen 329

Glass, Philip 330

Glover, Wally 294, 301

Goff, Barbara 217

Goff, Helen Lyndon 'Lindy' *see* Travers, Pamela Lyndon

Goff, Moya 217

Goff, Travers Lyndon 214–216

Goldberg, Danny 336

Goldstein, Vida 144–145, 146, 149

Goodman, David 296

Goodsir, Agnes 271

Goossens, Sir Eugene 296–297

Gordon, Charles 243

Gordon, Lady Duff 201

Gormondy (from Indigenous people near Fraser Island) 64

Gourielli-Tchkonia, Prince Artchil 135, 136

Graham, John 63–65

Greene, Alexander John 67, 68

Greenlees, Gavin 292–299

Greer, Germaine 320, 331, 336

Grice, Richard 179

Grimson, Ellen 261

Grimwade, Frederick Sheppard 122, 124

Guard, Betty 68

Guard, Captain John 68

Guinan, 'Texas' 251

Gurdjieff, George Ivanovich 224, 225, 227, 229

Guthrie, Woody 326

Ham, David 267

Ham, Ethel 267, 268, 270, 273

Harris, Max 277

Hart, Lyman Oatman 96

Hay, Josslyn, Earl of Erroll 182, 192, 243, 249

Hay, Rosemary 182

Heald, George Trafford 78–79, 82

Heald, Susanna 78–79

Heap, Jane 227

Hearst, William Randolph 244

Henrys, Catherine 'Jemmy the Rover' 91

Herman, Sali 184

Hermes, Gertrude 228–229

Hester, Joy 266, 277, 278, 279, 282

Hillier (Howe gang member) 39, 40

Hinch, Derryn 336

Hirschfeld, Magnus 325

Hodgson, Caroline (née Lohman) (Madame Brussels) 1, 108–117, 251, 256

Hodgson, Irene 115–116

Hodgson, Studholme 109, 117

Hoff, Rayner 287

Hoffman, Anna 295

Hollay, Rosa 130

Hollingsworth, Kim 252

Holt, Charles 197

Holt, Dame Zara 179

Hone, John Camillus 228–230

Hope, Neil 323, 327

Horne, Donald 326

Horseman, Mollie 288

Howe, Michael 2, 29, 31–44, 92

Hudson, George 259

Hughes, Billy, Prime Minister 147–148, 149
Hull, Patrick Purdy 82
Humphrey, Adolarias 36

Ingle, John 31–32
Isogawa, Akira 212

Jagger, Mick 335
James, Mrs Betty *see* Montez, Lola
James, Lieutenant Thomas 73, 74, 82
Jarrett, Pat 186, 188, 189, 190, 192
Javes, Nan 299
Jenkins, William 117
John, Cecilia 145, 146
Johnson, Amy 187
Johnson, Jacob 152
Johnson, Reverend Richard 10, 11, 13, 15
Johnston, Gae 308
Johnston, George 302, 307–319
Johnston, Jason 313
Johnston, John 308
Johnston, Martin 310, 319
Johnston, Minnie (née Wright) 308
Johnston, Shane 310, 318, 319
Jolson, Al 170
Joplin, Janis 330
Joyce, James 219, 289
Jung, Carl 289

Kahanamoku, Duke 158
Kann, Percy 202, 205
Kashif, Amer, Maharajah 199

Kaye, Elsie 254, 258
Kaye, Lenny 332
Kellermann, Annette 157–177
Kellermann, Frederick (brother of Annette) 159
Kellermann, Frederick (father of Annette) 159, 161, 165
Kellermann, Maurice 159, 165
Kellogg, Dr John Harvey 173
Kelly, Grace 176, 248
Kelly, James 34
Kenmare, Dowager Countess of 246
Kenmare, Lady Enid, Countess of *see* Lindeman, Enid
Kennedy, Jacqueline 327, 330
Kennedy, John F., President 236, 326
Kennedy, Joseph 236
Kennedy, Kathleen 'Kick' 236
Kennedy, Robert Jr 334
Kenny, Sister Elizabeth 171
Kenny, Leo 307
Kerr, Deborah 327
Khan, Aly 241
Kierly, Dr R. J. 298
Kingsmill, Anthony 316
Kneale, Bruce 307
Knopwood, Reverend Robert 33, 36, 44
Kreisler, Fritz 172
Krishnamurti, J. 231

Lakeman, Agnes 7
Lamington, Lord Charles Cochrane-Baillie 121, 122

Landau, Jon 332

Langley, Jean 283

Lanvin, Jeanne 134, 201

Latour, Loma 293

Lawlor, Adrian 273

Layton, Aviva (née Canton) 323, 324, 328, 334

Leary, Timothy 227, 329

Leigh, Kate 251, 252, 255, 256, 257, 258, 259, 260, 261, 264, 265

Leis, Peter 209

Lennie, David 211

Lennie, Helen 211

Lennox, Captain George 74

Letham, Isabel 158

Levi, Eliphas (Alphonse Constant) 290

Lewis, C. S. 294

Lewis, Leonard Lloyd (Leonard Lloyd-Lewis) 203, 206, 208

Lichtenstein, Roy 328

Lilley, Nathaniel 18, 21, 24, 26

Lindeman, Charles 234

Lindeman, Dr Henry 234

Lindeman, Lady Enid, Countess of Kenmare (also Enid Cameron, Enid Cavendish, Enid Furness and Enid Castlerosse) 2, 233–250

Lindeman, Grant 236, 245

Lindsay, Daryl 190

Lindsay, Joan (née Weigall) 182, 191

Lindsay, Norman 285, 287, 288

Liszt, Franz 75

Little, Barry 210

Lloyd George, David, Prime Minister 145

Lloyd-Lewis, Leonard see Lewis, Leonard Lloyd

Lloyd-Lewis, Robin 'Robert' 204, 207, 208, 211

London, Jack 288

Long, John 209

Loridan, Jean Baptiste 98

Louis, Prince of Monaco 248

Lowe, Barrie 301

Lucas, Vera 258

Ludwig I, King of Bavaria 71, 76, 77, 78, 79–80

Lyons, Joseph, Prime Minister 185

MacArthur, General Douglas 322

Mackellar, Dorothea 218

Macmillan, Harold, Prime Minister 188

Macnamara, Francis 227, 228

Macquarie, Governor Lachlan 35, 42, 44

Mahoney Griffin, Marion 153

Mailer, Norman 329

Major, John 53, 69

Malouf, David 324, 325

Mansfield, Katherine 227

Marden, Caroline 74

Marien, Frank 287

Markham, Beryl 249

Marquand, Julia 97–98

Martin, David 306

Martin, James 12, 18, 20, 21, 24

Martin, Shane (pseudonym of George Johnston) *see* Johnston, George
Mary, Queen 180, 182
Mature, Victor 166
Maugham, Somerset 198, 245
Maurice, Jean-Claude 314
McAuley, James 277
McCartney, Linda (née Eastman) 328, 329, 330–331, 335
McCartney, Paul 330, 335
McClelland, Annie 106
McCrae, Dr William 289
McCubbin, Frederick 184, 267, 274
McCulloch, Allan 280–281
McGuinness, Paddy 328
McIndoe, Sir Archibald 244
McKay, Margaret 102
McKay, William *see* Edwards, Marion 'Bill'
Melba, Dame Nellie (Helen Mitchell) 123, 159, 169, 180, 268, 334
Meissner, Franz 239
Meltzer, Richard 332
Menzies, Robert, Prime Minister 185
Mercier, Emile 288
Méthot, Yvan 210
Milbanke, Sir John Peniston 233
Milbanke, Sheila (née Chisholm) 233, 240
Miles, William 155, 156
Miller, Olga 54
Milne, A. A. 221

Milton, Reverend John 86
Minihan, Lucy 102–103, 105
Miró, Joan 289
Mitchell, Sir Edward 181
Mitchell, Helen *see* Melba, Dame Nellie 159
Molyneux, Captain Edward 203, 248
Moncrieff, Amy Wall 195
Moncrieff, Gladys 195, 196
Montez, Donna Lolah *see* Montez, Lola
Montez, Lola (Maria Delores Eliza Rosanna Gilbert, Mrs Betty James, Donna Lolah Montez, Maria de los Delores de Landsfeld, Countess Marie von Landsfeld) 71–89, 235
Moore, Sarah 97
Mora, George 279
Mora, Mirka 279
Morehead, Boyd Dunlop 214, 215
Morehead, Helen 'Aunt Ellie' 215, 216, 217, 219, 226, 227
Morehead, Margaret 215–217
Morehead, Maria 215
Morehead, Robert 215
Morgan, Mr 25
Morgan, Molly 26
Morrison, Jim 330
Morton, Frank 218, 219
Morton, William 18, 21
Mosley, Sir Oswald 153
Moyes, Helen Fraser 144
Mudie, Ian Mayleston 288
Munro, Peter 322

Murdoch, Keith 186
Murdoch, Rupert 325, 326
Murphy, Professor L. J. 290

Nepean, Evan 24
Neville, Richard 333, 335
Nicolls, General Lieutenant Sir
    Jasper 73
Niland, D'Arcy 310
Nin, Anaïs 135
Nolan, Amelda 276
Nolan, Cynthia (née Reed) 185,
    271, 273, 274, 278, 283
Nolan, Elizabeth (née Patterson)
    276
Nolan, Mary (née Boyd Perceval)
    283
Nolan, Sidney 49, 190, 210, 266,
    275, 277, 278–279, 281, 282,
    283
Northcote, Lord 162
Norton, Albert 286
Norton, Beena Salek (née
    Aschman) 286
Norton, Cecily see Boothman,
    Cecily
Norton, John 116
Norton, Phyllis 286
Norton, Richard 197
Norton, Rosaleen 1, 285–301
Nureyev, Rudolf 330

O'Berne, James 37
O'Higgins, Patrick 121
O'Keeffe, Georgia 227, 229
Oliver, Charles Silver 72

Oliver, Elizabeth 72
Oliver, Mary Green 72
Orage, Alfred 224, 225
Orage, Jessie 227, 229
O'Reilly, John 27
Osborne, Charles 322
Otter, Lieutenant Charles 63, 64,
    65

Packer, Frank 326
Palmer, Vance 218
Pankhurst, Adela Constantia Mary
    139–156, 292
Pankhurst, Christabel 141, 142,
    143, 144, 145, 152
Pankhurst, Emmeline Goulden
    139–142, 144, 152
Pankhurst, Estelle Sylvia 141, 144
Pankhurst, Frank 141
Pankhurst, Frank 'Harry'
    141–142, 144
Pankhurst, Dr Richard 139–141
Park, Ruth 252, 305, 310, 315
Parker, Bonnie 251
Parker-Bowles, Camilla 233
Parsons, Eric 262–263
Parsons, Mary 263
Pavlova, Anna 157, 172
Peck, Mary Ann 38
Peel, Robert 76
Peers, Sarah 179
Pellier, Madame 194, 203, 204,
    207
Perceval, John 266, 277, 279, 280,
    281, 283
Perceval, Mary Boyd 283

Phillip, Governor Arthur 9–10, 11, 15, 16, 24
Pitblado, Clare 268, 275
Pitt, Richard 32, 36
Pitt, Salome 31, 32
Plessis, Alphonsine 76
Plumpton, Alfred 115
Pohl, Jacob 115
Poiret, Paul 129, 208, 209
Pollock, 'Jigger' 103, 104
Pollock, Mr 24
Pond, Theron 123
Pow, Emma 267
Prichard, Katharine Susannah 218

Quinn, Leonard 269–270, 272

Rabin, Zell 325, 326, 327
Rainier, Prince of Monaco 248
Rauschenberg, Robert 328
Ready, Mr 95, 97
Reed, John 266, 271–284
Reed, Lou 330
Reed, Sunday (née Lelda Sunday Baillieu) 185, 266–284
Reid, Barrett 'Barrie' 279, 282, 323
Reynolds, Sir Joshua 180
Roberts, Tom 274
Robinson, George Augustus 46–47, 91
Robinson, Lisa 332, 336
Romanoff, Prince Dimitri 233
Roosevelt, Franklin, President 175, 188
Ropschitz, Liliana *see* Roxon, Lillian

Ross, Ethel 149
Ross, Major Robert 10
Ross, Robert 149
Rowan, Ellis (née Ryan) 180, 191
Roxon, Izydor 321
Roxon, Jacob 'Jack' 321, 336
Roxon, Lillian (née Liliana Ropschitz) 320–336
Roxon, Milo 321, 325
Rubinstein, Ceska 122, 124, 125, 128
Rubinstein, Helena (Chaja) 2, 118–138
Rubinstein, Hertzel 119
Rubinstein, Manka 132, 133
Rubinstein, Pauline 130
Russell, George 'AE' 219–226
Russell, Henry Stuart 69
Russell, William 81
Rutherford, Major General, Sir James 73
Ryan, Alice Elfrida (née Sumner) 179, 181, 183
Ryan, Charles (father of Sir Charles Snodgrass Ryan) 180
Ryan, Sir Charles Snodgrass 180–181, 182
Ryan, Ethel Marion Sumner *see* Casey, Lady Maie
Ryan, Patrick 184
Ryan, Rupert 181, 182, 183, 184
Ryan, T. J. 148

Sackville, Lady Idina 243
Sands, Dr S. G. 298
Saraset, Christina 217

Sargent, Dudley 167
Sassoon, Vidal 328
Sawyer, Ralph 196, 197
Schiaparelli, Elsa 134, 201, 245
Scott, Ada (née Ryan) 180
Scott, Lord Charles 180
Scott, Sergeant James 17
Scott, Rose 161
Seekamp, Henry 87
Septon (Howe gang member) 42
Sert, Misia Natanson 129
Shepard, Ernest 226
Shepard, Florence 226
Shepard, Mary 226
Shepherd, Jack 21
Shilton, Dean 300
Sholto, Phyllis 209
Shriver, Robert 334
Silberfeld, Gitel 119
Silberfeld, Louis 120
Sime, Dawn 280
Sime, Ian 280
Simms, John, Samuel Bird 18, 21
Simpson, Wallis 241
Sitwell, Dame Edith 219, 294
Smit, Detmer 15
Smith, Fern 280
Smith, Gray 278, 280
Smith, Peregrine 280
Smith, Tommy 249
Snowdon, Lord Anthony
    Armstrong-Jones 231, 331
Soeurs, Callot 201
Sorell, Lieutenant Governor
    William 38, 42–43
Sorensen, Rhyl 322, 335

Sousa, John Philip 172
Splitter, Helena Silberfeld 119
Standish, Frederick 112
Stawell, Sir Richard 182
Stephensen, Percy Reginald 156,
    292
Stewart, Harold 277
Stewart, Nellie 123
Street, Mr Justice 261
Streeton, Sir Arthur 267, 274, 300
Stynes, James 39
Sulkowski, Prince Ludwig 88
Sullivan, Jimmie 165, 166, 170,
    175, 176
Sumner, Theodotus 179
Sutherland, Graham 136
Sutherland, Dame Joan 297
Sutherland, Margaret 192
Swan, John 91
Sydney, Lord (Thomas
    Townshend) 9

Taylor, Elizabeth 327
Taylor, Elsie 308
Taylor, John 328
Tench, Captain Lieutenant
    Watkin 12, 15, 17, 18, 20
Tennant, Kylie 288
Thomas, Richard 26
Thompson, John 122
Tiffany, Anne Cameron 239, 249
Tissot, Berthe 181
Titus, Edward 118, 127–130, 132,
    133, 134, 135
Titus, Horace 130, 137
Titus, Roy 129

Tolokunganah (Indigenous leader in Tasmania) 34
Tonnson, Captain 41
Toscanini, Arturo 172
Travers, Pamela Lyndon (née Helen Lyndon 'Lindy' Goff) 213–232, 237
Tremaye, Ellen (Mrs De Lacy Evans, Edward De Lacy Evans) 1, 90–101
Trevor-Roper, Hugh 247
Troy, Richard 39
Tryon, Lord Anthony 233
Tryon, Dale (née Harper) 233
Tucker, Albert 266, 277, 278, 279
Tucker, Sweeney 277, 278, 279, 283
Turpin, Dick 21, 32
Twiss, Edward 253
Twiss, Matilda Mary 'Tilly' see Devine, Tilly

Vanderbilt, Gloria Morgan 240
Varley, Henry 108
Vassilieff, Danila 282
Vaughan Williams, Ralph 286
Victoria, Queen 71, 196
Vidal, Yves 247
Vincent, Lady Kitty Ogilvie 183
Vionnet, Madeleine 201
Vockins, Doris 227
von Landsfeld, Countess Marie see Montez, Lola

Waite, Arthur Edward 291, 292
Walford, Leslie 210, 212

Walker, Karen 212
Walsh, Faith 152
Walsh, Hannah 150
Walsh, Richard 150, 156
Walsh, Sylvia 151
Walsh, Tom 148, 149, 150–152, 156
Walyer (Tarenorerer) 44–47, 48
Wanjon, Timotheus 20
Ward, Fred 271, 273
Warhol, Andy 328, 329, 330
Watling, Thomas 26
Watt, Ernest 248
Waugh, Evelyn 201, 233
Webb, Captain Matthew 163
Weber, Lois 171
Wells, Thomas 38, 40
Westminster, Duke and Duchess of 240, 243, 244
White, John 11
White, Patrick 49, 64, 192
Williams, Esther 166, 175, 176
Williams, Fred 281
Williams, Tennessee 330
Wilson, Annie 114
Wilson, Group Captain Walter 236, 238
Winn, Godfrey 246
Wodehouse, P. G. 244
Wooster, Marcelle (née Kellermann) 160, 161, 165, 175, 177
Worrall, Thomas 29, 40, 43
Wren, John 114, 117
Wright, Judith 279, 322
Wright, Stevie 329

Wylie, Mina 158, 160
Wynne, David 329

Yeats, William Butler 213, 219,
    220, 226, 292
Yorke, John 40
Youlden, Henry 53, 54, 55, 56,
    58, 63

Zander, Clarice 271